POETRY FROM CRESCENT MOON

Walking In Cornwall
by Ursula Le Guin

Hymns To the Night
by Novalis

Hymns To the Night: In Translation
by Novalis

Flower Pollen: Selected Thoughts
by Novalis

Novalis: His Life, Thoughts and Works
by Novalis

Edmund Spenser: *Heavenly Love: Selected Poems*
selected and introduced by Teresa Page

Edmund Spenser: *Amoretti*
edited by Teresa Page

The Visions of Petrarch and Bellay: Early Sonnets
by Edmund Spenser

Robert Herrick: *Delight In Disorder: Selected Poems*
edited and introduced by M.K. Pace

Robert Herrick: *Hesperides*
edited and introduced by M.K. Pace

Robert Herrick: *Upon Julia's Breasts: Love Poems*
edited and introduced by M.K. Pace

Sir Thomas Wyatt: *Love For Love: Selected Poems*
selected and introduced by Louise Cooper

John Donne: *Air and Angels: Selected Poems*
selected and introduced by A.H. Ninham

D.H. Lawrence: *Being Alive: Selected Poems*
edited with an introduction by Margaret Elvy

D.H. Lawrence: *Amores*
edited with an introduction by Margaret Elvy

D.H. Lawrence: *Look! We Have Come Through!*
edited with an introduction by Margaret Elvy

D.H. Lawrence: *Love Poems and Others*
edited with an introduction by Margaret Elvy

D.H. Lawrence: *New Poems*
edited with an introduction by Margaret Elvy

D.H. Lawrence: Symbolic Landscapes
by Jane Foster

D.H. Lawrence: Infinite Sensual Violence
by M.K. Pace

Percy Bysshe Shelley: *Paradise of Golden Lights: Selected Poems*
selected and introduced by Charlotte Greene

Selected Poems
by William Shakespeare

Elizabethan Sonnet Cycles
by Daniel, Drayton, Sidney,
Spenser and Shakespeare

Elizabethan Sonnet Cycles (Volume
Two)
by Lodge, Griffin, Smith,
Constable and Fletcher

Three Metaphysical Poets
edited by A.H. Ninham

Three Romantic Poets
edited by Miriam Chalk

FIGURES OF SEVERAL CENTURIES

FIGURES OF SEVERAL CENTURIES

ARTHUR SYMONS

Edited by Jeremy Mark Robinson

CRESCENT MOON

First published 1916. This edition © 2024.

Set in Book Antiqua 10 on 14pt.
Designed by Radiance Graphics.

British Library Cataloguing in Publication data

ISBN-13 9781861718129
ISBN-13 9781861719089

CRESCENT MOON PUBLISHING
P.O. Box 1312, Maidstone, Kent, ME14 5XU
Great Britain, www.crmoon.com

CONTENTS

NOTE ON THE TEXT

The text is from *Figures of Several Centuries* by Arthur Symons, published by Constable and Company, 1916.

"Close to your hand lies a little volume, bound in some Nile-green skin that has been pounded with gilded nenuphars, and smoothed with hard ivory. It is the book that Gautier loved, it is Baudelaire's masterpiece."

OSCAR WILDE ("Intentions").

Arthur Symons, two portraits
(both National Portrait
Gallery, London).

TO
JOSEPH CONRAD
WITH A FRIEND'S ADMIRATION

SAINT AUGUSTINE

The *Confessions* of St. Augustine are the first autobiography, and they have this to distinguish them from all other autobiographies, that they are addressed directly to God. Rousseau's unburdening of himself is the last, most effectual manifestation of that nervous, defiant consciousness of other people which haunted him all his life. He felt that all the men and women whom he passed on his way through the world were at watch upon him, and mostly with no very favourable intentions. The exasperation of all those eyes fixed upon him, the absorbing, the protesting self-consciousness which they called forth in him, drove him, in spite of himself, to set about explaining himself to other people, to the world in general. His anxiety to explain, not to justify, himself was after all a kind of cowardice before his own conscience. He felt the silent voices within him too acutely to keep silence. Cellini wrote his autobiography because he heard within him such trumpeting voices of praise, exultation, and the supreme satisfaction of a violent man who has conceived himself to be always in the right, that it shocked him to think of going down into his grave without having made the whole world hear those voices. He hurls at you this book of his own deeds that it may smite you into acquiescent admiration. Casanova, at the end of a long life in which he had tasted all the forbidden fruits of the earth, with a simplicity of pleasure in which the sense of their being forbidden was only the least of their abounding flavours, looked back upon his past self with a slightly pathetic admiration, and set himself to go all over those successful adventures, in love and in other arts, firstly, in order that he might be amused by recalling them, and then because he thought the record would do him credit. He neither intrudes himself as a model, nor acknowledges that he was very often in the wrong. Always passionate after sensations, and for their own sake, the writing of an autobiography was the last, almost active, sensation that was left to him, and he accepted it energetically.

Probably St. Augustine first conceived of the writing of an autobiography as a kind of penance, which might be fruitful also to others. By its form it challenges the slight difficulty that it appears to be telling God what God knew already. But that is the difficulty which every prayer also challenges. To those we love, are we not fond of telling many things about ourselves which they know already? A prayer, such confessions as these, are addressed to God by one of those subterfuges by which it is necessary to approach the unseen and infinite, under at least a disguise of mortality. And the whole book, as no other such book has ever been, is lyrical. This prose, so simple, so familiar, has in it the exaltation of poetry. It can pass, without a change of tone, from the boy's stealing of pears: 'If aught of those pears came within my mouth, what sweetened it was the sin'; to a tender human affection: 'And now he lives in Abraham's bosom: whatever that be which is signified by that bosom, there lives my Nebridius, my sweet friend'; and from that to the saint's rare, last ecstasy: 'And sometimes Thou admittedst me to an affection, very unusual, in my inmost soul, rising to a strange sweetness, which if it were perfected in me, I know not what in it would not belong to the life to come.' And even self-analysis, of which there is so much, becoming at times a kind of mathematics, even those metaphysical subtleties which seem, to sharpen thought upon thought to an almost invisible fineness of edge, become also lyrical, inter-penetrated as they are with this sense of the divine.

To St. Augustine all life is seen only in its relation to the divine; looked at from any other side, it has no meaning, and, looked at even with this light upon it, is but for the most part seen as a blundering in the dark, a wandering from the right path. In so far as it is natural, it is evil. In so far as it is corrected by divine grace, it leaves the human actors in it without merit; since all virtue is God's, though all vice is man's.

This conception of life is certainly valuable in giving harmony to the book, presenting as it does a sort of background. It brings with it a very impressive kind of symbolism into its record of actual facts, to all of which it gives a value, not in themselves, if you please to put it so, or, perhaps more properly, their essential value. When nothing which happens, happens except under God's direct responsibility, when nothing is said which is not one of your 'lines' in the drama which is being played, not so much by as through you, there can be no exteriorities, nothing can be trivial, in a record of life so conceived. And this point of view also helps the writer to keep all his details in proportion; the auto-biographer's usual fault, artistically at least, being an inordinate valuation of small concerns, because they happened to him. To St. Augustine, while not the smallest human event is without significance, in its relation to eternity, not the greatest human event is of importance, in its relation to time; and his own share in it would but induce a special, it may seem an exaggerated, humility on his part. Thus, speaking of his early studies, his triumphs in them, not without a certain *naïveté*: 'Whatever was written, either in rhetoric or logic, geometry, music, and arithmetic, by myself without much difficulty or any instruction, I understood, Thou knowest, O Lord my God; because both quickness and understanding and acuteness in discerning is Thy gift.' Or, again, speaking of the youthful excellences ('excellently hadst Thou made him') of that son who was the son of his beloved mistress: 'I had no part in that boy, but the sin.'

Intellectual pride, one sees in him indeed, at all times, by the very force with which it is repressed into humility; and, in all that relates to that mistress, in the famous cry: 'Give me chastity, but not yet!' in all those insurgent memories of 'these various and shadowy loves,' we see the force of the flesh, in one who lived always with so passionate a life, alike of the spirit and the senses. Now, recalling what was sinful in him, in his confessions to God, he is reluctant to allow any value to the most honourable of human sentiments, to so much as forgive the most estimable of human weaknesses. 'And now, Lord, in writing I confess it unto Thee. Read it who will, and interpret it how he will: and if any finds sin therein, that I wept my mother for a small portion of an hour (the mother who for the time was dead to mine eyes, who had for many years wept for me that I might live in Thine eyes), let him not deride me; but rather, if he be one of large charity, let him weep for himself for my sins unto Thee, the Father of all the brethren of Thy Christ.' And yet it is of this mother that he writes his most tender, his most beautiful pages. 'The day was now approaching whereon she was to depart this life (which day Thou well knewest, we knew not), it came to pass, Thyself, as I believe, by Thy secret ways so ordering it, that she and I stood alone, leaning in a certain window, which looked into the garden of the house where we now lay, at Ostia…' It is not often that memory, in him, is so careful of 'the images of earth, and water, and air,' as to call up these delicate pictures. They too had become for him among the desirable things which are to be renounced for a more desirable thing.

That sense of the divine in life, and specially of the miracles which happen a certain number of times in every existence, the moments which alone count in the soul's summing-up of itself, St. Augustine has rendered with such significance, with such an absolute wiping out from the memory of everything else, just because he has come to that, it might seem, somewhat arid point of spiritual ascent. That famous moment of the *Tolle, lege*: 'I cast myself down I know not how, under a certain fig-tree, giving full vent to my tears … when lo! I heard from a neighbouring house a voice, as of boy or girl, I know not, chanting, and oft repeating, "Take up and read, take up and read"'; the Bishop's word to

Monnica ('as if it had sounded from heaven'), 'It is not possible that the son of those tears should perish'; the beggar-man, 'joking and joyous,' in the streets of Milan: it is by these, apparently trifling, these all-significant moments that his narrative moves, with a more reticent and effective symbolism than any other narrative known to me. They are the moments in which the soul has really lived, or has really seen; and the rest of life may well be a blindness and a troubled coming and going.

I said that the height from which St. Augustine apprehends these truths may seem a somewhat arid one. That is perhaps only because it is nearer the sky, more directly bathed in what he calls, beautifully, 'this queen of colours, the light.' There is a passage in the tenth book which may almost be called a kind of æsthetics. They are æsthetics indeed of renunciation, but a renunciation of the many beauties for the one Beauty, which shall contain as well as eclipse them; 'because those beautiful patterns which through men's souls are conveyed into their cunning hands, come from that Beauty, which is above our souls.' And it is not a renunciation by one who had never enjoyed what he renounces, or who feels himself, even now, quite safe from certain forms of its seduction. He is troubled especially by the fear that 'those melodies which Thy words breathe soul into, when sung with a sweet and attuned voice,' may come to move him 'more with the voice than with the words sung.' Yet how graciously he speaks of music, allowing 'that the several affections of our spirit, by a sweet variety, have their own proper measures in the voice and singing, by some hidden correspondence wherewith they are stirred up.' It is precisely because he feels so intimately the beauty of all things human, though it were but 'a dog coursing in the field, a lizard catching flies,' that he desires to pass through these to that passionate contemplation which is the desire of all seekers after the absolute, and which for him is God. He asks of all the powers of the earth: 'My questioning them, was my thoughts on them; and their form of beauty gave the answer.' And by how concrete a series of images does he strive to express the inexpressible, in that passage of pure poetry on the love of God! 'But what do I love, when I love thee? not beauty of bodies, nor the fair harmony of time, nor the brightness of the light, so gladsome to our eyes, nor sweet melodies of varied songs, nor the fragrant smell of flowers, and ointments, and spices, not manna and honey, not limbs acceptable to embracements of flesh. None of these I love, when I love my God; and yet I love a kind of light, and melody, and fragrance, and meat, and embracement, when I love my God, the light, melody, fragrance, meat, embracement of my inner man: where there shineth unto my soul what space cannot contain, and there soundeth what time beareth not away, and there smelleth what breathing disperseth not, and there tasteth what eating diminisheth not, and there clingeth what satiety divorceth not. This is it which I love when I love my God.'

Mentioning in his confessions only such things as he conceives to be of import to God, it happens, naturally, that St. Augustine leaves unsaid many things that would have interested most men, perhaps more. 'What, then, have I to do with men, that they should hear my confessions – as if they could heal my infirmities, – a race curious to know the lives of others, slothful to amend their own?' Finding, indeed, many significant mentions of things and books and persons, Faustus the Manichee, the 'Hortensius' of Cicero, the theatre, we shall find little pasture here for our antiquarian, our purely curious, researches. We shall not even find all that we might care to know, in St. Augustine himself, of the surface of the mind's action, which we call character, or the surface emotions, which we call temperament. Here is a soul, one of the supreme souls of humanity, speaking directly to that supreme soul which it has apprehended outside humanity. Be sure that, if it forgets many things which you, who overhear, would like it to have remembered, it will remember everything which it is important to remember, everything which the recording angel, who is the soul's finer criticism of itself, has already inscribed in the book of the last judgment.

1897.

CHARLES LAMB

I

There is something a little accidental about all Lamb's finest work. Poetry he seriously tried to write, and plays and stories; but the supreme criticism of the *Specimens of English Dramatic Poets* arose out of the casual habit of setting down an opinion of an extract just copied into one's note-book, and the book itself, because, he said, 'the book is such as I am glad there should be.' The beginnings of his miscellaneous prose are due to the 'ferreting' of Coleridge. 'He ferrets me day and night,' Lamb complains to Manning in 1800, 'to do something. He tends me, amidst all his own worrying and heart-oppressing occupations, as a gardener tends his young tulip... He has lugged me to the brink of engaging to a newspaper, and has suggested to me for a first plan the forgery of a supposed manuscript of Burton, the anatomist of melancholy'; which was done, in the consummate way we know, and led in its turn to all the rest of the prose. And Barry Cornwall tells us that 'he was almost teased into writing the *Elia* essays.'

He had begun, indeed, deliberately, with a story, as personal really as the poems, but, unlike them, set too far from himself in subject and tangled with circumstances outside his knowledge. He wrote *Rosamund Gray* before he was twenty-three, and in that 'lovely thing,' as Shelley called it, we see most of the merits and defects of his early poetry. It is a story which is hardly a story at all, told by comment, evasion, and recurrence, by 'little images, recollections, and circumstances of past pleasures' or distresses; with something vague and yet precise, like a dream partially remembered. Here and there is the creation of a mood and moment, almost like Coleridge's in the *Ancient Mariner*; but these flicker and go out. The style would be laughable in its simplicity if there were not in it some almost awing touch of innocence; some hint of that divine goodness which, in Lamb, needed the relief and savour of the later freakishness to sharpen it out of insipidity. There is already a sense of what is tragic and endearing in earthly existence, though no skill as yet in presenting it; and the moral of it is surely one of the morals or messages of *Elia*: 'God has built a brave world, but methinks he has left his creatures to bustle in it how they may.'

Lamb had no sense of narrative, or, rather, he cared in a story only for the moments when it seemed to double upon itself and turn into irony. All his attempts to write for the stage (where his dialogue might have been so telling) were foiled by his inability to 'bring three together on the stage at once,' as he confessed in a letter to Mrs. Shelley; 'they are so shy with me, that I can get no more than two; and there they stand till it is the time, without being the season, to withdraw them.' Narrative he could manage only when it was prepared for him by another, as in the *Tales from Shakespeare* and the *Adventures of Ulysses*. Even in *Mrs. Leicester's School*, where he came nearest to success in a plain narrative, the three stories, as stories, have less than the almost perfect art of the best of Mary Lamb's: of *Father's Wedding-Day*, which Landor, with wholly pardonable exaggeration, called 'with the sole exception of the *Bride of Lammermoor*, the most beautiful tale in prose composition in any language, ancient or modern.' There is something of an incomparable kind of story-telling in most of the best essays of *Elia*, but it is a kind which he had to find out, by accident and experiment, for himself; and chiefly through letter-writing. 'Us dramatic geniuses,' he speaks of, in a letter to Manning against the taking of all words in a literal sense; and it was this wry dramatic genius in him that was, after all, the quintessential part of himself. 'Truth,' he says in this letter, 'is one and poor, like the cruse of Elijah's widow. Imagination is the bold face that multiplies its oil: and thou, the old cracked pipkin, that could not believe it could be put to such purposes.' It was to his correspondents, indeed to the incitement of their wakeful friendship, that he owes more perhaps than the mere materials of his miracles.

To be wholly himself, Lamb had to hide himself under some disguise, a name, 'Elia,' taken literally as a pen name, or some more roundabout borrowing, as of an old fierce critic's, Joseph Ritson's, to heighten and soften the energy of marginal annotations on a pedant scholar. In the letter in which he announces the first essays of *Elia*, he writes to Barron Field: 'You shall soon have a tissue of truth and fiction, impossible to be extricated, the interleavings shall be so delicate, the partitions perfectly invisible.' The correspondents were already accustomed to this 'heavenly mingle.' Few of the letters, those works of nature, and almost more wonderful than works of art, are to be taken on oath. Those elaborate lies, which ramify through them into patterns of sober-seeming truth, are in anticipation, and were of the nature of a preliminary practice for the innocent and avowed fiction of the essays. What began in mischief ends in art.

II

'I am out of the world of readers,' Lamb wrote to Coleridge, 'I hate all that do read, for they read nothing but reviews and new books. I gather myself up into the old things.' 'I am jealous for the actors who pleased my youth,' he says elsewhere. And again:

'For me, I do not know whether a constitutional imbecility does not incline me too obstinately to cling to the remembrances of childhood; in an inverted ratio to the usual sentiment of mankind, nothing that I have been engaged in since seems of any value or importance compared to the colours which imagination gave to everything then.' In Lamb this love of old things, this willing recurrence to childhood, was the form in which imagination came to him. He is the grown-up child of letters, and he preserves all through his life that child's attitude of wonder, before 'this good world, which he knows – which was created so lovely, beyond his deservings.' He loves the old, the accustomed, the things that people have had about them since they could remember. 'I am in love,' he says in the most profoundly serious of his essays, 'with this green earth; the face of town and country; and the sweet security of streets.' He was a man to whom mere living had zest enough to make up for everything that was contrary in the world. His life was tragic, but not unhappy. Happiness came to him out of the little things that meant nothing to others, or were not so much as seen by them. He had a genius for living, and his genius for writing was only a part of it, the part which he left to others to remember him by.

Lamb's religion, says Pater, was 'the religion of men of letters, religion as understood by the soberer men of letters in the last century'; and Hood says of him: 'As he was in spirit an Old Author, so was he in faith an Ancient Christian.' He himself tells Coleridge that he has 'a taste for religion rather than a strong religious habit,' and, later in life, writes to a friend: 'Much of my seriousness has gone off.' On this, as on other subjects, he grew shyer, withdrew more into himself; but to me it seems that a mood of religion was permanent with him. 'Such religion as I have,' he said, 'has always acted on me more by way of sentiment than argumentative process'; and we find him preferring churches when they are empty, as many really religious people have done. To Lamb religion was a part of human feeling, or a kindly shadow over it. He would have thrust his way into no mysteries. And it was not lightly, or with anything but a strange-complexioned kind of gratitude, that he asked: 'Sun, and sky, and breeze, and solitary walks, and summer holidays, and the greenness of fields, and the delicious juices of meats and fishes, and society, and the cheerful glass, and candle-light, and fire-side conversations, and innocent vanities, and jests, and *irony itself* – do these things go out with life?'

It was what I call Lamb's religion that helped him to enjoy life so humbly, heartily, and delicately, and to give to others the sensation of all that is most enjoyable in the things about us. It may be said of him, as he says of the fox in the fable: 'He was an adept in that species of moral alchemy, which turns everything into gold.' And this moral alchemy of his was no reasoned and arguable optimism, but a 'spirit of youth in everything,' an irrational, casuistical, 'matter-of-lie' persistence in the face of all logic, experience, and sober judgment; an upsetting of truth grown tedious and custom gone stale. And for a truth of the letter it substituted a new, valiant truth of the spirit; for dead things, living ideas; and gave birth to the most religious sentiment of which man is capable: grateful joy.

Among the innumerable objects and occasions of joy which Lamb found laid out before him, at the world's feast, books were certainly one of the most precious, and after books came pictures. 'What any man can write, surely I may read!' he says to Wordsworth, of Caryl on Job, six folios. 'I like books about books,' he confesses, the test of the book-lover. 'I love,' he says, 'to lose myself in other men's minds. When I am not walking, I am reading; I cannot sit and think. Books think for me.' He was the finest of all readers, far more instant than Coleridge; not to be taken unawares by a Blake ('I must look on him as one of the most extraordinary persons of the age,' he says of him, on but a slight and partial acquaintance), or by Wordsworth when the *Lyrical Ballads* are confusing all judgments, and he can pick out at sight 'She Dwelt Among the Untrodden Ways' as 'the best piece in it,' and can define precisely the defect of much of the book, in one of those incomparable letters of escape, to Manning: 'It is full of original thought, but it does not often make you laugh or cry. It too artfully aims at simplicity of expression.' I choose these instances because the final test of a critic is in his reception of contemporary work; and Lamb must have found it much easier to be right, before every one else, about Webster, and Ford, and Cyril Tourneur, than to be the accurate critic that he was of Coleridge, at the very time when he was under the 'whiff and wind' of Coleridge's influence. And in writing of pictures, though his knowledge is not so great nor his instinct so wholly 'according to knowledge,' he can write as no one has ever written in praise of Titian (so that his very finest sentence describes a picture of Titian) and can instantly detect and minutely expose the swollen contemporary delusion of a would-be Michael Angelo, the portentous Martin.

Then there were the theatres, which Lamb loved next to books. There has been no criticism of acting in English like Lamb's, so fundamental, so intimate and elucidating. His style becomes quintessential when he speaks of the stage, as in that tiny masterpiece, *On the Acting of Munden*, which ends the book of *Elia*, with its great close, the Beethoven soft wondering close, after all the surges: 'He understands a leg of mutton in its quiddity. He stands wondering, amid the commonplace materials of life, like primeval man with the sun and stars about him.' He is equally certain of Shakespeare, of Congreve, and of Miss Kelly. When he defines the actors, his pen seems to be plucked by the very wires that work the puppets. And it is not merely because he was in love with Miss Kelly that he can write of her acting like this, in words that might apply with something of truth to himself. He has been saying of Mrs. Jordan, that 'she seemed one whom care could not come near; a privileged being, sent to teach mankind what it most wants, joyousness.' Then he goes on: 'This latter lady's is the joy of a freed spirit, escaping from care, as a bird that had been limed; her smiles, if I may use the expression, seemed saved out of the fire, relics which a good and innocent heart had snatched up as most portable; her contents are visitors, not inmates: she can lay them by altogether; and when she does so, I am not sure that she is not greatest.' Is not this, with all its precise good sense, the rarest poetry of prose, a poetry made up of no poetical epithets, no fanciful similes, but 'of imagination all compact,' poetry in substance?

Then there was London. In Lamb London found its one poet. 'The earth, and sea, and sky (when all is said),' he admitted, 'is but as a house to live in'; and, 'separate from the pleasure of your company,' he assured Wordsworth, 'I don't much care if I never see a mountain in my life. I have passed all my days in London, until I have formed as many and intense local attachments as any of your mountaineers can have done with dead nature. The lighted shops of the Strand and Fleet Street, the innumerable trades, tradesmen, and customers, coaches, waggons, play-houses, all the bustle and wickedness round about Covent Garden, the very women of the town, the watchmen, drunken scenes, rattles – life awake, if you awake, at all hours of the night, the impossibility of being dull in Fleet Street, the crowds, the very dirt and mud, the sun shining upon houses and pavements, the print shops, the old bookstalls, parsons cheapening books, coffee-houses, steams of soups from kitchens, the pantomime, London itself a pantomime and a masquerade – all these things work themselves into my mind and feed me, without a power of satiating me. The wonder of these sights impels me into night-walks about her crowded streets, and I often shed tears in the motley Strand from fulness of joy at so much life.' There, surely, is the poem of London, and it has almost more than the rapture, in its lover's catalogue, of Walt Whitman's poems of America. Almost to the end, he could say (as he does again to Wordsworth, not long before his death), 'London streets and faces cheer me inexpressibly, though of the latter not one known one were remaining.' He traces the changes in streets, their distress or disappearance, as he traces the dwindling of his friends, 'the very streets, he says,' writes Mary, 'altering every day.' London was to him the new, better Eden. 'A garden was the primitive prison till man with Promethean felicity and boldness sinned himself out of it. Thence followed Babylon, Nineveh, Venice, London, haberdashers, goldsmiths, taverns, play-houses, satires, epigrams, puns – these all came in on the town part, and thither side of innocence.' To love London so was part of his human love, and in his praise of streets he has done as much for the creation and perpetuating of joy as Wordsworth ('by whose system,' Mary Lamb conjectured, 'it was doubtful whether a liver in towns had a soul to be saved') has done by his praise of flowers and hills.

And yet, for all his 'disparagement of heath and highlands,' as he confessed to Scott, Lamb was as instant and unerring in his appreciation of natural things, once brought before them, as he was in his appreciation of the things of art and the mind and man's making. He was a great walker, and sighs once, before his release from the desk: 'I wish I were a caravan driver or a penny post man, to earn my bread in air and sunshine.' We have seen what he wrote to Wordsworth about his mountains, before he had seen them. This is what he writes of them to Manning, after he has seen them: 'Such an impression I never received from objects of sight before, nor do I suppose I can ever again... In fine, I have satisfied myself that there is such a thing as that which tourists call *romantic*, which I very much suspected before.' And to Coleridge he writes: 'I feel that I shall remember your mountains to the last day I live. They haunt me perpetually.' All this Lamb saw and felt, because no beautiful thing could ever appeal to him in vain. But he wrote of it only in his letters, which were all of himself; because he put into his published writings only the best or the rarest or the accustomed and familiar part of himself, the part which he knew by heart.

III

Beyond any writer pre-eminent for charm, Lamb had salt and sting. There is hardly a known grace or energy of prose which he has not somewhere exemplified; as often in his letters as in his essays; and always with something final about it. He is never more himself than when he says, briefly: 'Sentiment came in with Sterne, and was a child he had by Affectation'; but then he is also never more himself than when he expands and develops, as in this rendering of the hisses which damned his play in Drury Lane:

> It was not a hiss neither, but a sort of a frantic yell, like a congreg-
> ation of mad geese, with roaring something like bears, mows and
> mops like apes, sometimes snakes, that hissed me into madness.
> 'Twas like St. Anthony's temptations. Mercy on us, that God should
> give His favourite children, men, mouths to speak with, to discourse
> rationally, to promise smoothly, to flatter agreeably, to encourage
> warmly, to counsel wisely: to sing with, to drink with, and to kiss
> with: and that they should turn them into the mouths of adders, bears,
> wolves, hyenas, and whistle like tempests, and emit breath through
> them like distillations of aspic poison, to asperse and vilify the
> innocent labours of their fellow creatures who are desirous to please
> them!

Or it may be a cold in the head which starts the heroic agility of his tongue, and he writes a long letter without a full stop, which is as full of substance as one of his essays. His technique is so incredibly fine, he is such a Paganini of prose, that he can invent and reverse an idea of pyramidal wit, as in this burlesque of a singer: 'The shake, which most fine singers reserve for the close or cadence, by some unaccountable flexibility, or tremul-ousness of pipe, she carrieth quite through the composition; so that the time, to a common air or ballad, keeps double motion, like the earth – running the primary circuit of the tune, and still revolving upon its own axis'; and he can condense into six words the whole life-history and the soul's essential secret of Coleridge, when he says of him, in almost the last fragment of prose that he wrote, 'he had a hunger for eternity.'

To read Lamb makes a man more humane, more tolerant, more dainty; incites to every natural piety, strengthens reverence; while it clears his brain of whatever dull fumes may have lodged there, stirs up all his senses to wary alertness, and actually quickens his vitality, like high pure air. It is, in the familiar phrase, 'a liberal education'; but it is that finer education which sets free the spirit. His natural piety, in the full sense of the word, seems to me deeper and more sensitive than that of any other English writer. Kindness, in him, embraces mankind, not with the wide engulfing arms of philanthropy, but with an individual caress. He is almost the sufficient type of virtue, so far as virtue can ever be loved; for there is not a weakness in him which is not the bastard of some good quality, and not an error which had an unsocial origin. His jests add a new reverence to lovely and noble things, or light up an unsuspected 'soul of goodness in things evil.'

No man ever so loved his friends, or was so honest with them, or made such a religion of friendship. His character of Hazlitt in the 'Letter to Southey' is the finest piece of emotional prose which he ever wrote, and his pen is inspired whenever he speaks of Coleridge. 'Good people, as they are called,' he writes to Wordsworth, 'won't serve. I want individuals. I am made up of queer points and want so many answering needles.' He counts over his friends in public, like a child counting over his toys, when some one has offered an insult to one of them. He has delicacies and devotions towards his friends, so subtle and so noble that they make every man his friend. And, that love may deepen into awe, there is the tragic bond, that protecting love for his sister which was made up of so many strange components: pity for madness, sympathy with what came so close to him in it, as well as mental comradeship, and that paradox of his position, by which he supports that by which he is supported.

It is, then, this 'human, too human' creature, who comes so

close to our hearts, whom we love and reverence, who is also, and above all, or at least in the last result, that great artist in prose, faultless in tact, flawless in technique, that great man of letters, to whom every lover of 'prose as a fine art' looks up with an admiration which may well become despair. What is it in this style, this way of putting things, so occasional, so variegated, so like his own harlequin in his 'ghastly vest of white patchwork,' 'the apparition of a dead rainbow'; what is it that gives to a style, which no man can analyse, its 'terseness, its jocular pathos, which makes one feel in laughter?' Those are his own words, not used of himself; but do they not do something to define what can, after all, never be explained?

IV

Lamb's defects were his qualities, and nature drove them inward, concentrating, fortifying, intensifying them; to a not wholly normal or healthy brain, freakish and without consecution, adding a stammering tongue which could not speak evenly, and had to do its share, as the brain did, 'by fits.' 'You,' we find Lamb writing to Godwin,

> 'cannot conceive of the desultory and uncertain way in which I (an author by fits) sometimes cannot put the thoughts of a common letter into sane prose... Ten thousand times I have confessed to you, talking of my talents, my utter inability to remember in any comprehensive way what I have read. I can vehemently applaud, or perversely stickle, at parts; but I cannot grasp at a whole. This infirmity (which is nothing to brag of) may be seen in my two little compositions, the tale and my play, in both which no reader, however partial, can find any story.'

'My brain,' he says, in a letter to Wordsworth, 'is desultory, and snatches off hints from things.' And, in a wise critical letter to Southey, he says, summing up himself in a single phrase: 'I never judge system-wise of things, but fasten upon particulars.'

Is he, in these phrases that are meant to seem so humble, really apologising for what was the essential quality of his genius? Montaigne, who (it is Lamb that says it) 'anticipated all the discoveries of succeeding essayists,' affected no humility in the statement of almost exactly the same mental complexion. 'I take the first argument that fortune offers me,' he tells us; 'they are all equally good for me; I never design to treat them in their totality, for I never see the whole of anything, nor do those see it who promise to show it to me... In general I love to seize things by some unwonted lustre.' There, in the two greatest of the essayists, one sees precisely what goes to the making of the essayist. First, a beautiful disorder: the simultaneous attack and appeal of contraries, a converging multitude of dreams, memories, thoughts, sensations, without mental preference, or conscious guiding of the judgment; and then, order in disorder, a harmony more properly musical than logical, a separating and return of many elements, which end by making a pattern. Take that essay of *Elia* called *Old China*, and, when you have recovered from its charm, analyse it. You will see that, in its apparent lawlessness and wandering like idle memories, it is constructed with the minute care, and almost with the actual harmony, of poetry; and that vague, interrupting, irrelevant, lovely last sentence is like the refrain which returns at the end of a poem.

Lamb was a mental gipsy, to whom books were roads open to adventures; he saw skies in books, and books in skies, and in every orderly section of social life magic possibilities of vagrancy. But he was also a Cockney, a lover of limit, civic tradition, the uniform of all ritual. He liked exceptions, because, in every other instance, he would approve of the rule. He broke bounds with exquisite decorum. There was in all his excesses something of 'the good clerk.'

Lamb seemed to his contemporaries notably eccentric, but he

was nearer than them all to the centre. His illuminating rays shot out from the very heart of light, and returned thither after the circuit. Where Coleridge lost himself in clouds or in quicksands, Lamb took the nearest short-cut, and, having reached the goal, went no step beyond it.

And he was a bee for honey, not, like Coleridge, a browsing ox. To him the essence of delight was choice; and choice, with him, was readier when the prize was far-fetched and dear bought: a rarity of manners, books, pictures, or whatever was human or touched humanity. 'Opinion,' he said, 'is a species of property; and though I am always desirous to share with my friends to a certain extent, I shall ever like to keep some tenets and some property properly my own.' And then he found, in rarity, one of the qualities of the best; and was never, like most others, content with the good, or in any danger of confusing it with the best. He was the only man of that great age, which had Coleridge, and Wordsworth, and Shelley, and the rest, whose taste was flawless. All the others, who seemed to be marching so straight to so determined a goal, went astray at one time or other; only Lamb, who was always wandering, never lost sense of direction, or failed to know how far he had strayed from the road.

The quality which came to him from that germ of madness which lay hidden in his nature had no influence upon his central sanity. It gave him the tragic pathos and mortal beauty of his wit, its dangerous nearness to the heart, its quick sense of tears, its at times desperate gaiety; and, also, a hard, indifferent levity, which, to brother and sister alike, was a rampart against obsession, or a stealthy way of temporising with the enemy. That tinge is what gives its strange glitter to his fooling; madness playing safely and lambently around the stoutest common sense. In him reason always justifies itself by unreason, and if you consider well his quips and cranks you will find them always the play of the intellect. I know one who read the essays of *Elia* with intense delight, and was astonished when I asked her if she had been amused. She had seen so well through the fun to its deep inner meaning that the fun had not detained her. She had found in all of it nothing but a pure intellectual reason, beyond logic, where reason is one with intuition.

1905.

VILLON

Villon was the first modern poet; he remains the most modern of poets. One requires a certain amount of old French, together with some acquaintance with the argot of the time, to understand the words in which he has written down his poems; many allusions to people and things have only just begun to be cleared up, but, apart from these things, no poet has ever brought himself closer to us, taken us into his confidence more simply, than this *personnage peu recommandable, fainéant, ivrogne, joueur, débauché, écornifleur, et, qui pis est, souteneur de filles, escroc, voleur, crocheteur de portes et de coffres*. The most disreputable of poets, he confesses himself to us with a frankness in which shamelessness is difficult to distinguish from humility. M. Gaston Paris, who for the most part is content to take him as he is, for better for worse, finds it necessary to apologise for him when he comes to the ballad of *La Grosse Margot*: this, he professes, we need not take as a personal confession, but as a mere exercise in composition! But if we are to understand Villon rightly, we must not reject even *la grosse Margot* from her place in his life. He was no dabbler in infamy, but one who loved infamous things for their own sake. He loved everything for its own sake: *la grosse Margot* in the flesh, *les dames du temps jadis* in the spirit,

> Sausses, brouets et gros poissons,
> Tartes, flaons, œfs frits et pochez,

Perdus, et en toutes façons,

his mother, *le bon royaume de France*, and above all, Paris. *Il a parcouru toute la France sans rapporter une seule impression de campagne. C'est un poète de ville, plus encore: un poète de quartier. Il n'est vraiment chez lui que sur la Montague Sainte-Geneviève, entre le Palais, les collèges, le Châtelet, les tavernes, les rotisseries, les tripots et les rues où Marion l'Idole et la grande Jeanne de Bretagne tiennent leur 'publique école'.* It is in this world that he lived, for this world that he wrote. *Fils du peuple, entré par l'instruction dans la classe lettrée, puis déclassé par ses vices, il dut à son humble origine de rester en communication constante avec les sources éternelles de toute vraie poésie.* And so he came into a literature of formalists, like a child, a vigorous, unabashed, malicious child, into a company of grey-beards.

Villon, before any one in French literature, called things by their names, made poetry as Homer made it, with words that meant facts. He was a thief and a vagabond who wrote in the 'grand style' by daring to be sincere to himself, to the aspect under which human things came to him, to the precise names of precise things. He had a sensitiveness in his soul which perhaps matched the deftness of his fingers, in their adroit, forbidden trade: his soul bent easily from his mother praying in the cloister to the fat Margot drinking in the tavern; he could dream exquisitely over the dead ladies who had once been young, and who had gone like last year's snow, and then turn to the account-book of his satirical malice against the clerks and usurers for whom he was making the testament of his poverty. He knew winter, 'when the wolves live on wind,' and how the gallows looks when one stands under it. And he knew all the secrets of the art of verse-making which courtly poets, like the King, used for the stringing together of delicate trifles, ornamental evasions of facts. He was no poet of the people, but a scholar vagabond, loving the gutter; and so he has the sincerity of the artist as well as the only half-convincing sincerity of the man. There has been no greater artist in French verse, as there has been no greater poet; and the main part of the history of poetry in France is the record of a long forgetting of all that Villon found out for himself.

1901.

CASANOVA AT DUX:
AN UNPUBLISHED CHAPTER
OF HISTORY

I

The *Memoirs* of Casanova, though they have enjoyed the popularity of a bad reputation, have never had justice done to them by serious students of literature, of life, and of history. One English writer, indeed, Mr. Havelock Ellis, has realised that 'there are few more delightful books in the world,' and he has analysed them in an essay on Casanova, published in *Affirmations*, with extreme care and remarkable subtlety. But this essay stands alone, at all events in English, as an attempt to take Casanova seriously, to show him in his relation to his time, and in his relation to human problems. And yet these *Memoirs* are perhaps the most valuable document which we possess on the society of the eighteenth century; they are the history of a unique life, a unique personality, one of the greatest of autobiographies; as a record of adventures, they are more entertaining than *Gil Blas*, or *Monte Cristo*, or any of the imaginary travels, and escapes, and masquerades in life, which have been written in imitation of them. They tell the story of a man who loved life passionately for its own sake: one to whom woman was, indeed, the most important thing in the world, but to whom nothing in the world was indifferent. The bust which gives us the most lively notion of him shows us a great, vivid, intellectual face, full of fiery energy and calm resource, the face of a thinker and a fighter in one. A scholar, an adventurer, perhaps a Cabalist, a busy stirrer in politics, a gamester, one 'born for the fairer sex,' as he tells us, and born also to be a vagabond; this man, who is remembered now for his written account of his own life, was that rarest kind of autobiographer, one who did not live to write, but wrote because he had lived, and when he could live no longer.

And his *Memoirs* take one all over Europe, giving sidelights, all the more valuable in being almost accidental, upon many of the affairs and people most interesting to us during two-thirds of the eighteenth century. Giacomo Casanova was born in Venice, of Spanish and Italian parentage, on April 2, 1725; he died at the Château of Dux, in Bohemia, on June 4, 1798. In that lifetime of seventy-three years he travelled, as his *Memoirs* show us, in Italy, France, Germany, Austria, England, Switzerland, Belgium, Russia, Poland, Spain, Holland, Turkey; he met Voltaire at Ferney, Rousseau at Montmorency, Fontenelle, d'Alembert and Crébillon at Paris, George III. in London, Louis XV. at Fontainebleau, Catherine the Great at St. Petersburg, Benedict XII. at Rome, Joseph II. at Vienna, Frederick the Great at Sans-Souci. Imprisoned by the Inquisitors of State in the *Piombi* at Venice, he made, in 1755, the most famous escape in history. His *Memoirs*, as we have them, break off abruptly at the moment when he is expecting a safe conduct, and the permission to return to Venice after twenty years' wanderings. He did return, as we know from documents in the Venetian archives; he returned as secret agent of the Inquisitors, and remained in their service from 1774 until 1782. At the end of 1782 he left Venice; and next year we find him in Paris, where, in 1784, he met Count Waldstein at the Venetian Ambassador's, and was invited by him to become his librarian at Dux. He accepted, and for the fourteen remaining years of his life lived at Dux, where he wrote his *Memoirs*.

Casanova died in 1798, but nothing was heard of the *Memoirs* (which the Prince de Ligne, in his own *Memoirs*, tells us that Casanova had read to him, and in which he found *du dramatique, de la rapidité, du comique, de la philosophie, des choses neuves, sublimes, inimitables même*) until the year 1820, when a certain Carlo Angiolini brought to the publishing house of Brockhaus, in Leipzig, a manuscript entitled *Histoire de ma vie jusqu'à l'an* 1797, in the handwriting of Casanova. This manuscript, which I have examined at Leipzig, is written on foolscap paper, rather rough and yellow; it is written on both sides of the page, and in sheets or quires; here and there the paging shows that some pages have been omitted, and in their place are smaller sheets of thinner and whiter paper, all in Casanova's handsome, unmistakable handwriting. The manuscript is done up in twelve bundles, corresponding with the twelve volumes of the original edition; and only in one place is there a gap. The fourth and fifth chapters of the twelfth volume are missing, as the editor of the original edition points out, adding: 'It is not probable that these two chapters have been withdrawn from the manuscript of Casanova by a strange hand; everything leads us to believe that the author himself suppressed them, in the intention, no doubt, of re-writing them, but without having found time to do so.' The manuscript ends abruptly with the year 1774, and not with the year 1797, as the title would lead us to suppose.

This manuscript, in its original state, has never been printed. Herr Brockhaus, on obtaining possession of the manuscript, had it translated into German by Wilhelm Schütz, but with many omissions and alterations, and published this translation, volume by volume, from 1822 to 1828, under the title, *Aus den Memoiren des Venetianers Jacob Casanova de Seingalt*. While the German edition was in course of publication, Herr Brockhaus employed a certain Jean Laforgue, a professor of the French language at Dresden, to revise the original manuscript, correcting Casanova's vigorous, but at times incorrect, and often somewhat Italian, French according to his own notions of elegant writing, suppressing passages which seemed too free-spoken from the point of view of morals and of politics, and altering the names of some of the persons referred to, or replacing those names by initials. This revised text was published in twelve volumes, the first two in 1826, the third and fourth in 1828, the fifth to the eighth in 1832, and the ninth to the twelfth in 1837; the first four bearing the imprint of Brockhaus at Leipzig and Ponthieu et Cie at Paris; the next four the imprint of Heideloff et Campé at Paris; and the last four nothing but *À Bruxelles*. The volumes are all uniform, and were all really printed for the firm of Brockhaus. This, however far from representing the real text, is the only authoritative edition, and my references throughout this article will always be to this edition.

In turning over the manuscript at Leipzig, I read some of the suppressed passages, and regretted their suppression; but Herr Brockhaus, the present head of the firm, assured me that they are not really very considerable in number. The damage, however, to the vivacity of the whole narrative, by the persistent alterations of M. Laforgue, is incalculable. I compared many passages, and found scarcely three consecutive sentences untouched. Herr Brockhaus (whose courtesy I cannot sufficiently acknowledge) was kind enough to have a passage copied out for me, which I afterwards read over, and checked word by word. In this passage Casanova says, for instance: *Elle venoit presque tous les jours lui faire une belle visite.* This is altered into: *Cependant chaque jour Thérèse venait lui faire une visite.* Casanova says that some one *avoit, comme de raison, formé le projet d'allier Dieu avec le diable.* This is made to read: *Qui, comme de raison, avait saintement formé le projet d'allier les intérêts du ciel aux œuvres de ce monde.* Casanova tell us that Thérèse would not commit a mortal sin *pour devenir reine du monde*: *pour une couronne*, corrects the indefatigable Laforgue. *Il ne savoit que lui dire* becomes *Dans cet état de perplexité*; and so forth. It must, therefore, be realised that the *Memoirs*, as we have them, are only a kind of pale tracing of the vivid colours of the original.

When Casanova's *Memoirs* were first published, doubts were expressed as to their authenticity, first by Ugo Foscolo (in the *Westminster Review*, 1827), then by Quérard, supposed to be an authority in regard to anonymous and pseudonymous writings, finally by Paul Lacroix, *le bibliophile Jacob*, who suggested, or rather expressed his 'certainty,' that the real author of the *Memoirs* was Stendhal, whose 'mind, character, ideas and style' he seemed to recognise on every page. This theory, as foolish and as unsupported as the Baconian theory of Shakespeare, has been carelessly accepted, or at all events accepted as possible, by many good scholars who have never taken the trouble to look into the matter for themselves. It was finally disproved by a series of articles of Armand Baschet, entitled *Preuves curieuses de l'authenticité des Mémoires de Jacques Casanova de Seingalt*, in *Le Livre*, January, February, April and May, 1881; and these proofs were further corroborated by two articles of Alessandro d'Ancona, entitled *Un Avventuriere del Secolo XVIII.*, in the *Nuova Antologia*, February 1 and August 1, 1882. Baschet had never himself seen the manuscript of the *Memoirs*, but he had learnt all the facts about it from Messrs. Brockhaus, and he had himself examined the numerous papers relating to Casanova in the Venetian archives. A similar examination was made at the Frari at about the same time by the Abbé Fulin; and I myself, in 1894, not knowing at the time that the discovery had been already made, made it over again for myself. There the arrest of Casanova, his imprisonment in the *Piombi*, the exact date of escape, the name of the monk who accompanied him, are all authenticated by documents contained in the *riferte* of the Inquisition of State; there are the bills for the repairs of the roof and walls of the cell from which he escaped; there are the reports of the spies on whose information he was arrested, for his too dangerous free-spokenness in matters of religion and morality. The same archives contain forty-eight letters of Casanova to the Inquisitors of State, dating from 1763 to 1782, among the *Riferte dei Confidenti*, or reports of secret agents; the earliest asking permission to return to

Venice, the rest giving information in regard to the immoralities of the city, after his return there; all in the same handwriting as the *Memoirs*. Further proof could scarcely be needed, but Baschet has done more than prove the authenticity, he has proved the extraordinary veracity, of the *Memoirs*. F. W. Barthold, in *Die Geschichtlichen Persönlichkeiten in J. Casanova's Memoiren*, 2 vols., 1846, had already examined about a hundred of Casanova's allusions to well-known people, showing the perfect exactitude of all but six or seven, and out of these six or seven inexactitudes ascribing only a single one to the author's intention. Baschet and d'Ancona both carry on what Barthold had begun; other investigators, in France, Italy and Germany, have followed them; and two things are now certain, first, that Casanova himself wrote the *Memoirs* published under his name, though not textually in the precise form in which we have them; and, second, that as their veracity becomes more and more evident as they are confronted with more and more independent witnesses, it is only fair to suppose that they are equally truthful where the facts are such as could only have been known to Casanova himself.

II

For more than two-thirds of a century it has been known that Casanova spent the last fourteen years of his life at Dux, that he wrote his *Memoirs* there, and that he died there. During all this time people have been discussing the authenticity and the truthfulness of the *Memoirs*, they have been searching for information about Casanova in various directions, and yet hardly any one has ever taken the trouble, or obtained the permission, to make a careful examination in precisely the one place where information was most likely to be found. The very existence of the manuscripts at Dux was known only to a few, and to most of these only on hearsay; and thus the singular good fortune was reserved for me, on my visit to Count Waldstein in September 1899, to be the first to discover the most interesting things contained in these manuscripts. M. Octave Uzanne, though he had not himself visited Dux, had indeed procured copies of some of the manuscripts, a few of which were published by him in *Le Livre*, in 1887 and 1889. But with the death of *Le Livre* in 1889 the *Casanova inédit* came to an end, and has never, so far as I know, been continued elsewhere. Beyond the publication of these fragments, nothing has been done with the manuscripts at Dux, nor has an account of them ever been given by any one who has been allowed to examine them.

For five years, ever since I had discovered the documents in the Venetian archives, I had wanted to go to Dux; and in 1899, when I was staying with Count Lützow at Zampach, in Bohemia, I found the way kindly opened for me. Count Waldstein, the present head of the family, with extreme courtesy, put all his manuscripts at my disposal, and invited me to stay with him. Unluckily, he was called away on the morning of the day that I reached Dux. He had left everything ready for me, and I was shown over the castle by a friend of his, Dr. Kittel, whose courtesy I should like also to acknowledge. After a hurried visit to the castle we started on the long drive to Oberleutensdorf, a smaller Schloss near Komotau, where the Waldstein family was then staying. The air was sharp and bracing; the two Russian horses flew like the wind; I was whirled along in an unfamiliar darkness, through a strange country, black with coal mines, through dark pine woods, where a wild peasantry dwelt in little mining towns. Here and there, a few men and women passed us on the road, in their Sunday finery; then a long space of silence, and we were in the open country, galloping between broad fields; and always in a haze of lovely hills, which I saw more distinctly as we drove back next morning.

The return to Dux was like a triumphal entry, as we dashed

through the market-place filled with people come for the Monday market, pots and pans and vegetables strewn in heaps all over the ground, on the rough paving stones, up to the great gateway of the castle, leaving but just room for us to drive through their midst. I had the sensation of an enormous building: all Bohemian castles are big, but this one was like a royal palace. Set there in the midst of the town, after the Bohemian fashion, it opens at the back upon great gardens, as if it were in the midst of the country. I walked through room after room, along corridor after corridor; everywhere there were pictures, everywhere portraits of Wallenstein, and battle-scenes in which he led on his troops. The library, which was formed, or at least arranged, by Casanova, and which remains as he left it, contains some 25,000 volumes, some of them of considerable value; one of the most famous books in Bohemian literature, Skála's *History of the Church*, exists in manuscript at Dux, and it is from this manuscript that the two published volumes of it were printed. The library forms part of the Museum, which occupies a ground-floor wing of the castle. The first room is an armoury, in which all kinds of arms are arranged, in a decorative way, covering the ceiling and the walls with strange patterns. The second room contains pottery, collected by Casanova's Waldstein on his Eastern travels. The third room is full of curious mechanical toys, and cabinets, and carvings in ivory. Finally, we come to the library, contained in the two innermost rooms. The book-shelves are painted white, and reach to the low-vaulted ceilings, which are white-washed. At the end of a bookcase, in the corner of one of the windows, hangs a fine engraved portrait of Casanova.

After I had been all over the castle, so long Casanova's home, I was taken to Count Waldstein's study, and left there with the manuscripts. I found six huge cardboard cases, large enough to contain foolscap paper, lettered on the back: *Gräfl. Waldstein-Wartenberg'sches Real Fideicommiss. Dux-Oberleutensdorf: Handschriftlicher Nachlass Casanova*. The cases were arranged so as to stand like books; they opened at the side; and on opening them, one after another, I found series after series of manuscripts roughly thrown together, after some pretence at arrangement, and lettered with a very generalised description of contents. The greater part of the manuscripts were in Casanova's handwriting, which I could see gradually beginning to get shaky with years. Most were written in French, a certain number in Italian. The beginning of a catalogue in the library, though said to be by him, was not in his handwriting. Perhaps it was taken down at his dictation. There were also some copies of Italian and Latin poems not written by him. Then there were many big bundles of letters addressed to him, dating over more than thirty years. Almost all the rest was in his own handwriting.

I came first upon the smaller manuscripts, among which I found, jumbled together on the same and on separate scraps of paper, washing-bills, accounts, hotel bills, lists of letters written, first drafts of letters with many erasures, notes on books, theological and mathematical notes, sums, Latin quotations, French and Italian verses, with variants, a long list of classical names which have and have not been *francisés*, with reasons for and against; 'what I must wear at Dresden'; headings without anything to follow, such as: 'Reflexions on respiration, on the true cause of youth – the crows'; a new method of winning the lottery at Rome; recipes, among which is a long printed list of perfumes sold at Spa; a newspaper cutting, dated Prague, 25th October 1790, on the thirty-seventh balloon ascent of Blanchard; thanks to some 'noble donor' for the gift of a dog called 'Finette'; a passport for *Monsieur de Casanova, Vénitien, allant d'ici en Hollande*, October 13, 1758 (*Ce Passeport bon pour quinze jours*), together with an order for post-horses, gratis, from Paris to Bordeaux and Bayonne.[1]

Occasionally, one gets a glimpse into his daily life at Dux, as in this note, scribbled on a fragment of paper (here and always I translate the French literally): 'I beg you to tell my servant what the biscuits are that I like to eat, dipped in wine, to fortify my stomach. I believe that they can all be found at Roman's.'

Usually, however, these notes, though often suggested by something closely personal, branch off into more general considerations; or else begin with general considerations, and end with a case in point. Thus, for instance, a fragment of three pages begins: 'A compliment which is only made to gild the pill is a positive impertinence, and Monsieur Bailli is nothing but a charlatan; the monarch ought to have spit in his face, but the monarch trembled with fear.' A manuscript entitled *Essai d'Égoïsme*, dated, 'Dux, this 27th June, 1769,' contains, in the midst of various reflections, an offer to let his *appartement* in return for enough money to 'tranquillise for six months two Jew creditors at Prague.' Another manuscript is headed 'Pride and Folly,' and begins with a long series of antitheses, such as: 'All fools are not proud, and all proud men are fools. Many fools are happy, all proud men are unhappy.' On the same sheet follows this instance or application:

> Whether it is possible to compose a Latin distich of the greatest beauty without knowing either the Latin language or prosody. We must examine the possibility and the impossibility, and afterwards see who is the man who says he is the author of the distich, for there are extraordinary people in the world. My brother, in short, ought to have composed the distich, because he says so, and because he confided it to me tête-à-tête. I had, it is true, difficulty in believing him; but what is one to do? Either one must believe, or suppose him capable of telling a lie which could only be told by a fool; and that is impossible, for all Europe knows that my brother is not a fool.

Here, as so often in these manuscripts, we seem to see Casanova thinking on paper. He uses scraps of paper (sometimes the blank page of a letter, on the other side of which we see the address) as a kind of informal diary; and it is characteristic of him, of the man of infinitely curious mind, which this adventurer really was, that there are so few merely personal notes among these casual jottings. Often, they are purely abstract; at times, metaphysical *jeux d'esprit*, like the sheet of fourteen 'Different Wagers,' which begins:

I wager that it is not true that a man who weighs a hundred pounds will weigh more if you kill him. I wager that if there is any difference, he will weigh less. I wager that diamond powder has not sufficient force to kill a man.

Side by side with these fanciful excursions into science, come more serious ones, as in the note on Algebra, which traces its progress since the year 1494, before which 'it had only arrived at the solution of problems of the second degree, inclusive.' A scrap of paper tells us that Casanova 'did not like regular towns.' 'I like,' he says, 'Venice, Rome, Florence, Milan, Constantinople, Genoa.' Then he becomes abstract and inquisitive again, and writes two pages, full of curious, out-of-the-way learning, on the name of Paradise:

> The name of Paradise is a name in Genesis which indicates a place of pleasure (*lieu voluptueux*): this term is Persian. This place of pleasure was made by God before he had created man.

It may be remembered that Casanova quarrelled with Voltaire, because Voltaire had told him frankly that his translation of *L'Écossaise* was a bad translation. It is piquant to read another note written in this style of righteous indignation:

> Voltaire, the hardy Voltaire, whose pen is without bit or bridle; Voltaire, who devoured the Bible, and ridiculed our dogmas, doubts, and after having made proselytes to impiety, is not ashamed, being reduced to the extremity of life, to ask for the sacraments, and to cover his body with more relics than St. Louis had at Amboise.

Here is an argument more in keeping with the tone of the *Memoirs*:

> A girl who is pretty and good, and as virtuous as you please, ought not to take it ill that a man, carried away by her charms, should set himself to the task of making their conquest. If this man cannot please her by any means, even if his passion be criminal, she ought never to

take offence at it, nor treat him unkindly; she ought to be gentle, and pity him, if she does not love him, and think it enough to keep invincibly hold upon her own duty.

Occasionally he touches upon æsthetical matters, as in a fragment which begins with liberal definition of beauty:

Harmony makes beauty, says M. de S. P. (Bernardin de St. Pierre), but the definition is too short, if he thinks he has said everything. Here is mine. Remember that the subject is metaphysical. An object really beautiful ought to seem beautiful to all whose eyes fall upon it. That is all; there is nothing more to be said.

At times we have an anecdote and its commentary, perhaps jotted down for use in that latter part of the *Memoirs* which was never written, or which has been lost. Here is a single sheet, dated 'this 2nd September, 1791,' and headed *Souvenir*:

The Prince de Rosenberg said to me, as we went down stairs, that Madame de Rosenberg was dead, and asked me if the Comte de Waldstein had in the library the illustration of the Villa d'Altichiero, which the Emperor had asked for in vain at the city library of Prague, and when I answered 'yes,' he gave an equivocal laugh. A moment afterwards, he asked me if he might tell the Emperor. 'Why not, monseigneur? It is not a secret.' 'Is His Majesty coming to Dux?' 'If he goes to Oberlaitensdorf (*sic*) he will go to Dux, too; and he may ask you for it, for there is a monument there which relates to him when he was Grand Duke.' 'In that case, His Majesty can also see my critical remarks on the Egyptian prints.'

The Emperor asked me this morning, 6th October, how I employed my time at Dux, and I told him that I was making an Italian anthology. 'You have all the Italians, then?' 'All, sire.' See what a lie leads to. If I had not lied in saying that I was making an anthology, I should not have found myself obliged to lie again in saying that we have all the Italian poets. If the Emperor comes to Dux, I shall kill myself.

'They say that this Dux is a delightful spot,' says Casanova in one of the most personal of his notes, 'and I see that it might be for many; but not for me, for what delights me in my old age is independent of the place which I inhabit. When I do not sleep I dream, and when I am tired of dreaming I blacken paper, then I read, and most often reject all that my pen has vomited.' Here we see him blackening paper, on every occasion, and for every purpose. In one bundle I found an unfinished story about Roland, and some adventure with women in a cave; then a 'Meditation on arising from sleep, 19th May 1789'; then a 'Short Reflection of a Philosopher who finds himself thinking of procuring his own death. At Dux, on getting out of bed on 13th October 1793, day dedicated to St. Lucy, memorable in my too long life.' A big budget, containing cryptograms, is headed 'Grammatical Lottery'; and there is the title-page of a treatise on *The Duplication of the Hexahedron, demonstrated geometrically to all the Universities and all the Academies of Europe.*[2] There are innumerable verses, French and Italian, in all stages, occasionally attaining the finality of these lines, which appear in half a dozen tentative forms:

> *Sans mystère point de plaisirs,*
> *Sans silence point de mystère.*
> *Charme divin de mes loisirs,*
> *Solitude! que tu m'es chère!*

Then there are a number of more or less complete manuscripts of some extent. There is the manuscript of the translation of Homer's *Iliad, in ottava rima* (published in Venice, 1775-8); of the *Histoire de Venise*, of the *Icosameron*, a curious book published in 1787, purporting to be 'translated from English,' but really an original work of Casanova; *Philocalies sur les Sottises des Mortels*, a long manuscript never published; the sketch and beginning of *Le Polémarque, ou la Calomnie démasquée par la présence d'esprit. Tragicomédie en trois actes, composée à Dux dans le mois de Juin de l'Année, 1791*, which recurs again under the form of the *Polémoscopé: La Lorgnette menteuse ou la Calomnie démasquée*, acted before the Princess de Ligne, at her château at Teplitz, 1791. There is a treatise in Italian, *Delle Passioni*; there are long dialogues, such as *Le Philosophe et le Théologien*, and *Rêve: Dieu-*

Moi; there is the *Songe d'un Quart d'Heure*, divided into minutes; there is the very lengthy criticism of *Bernardin de Saint-Pierre*; there is the *Confutation d'une Censure indiscrète qu'on lit dans la Gazette de Iéna, 19 Juin 1789*; with another large manuscript, unfortunately imperfect, first called *L'Insulte*, and then *Placet au Public*, dated 'Dux, this 2nd March, 1790,' referring to the same criticism on the *Icosameron* and the *Fuite des Prisons*. *L'Histoire de ma Fuite des Prisons de la République de Venise, qu'on appelle les Plombs*, which is the first draft of the most famous part of the *Memoirs*, was published at Leipzig in 1788; and, having read it in the Marcian Library at Venice, I am not surprised to learn from this indignant document that it was printed 'under the care of a young Swiss, who had the talent to commit a hundred faults of orthography.'

III

We come now to the documents directly relating to the *Memoirs*, and among these are several attempts at a preface, in which we see the actual preface coming gradually into form. One is entitled *Casanova au Lecteur*, another *Histoire de mon Existence*, and a third *Preface*. There is also a brief and characteristic *Précis de ma vie*, dated November 17, 1797. Some of these have been printed in *Le Livre*, 1887. But by far the most important manuscript that I discovered, one which, apparently, I am the first to discover, is a manuscript entitled *Extrait du Chapitre 4 et 5*. It is written on paper similar to that on which the *Memoirs* are written; the pages are numbered 104-148; and though it is described as *Extrait*, it seems to contain, at all events, the greater part of the missing chapters to which I have already referred, Chapters iv. and v. of the last volume of the *Memoirs*. In this manuscript we find Armelline and

Scolastica, whose story is interrupted by the abrupt ending of Chapter iii.; we find Mariuccia of Vol. vii., Chapter ix., who married a hairdresser; and we find also Jaconine, whom Casanova recognises as his daughter, 'much prettier than Sophia, the daughter of Thérèse Pompeati, whom I had left at London.'[3] It is curious that this very important manuscript, which supplies the one missing link in the *Memoirs*, should never have been discovered by any of the few people who have had the opportunity of looking over the Dux manuscripts. I am inclined to explain it by the fact that the case in which I found this manuscript contains some papers not relating to Casanova. Probably, those who looked into this case looked no further. I have told Herr Brockhaus of my discovery, and I hope to see Chapters iv. and v. in their places when the long-looked-for edition of the complete text is at length given to the world.

Another manuscript which I found tells with great piquancy the whole story of the Abbé de Brosses' ointment, the curing of the Princess de Conti's pimples, and the birth of the Duc de Montpensier, which is told very briefly, and with much less point, in the *Memoirs* (vol. iii., p. 327). Readers of the *Memoirs* will remember the duel at Warsaw with Count Branicki in 1766 (vol. x., pp. 274-320), an affair which attracted a good deal of attention at the time, and of which there is an account in a letter from the Abbé Taruffi to the dramatist, Francesco Albergati, dated Warsaw, March 19, 1766, quoted in Ernesto Masi's *Life of Albergati*, Bologna, 1878. A manuscript at Dux in Casanova's handwriting gives an account of this duel in the third person; it is entitled, *Description de l'affaire arrivée à Varsovie le 5 Mars, 1766.* D'Ancona, in the *Nuova Antologia* (vol. lxvii., p. 412), referring to the Abbé Taruffi's account, mentions what he considers to be a slight discrepancy: that Taruffi refers to the *danseuse*, about whom the duel was fought, as La Casacci, while Casanova refers to her as La Catai. In this manuscript Casanova always refers to her as La Casacci; La Catai is evidently one of M. Laforgue's arbitrary alterations of the text.

In turning over another manuscript, I was caught by the name Charpillon, which every reader of the *Memoirs* will remember as the name of the harpy by whom Casanova suffered so much in London, in 1763-4. This manuscript begins by saying: 'I have been in London for six months and have been to see them (that is, the mother and daughter) in their own house,' where he finds nothing but 'swindlers, who cause all who go there to lose their money in gambling.' This manuscript adds some details to the story told in the ninth and tenth volumes of the *Memoirs*, and refers to the meeting with the Charpillons four and a half years before, described in Volume v., pages 482-485. It is written in a tone of great indignation. Elsewhere, I found a letter written by Casanova, but not signed, referring to an anonymous letter which he had received in reference to the Charpillons, and ending: 'My handwriting is known.' It was not until the last that I came upon great bundles of letters addressed to Casanova, and so carefully preserved that little scraps of paper, on which postscripts are written, are still in their places. One still sees the seals on the backs of many of the letters, on paper which has slightly yellowed with age, leaving the ink, however, almost always fresh. They come from Venice, Paris, Rome, Prague, Bayreuth, The Hague, Genoa, Fiume, Trieste, etc., and are addressed to as many places, often *poste restante*. Many are letters from women, some in beautiful handwriting, on thick paper; others on scraps of paper, in painful hands, ill-spelt. A Countess writes pitifully, imploring help; one protests her love, in spite of the 'many chagrins' he has caused her; another asks 'how they are to live together'; another laments that a report has gone about that she is secretly living with him, which may harm *his* reputation. Some are in French, more in Italian. *Mon cher Giacometto*, writes one woman, in French; *Carissimo e Amatissimo*, writes another, in Italian. These letters from women are in some confusion, and are in need of a good deal of sorting over and rearranging before their full extent can be realised. Thus I found letters in the same handwriting separated by letters in other handwritings; many are unsigned, or signed only by a single initial; many are undated, or dated only with the day of the week or month. There are a great many letters, dating from 1779 to 1786, signed 'Francesca Buschini,' a name which I cannot identify; they are written in Italian, and one of them begins: *Unico Mio vero Amico* ('my only true friend'). Others are signed 'Virginia B.'; one of these is dated, 'Forli, October 15, 1773.' There is also a 'Theresa B.,' who writes from Genoa. I was at first unable to identify the writer of a whole series of letters in French, very affectionate and intimate letters, usually unsigned, occasionally signed 'B.' She calls herself *votre petite amie*; or she ends with a half-smiling, half-reproachful 'good-night, and sleep better than I.' In one letter, sent from Paris in 1759, she writes: 'Never believe me, but when I tell you that I love you, and that I shall love you always.' In another letter, ill-spelt, as her letters often are, she writes: 'Be assured that evil tongues, vapours, calumny, nothing can change my heart, which is yours entirely, and has no will to change its master.' Now, it seems to me that these letters must be from Manon Baletti, and that they are the letters referred to in the sixth volume of the *Memoirs*. We read there (page 60) how on Christmas Day, 1759, Casanova receives a letter from Manon in Paris, announcing her marriage with 'M. Blondel, architect to the King, and member of his Academy'; she returns him his letters, and begs him to return hers, or burn them. Instead of doing so he allows Esther to read them, intending to burn them afterwards. Esther begs to be allowed to keep the letters, promising to 'preserve them religiously all her life.' 'These letters,' he says, 'numbered more than two hundred, and the shortest were of four pages.' Certainly there are not two hundred of them at Dux, but it seems to me highly probable that Casanova made a final selection from Manon's letters, and that it is these which I have found.

But, however this may be, I was fortunate enough to find the set of letters which I was most anxious to find: the letters from Henriette, whose loss every writer on Casanova has lamented. Henriette, it will be remembered, makes her first appearance at

Cesena, in the year 1748; after their meeting at Geneva, she reappears, romantically *à propos*, twenty-two years later, at Aix in Provence; and she writes to Casanova proposing *un commerce épistolaire*, asking him what he has done since his escape from prison, and promising to do her best to tell him all that has happened to her during the long interval. After quoting her letter, he adds: 'I replied to her, accepting the correspondence that she offered me, and telling her briefly all my vicissitudes. She related to me in turn, in some forty letters, all the history of her life. If she dies before me, I shall add these letters to these *Memoirs*; but to-day she is still alive, and always happy, though now old.' It has never been known what became of these letters, and why they were not added to the *Memoirs*. I have found a great quantity of them, some signed with her married name in full, 'Henriette de Schnetzmann,' and I am inclined to think that she survived Casanova, for one of the letters is dated Bayreuth, 1798, the year of Casanova's death. They are remarkably charming, written with a mixture of piquancy and distinction; and I will quote the characteristic beginning and end of the last letter I was able to find. It begins: 'No, it is impossible to be sulky with you!' and ends: 'If I become vicious, it is you, my Mentor, who make me so, and I cast my sins upon you. Even if I were damned I should still be your most devoted friend, Henriette de Schnetzmann.' Casanova was twenty-three when he met Henriette; now, herself an old woman, she writes to him when he is seventy-three, as if the fifty years that had passed were blotted out in the faithful affection of her memory. How many more discreet and less changing lovers have had the quality of constancy in change, to which this life-long correspondence bears witness? Does it not suggest a view of Casanova not quite the view of all the world? To me it shows the real man, who perhaps of all others best understood what Shelley meant when he said:

True love in this differs from gold or clay,
That to divide is not to take away.

But, though the letters from women naturally interested me the most, they were only a certain proportion of the great mass of correspondence which I turned over. There were letters from Carlo Angiolini, who was afterwards to bring the manuscript of the *Memoirs* to Brockhaus; from Balbi, the monk with whom Casanova escaped from the *Piombi*; from the Marquis Albergati, playwright, actor, and eccentric, of whom there is some account in the *Memoirs*; from the Marquis Mosca, 'a distinguished man of letters whom I was anxious to see,' Casanova tells us in the same volume in which he describes his visit to the Moscas at Pesaro; from Zulian, brother of the Duchess of Fiano; from Richard Lorrain, *bel homme, ayant de l'esprit, le ton et le goût de la bonne société*, who came to settle at Gorizia in 1773, while Casanova was there; from the Procurator Morosini, whom he speaks of in the *Memoirs* as his 'protector,' and as one of those through whom he obtained permission to return to Venice. His other 'protector,' the *avogador* Zaguri, had, says Casanova, 'since the affair of the Marquis Albergati, carried on a most interesting correspondence with me'; and in fact I found a bundle of no less than a hundred and thirty-eight letters from him, dating from 1784 to 1798. Another bundle contains one hundred and seventy-two letters from Count Lamberg. In the *Memoirs* Casanova says, referring to his visit to Augsburg at the end of 1761:

I used to spend my evenings in a very agreeable manner at the house of Count Max de Lamberg, who resided at the court of the Prince-Bishop with the title of Grand Marshal. What particularly attached me to Count Lamberg was his literary talent. A first-rate scholar, learned to a degree, he has published several much esteemed works. I carried on an exchange of letters with him which ended only with his death four years ago in 1792.

Casanova tells us that, at his second visit to Augsburg in the early part of 1767, he 'supped with Count Lamberg two or three times a week,' during the four months he was there. It is with this year that the letters I have found begin: they end with the year of his death, 1792. In his *Mémorial d'un Mondain* Lamberg refers to Casanova as 'a man known in literature, a man of profound knowledge.' In the first edition of 1774, he laments that 'a man such as M. de S. Galt' should not yet have been taken back into favour by the Venetian government, and in the second edition, 1775, rejoices over Casanova's return to Venice. Then there are letters from Da Ponte, who tells the story of Casanova's curious relations with Mme. d'Urfé, in his *Memorie scritte da esso*, 1829; from Pittoni, Bono, and others mentioned in different parts of the *Memoirs*, and from some dozen others who are not mentioned in them. The only letters in the whole collection that have been published are those from the Prince de Ligne and from Count Koenig.

IV

Casanova tells us in his *Memoirs* that, during his later years at Dux, he had only been able to 'hinder black melancholy from devouring his poor existence, or sending him out of his mind,' by writing ten or twelve hours a day. The copious manuscripts at Dux show us how persistently he was at work on a singular variety of subjects, in addition to the *Memoirs*, and to the various books which he published during those years. We see him jotting down everything that own amusement, and certainly without any thought of publication; engaging in learned controversies, writing treatises on abstruse mathematical problems, composing comedies to be acted before Count Waldstein's neighbours, practising verse-writing in two languages, indeed with more patience than success, writing philosophical dialogues in which God and himself are the speakers, and keeping up an extensive correspondence, both with distinguished men and with delightful women. His mental activity, up to the age of seventy-three, is as prodigious as the activity which he had expended in living a multiform and incalculable life. As in life everything living had interested him, so in his retirement from life every idea makes its separate appeal to him; and he welcomes ideas with the same impartiality with which he had welcomed adventures. Passion has intellectualised itself, and remains not less passionate. He wishes to do everything, to compete with every one; and it is only after having spent seven years in heaping up miscellaneous learning, and exercising his faculties in many directions, that he turns to look back over his own past life, and to live it over again in memory, as he writes down the narrative of what had interested him most in it. 'I write in the hope that my history will never see the broad daylight of publication,' he tells us, scarcely meaning it, we may be sure, even in the moment of hesitancy which may naturally come to him. But if ever a book was written for the pleasure of writing it, it was this one; and an autobiography written for oneself is not likely to be anything but frank.

'Truth is the only God I have ever adored,' he tells us: and we now know how truthful he was in saying so. I have only summarised in this article the most important confirmations of his exact accuracy in facts and dates; the number could be extended indefinitely. In the manuscripts we find innumerable further confirmations; and their chief value as testimony is that they tell us nothing which we should not have already known, if we had merely taken Casanova at his word. But it is not always easy to take people at their own word, when they are writing about themselves; and the world has been very loth to believe in Casanova as he represents himself. It has been specially loth to believe that he is telling the truth when he tells us about his adventures with women. But the letters contained among these manuscripts show us the women of Casanova writing to him with all the fervour and all the fidelity which he attributes to them; and they show him to us in the character of as fervid and faithful a lover. In every fact, every detail, and in the whole mental impression which they convey, these manuscripts bring before us the Casanova of the *Memoirs*. As I seemed to come upon Casanova at home, it was as if I came upon an old friend, already perfectly known to me, before I had made my pilgrimage to Dux.

1902.

FOOTNOTES

1. See the account of this visit to Holland, and the reference to taking a passport, *Memoirs*, v. 238.
2. See Charles Henry, *Les Connaissances Mathématiques de Casanova.* Rome 1883.
3. See *Memoirs*, ix. 272, *et seq.*

JOHN DONNE

I

Biography as a fine art can go no further than Walton's *Life and Death of Dr. Donne*. From the 'good and virtuous parents' of the first line to the 'small quantity of Christian dust' of the last, every word is the touch of a cunning brush painting a picture. The picture lives, and with so vivid and gracious a life that it imposes itself upon us as the portrait of a real man, faithfully copied from the man as he lived. But that is precisely the art of the painter. Walton's picture is so beautiful because everything in it is sacrificed to beauty; because it is a convention, a picture in which life is treated almost as theme for music. And so there remains an opportunity, even after this masterpiece, for a life of Donne which shall make no pretence to harmonise a sometimes discordant existence, or indeed to produce, properly speaking, a piece of art at all; but which shall be faithful to the document, a piece of history. Such a book has now been written by Mr. Gosse, in his *Life and Letters of John Donne, Dean of St. Paul's*. It is perhaps the most solid and serious contribution which Mr. Gosse has made to English literature, and we may well believe that it will remain the final authority on so interesting and so difficult a subject. For the first time, in the light of this clear analysis, and of these carefully arranged letters, we are able, if not indeed to see Donne as he really was, at all events to form our own opinion about every action of his life. This is one of the merits of Mr. Gosse's book; he has collected his documents, and he has given them to us as they are, guiding us adroitly along the course of the life which they illustrate, but not allowing himself to dogmatise on what must still remain conjectural. And he has given us a series of reproductions of portraits, of the highest importance in the study of one who is not merely a difficult poet, but a very ambiguous human being. They begin with the eager, attractive, somewhat homely youth of eighteen, grasping the hilt of his sword so tightly that his knuckles start out from the thin covering of flesh; passing into the mature Donne as we know him, the lean, humorous, large-browed, courtly thinker, with his large intent eyes, a cloak folded elegantly about his uncovered throat, or the ruff tightening about his carefully trimmed beard; and ending with the ghastly emblem set as a frontispiece to *Death's Duel*, the dying man wrapped already in his shroud, which gathers into folds above his head, as if tied together like the mouth of a sack, while the sunken cheeks and hollow closed eyelids are mocked by the shapely moustache, brushed upwards from the lips. In the beautiful and fanciful monument in St. Paul's done after the drawing from which this frontispiece was engraved, there is less ghastliness and a more harmonious beauty in the brave attitude of a man who dresses for death as he would dress for Court, wearing the last livery with an almost foppish sense of propriety. Between them these portraits tell much, and Mr. Gosse, in his narrative, tells us everything else that there is to tell, much of it for the first time; and the distinguished and saintly person of Walton's narrative, so simple, so easily explicable, becomes more complex at every moment, as fresh light makes the darkness more and more visible. At the end we seem to have become singularly intimate with a fascinating and puzzling creature, whom each of us may try to understand after his fashion, as we try to understand the real secrets of the character of our friends.

Donne's mind, then, if I may make my own attempt to

understand him, was the mind of the dialectician, of the intellectual adventurer; he is a poet almost by accident, or at least for reasons with which art in the abstract has but little to do. He writes verse, first of all, because he has observed keenly, and because it pleases the pride of his intellect to satirise the pretensions of humanity. Then it is the flesh which speaks in his verse, the curiosity of woman, which he has explored in the same spirit of adventure; then passion, making a slave of him for love's sake, and turning at last to the slave's hatred; finally, religion, taken up with the same intellectual interest, the same subtle indifference, and, in its turn, passing also into passionate reality. A few poems are inspired in him by what he has seen in remote countries; some are marriage songs and funeral elegies, written for friendship or for money. But he writes nothing 'out of his own head,' as we say; nothing lightly, or, it would seem, easily; nothing for the song's sake. He speaks, in a letter, of 'descending to print anything in verse'; and it is certain that he was never completely absorbed by his own poetry, or at all careful to measure his achievements against those of others. He took his own poems very seriously, he worked upon them with the whole force of his intellect; but to himself, even before he became a divine, he was something more than a poet. Poetry was but one means of expressing the many-sided activity of his mind and temperament. Prose was another, preaching another; travel and contact with great events and persons scarcely less important to him, in the building up of himself.

And he was interested in everything. At one moment he is setting himself to study Oriental languages, a singularly difficult task in those days. Both in poetry and divinity he has more Spanish than English books in his library. Scientific and technical terms are constantly found in his verse, where we should least expect them, where indeed they are least welcome. In *Ignatius – his Conclave* he speaks with learned enthusiasm of Copernicus and Tycho Brahe, and of his own immediate contemporaries, then but just become famous, Galileo ('who of late hath summoned the other worlds, the stars, to come nearer to him, and to give an account of themselves') and Kepler ('who hath received it into his care, that no new thing should be done in heaven without his knowledge'). He rebukes himself for his abandonment to 'the worst voluptuousness, which is an hydroptic, immoderate desire of human learning and languages.' At twenty-three he was a soldier against Spain under Raleigh, and went on the 'Islands Voyage'; later on, at different periods, he travelled over many parts of the Continent, with rich patrons or on diplomatic offices. Born a Catholic, he became a Protestant, deliberately enough; wrote books on controversial subjects, agains his old party, before he had taken orders in the Church of England; besides a strange, morbid speculation on the innocence of suicide. He used his lawyer's training for dubious enough purposes, advising the Earl of Somerset in the dark business of his divorce and re-marriage. And, in a mournful pause in the midst of many harrowing concerns, he writes to a friend: 'When I must shipwreck, I would fain do it in a sea where mine own impotency might have some excuse; not in a sullen, weedy lake, where I could not have so much as exercise for my swimming. Therefore I would fain do something, but that I cannot tell what is no wonder.' 'Though I be in such a planetary and erratic fortune that I can do nothing constantly,' he confesses later in the same letter.

No doubt some of this feverish activity, this uncertainty of aim, was a matter of actual physical health. It is uncertain at what time the wasting disease, of which he died, first settled upon him; but he seems to have been always somewhat sickly of body, and with just that at times depressing, at times exciting, malady which tells most upon the whole organisation. That preoccupation with death, which in early life led him to write his *Biathanatos*, with its elaborate apology for suicide, and at the end of his life to prepare so spectacularly for the act of dying, was but one symptom of a morbid state of body and brain and nerves, to which so many of his poems and so many of his letters bear witness. 'Sometimes,' he writes, in a characteristic letter, 'when I find myself transported with jollity and love of company, I hang lead to my heels, and reduce to my thoughts my fortunes, my years, the duties of a man, of a friend, of a husband, of a father, and all the incumbencies of a family; when sadness dejects me, either I countermine it with another sadness, or I kindle squibs about me again, and fly into sportfulness and company.'

At the age of thirty-five he writes from his bed describing every detail of what he frantically calls 'a sickness which I cannot name or describe,' and ends his letter: 'I profess to you truly, that my loathness to give over now, seems to myself an ill sign that I shall write no more.' It was at this time that he wrote the *Biathanatos*, with its explicit declaration in the preface: 'Whensoever any affliction assails me, methinks I have the keys of my prison in mine own hand, and no remedy presents itself so soon to my heart as mine own sword.' Fifteen years later, when one of his most serious illnesses was upon him, and his life in real danger, he notes down all his symptoms as he lies awake night after night, with an extraordinary and, in itself, morbid acuteness. 'I observe the physician with the same diligence as he the disease; I see he fears, and I fear with him; I overtake him, I over-run him in his fear, because he makes his pace slow; I fear the more because he disguises his fear, and I see it with the more sharpness because he would not have me see it.' As he lies in bed, he realises 'I am mine own ghost, and rather affright my beholders than instruct them. They conceive the worst of me now, and yet fear worse; they give me for dead now, and yet wonder how I do when they wake at midnight, and ask how I do to-morrow. Miserable and inhuman posture, where I must practise my lying in the grave by lying still.' This preying upon itself of the brain is but one significant indication of a temperament, neurotic enough indeed, but in which the neurosis is still that of the curious observer, the intellectual casuist, rather than of the artist. A wonderful piece of self-analysis, worthy of St. Augustine, which occurs in one of his funeral sermons, gives poignant expression to what must doubtless have been a common condition of so sensitive a brain. 'I throw myself down in my chamber, and I call in and invite God and His angels together; and when they are there, I neglect God and his angels for the noise of a fly, for the rattling of a coach, for the whining of a door; I talk on in the same posture of prayer, eyes lifted up, knees bowed down, as though I prayed to God; and if God should ask me when I last thought of God in that prayer, I cannot tell. Sometimes I find that I forgot what I was about; But when I began to forget it, I cannot tell. A memory of yesterday's pleasures, a fear of to-morrow's dangers, a straw under my knee, a noise in mine ear, a chimera in my brain, troubles me in my prayer.' It is this brain, turned inward upon itself, and darting out on every side in purely random excursions, that was responsible, I cannot doubt, for all the contradictions of a career in which the inner logic is not at first apparent.

Donne's career divides itself sharply into three parts: his youth, when we see him a soldier, a traveller, a lover, a poet, unrestrained in all the passionate adventures of youth; then a middle period, in which he is a lawyer and a theologian, seeking knowledge and worldly advancement, without any too restraining scruple as to the means which come to his hand; and then a last stage of saintly living and dying. What then is the link between these successive periods, the principle of development, the real Donne in short? 'He was none of these, or all of these, or more,' says Mr. Gosse. But, surely, he was indeed all of these, and his individuality precisely the growth from one stage to another, the subtle intelligence being always there, working vividly, but in each period working in a different direction. 'I would fain do something, but that I cannot tell what is no wonder.' Everything in Donne seems to me to explain itself in that fundamental uncertainty of aim, and his uncertainty of aim partly by a morbid physical condition. He searches, nothing satisfies him, tries everything, in vain; finding satisfaction at last in the Church, as in a haven of rest. Always it is the curious, insatiable brain searching. And he is always wretchedly aware that he 'can do nothing constantly.'

His three periods, then, are three stages in the search after a way to walk in, something worthy of himself to do. Thus, of his one printed collection of verse he writes: 'Of my *Anniversaries*, the fault which I acknowledge in myself is to have descended to print anything in verse, which, though it have excuse, even in our times, by example of men, which one would think should as little have done it as I, yet I confess I wonder how I declined to it, and do not pardon myself.' Of his legal studies he writes in the same letter: 'For my purpose of proceeding in the profession of the law, so far as to a title, you may be pleased to correct that imagination where you find it. I ever thought the study of it my best entertainment and pastime, but I have no ambition nor design upon the style.' Until he accepts religion, with all its limitations and encouragements, he has not even sure landmarks on his way. So speculative a brain, able to prove, and proving for its own uneasy satisfaction, that even suicide is 'not so naturally sin, that it may never be otherwise,' could allow itself to be guided by no fixed rules; and to a brain so abstract, conduct must always have seemed of less importance than it does to most other people, and especially conduct which is argument, like the demonstrations on behalf of what seems, on the face of it, a somewhat iniquitous divorce and re-marriage, or like those unmeasured eulogies, both of this 'blest pair of swans,' and of the dead child of a rich father. He admits, in one of his letters, that in his elegies, 'I did best when I had least truth for my subjects'; and of the *Anniversaries* in honour of little Mistress Drury, 'But for the other part of the imputation of having said so much, my defence is, that my purpose was to say as well as I could; for since I never saw the gentlewoman, I cannot be understood to have bound myself to have spoken the just truth.' He is always the casuist, always mentally impartial in the face of a moral problem, reserving judgment on matters which, after all, seem to him remote from an unimpassioned contemplation of things; until that moment of crisis comes, long after he has become a clergyman, when the death of his wife changed the world for him, and he became, in the words of Walton, 'crucified to the world, and all those vanities, those imaginary pleasures, that are daily acted on that restless stage; and they were as perfectly crucified to him.' From that time to the end of his life he had found what he had all the while been seeking: rest for the restlessness of his mind, in a meditation upon the divine nature; occupation, in being 'ambassador of God,' through the pulpit; himself, as it seemed to him, at his fullest and noblest. It was himself, really, that he had been seeking all the time, conscious at least of that in all the deviations of the way; himself, the ultimate of his curiosities.

II

And yet, what remains to us out of this life of many purposes, which had found an end satisfying to itself in the Deanery of St. Paul's, is simply a bundle of manuscript verses, which the writer could bring himself neither to print nor to destroy. His first satire speaks contemptuously of 'giddy fantastic poets,' and, when he allowed himself to write poetry, he was resolved to do something different from what anybody had ever done before, not so much from the artist's instinctive desire of originality, as from a kind of haughty, yet really bourgeois, desire to be indebted to nobody. With what care he wrote is confessed in a passage of one of his letters, where, speaking of a sermon, he says: 'For, as Cardinal Cusanus wrote a book, *Cribratio Alchorani*, I have cribrated, and re-cribrated, and post-cribrated the sermon, and must necessarily say, the King, who hath let fall his eye upon some of my poems, never saw, of mine, a hand, or an eye, or an affection, set down with so much study and diligence, and labour of syllables, as in this sermon I expressed those two points.' But he thought there were other things more important than being a poet, and this very labour of his was partly a sign of it. 'He began,' says Mr. Gosse with truth, 'as if poetry had never been written before.'

To the people of his time, to those who came immediately after him, he was the restorer of English poetry.

> The Muses' garden, with pedantic weeds
> O'erspread, was purged by thee,

says Carew, in those memorial verses in which the famous lines occur:

> Here lies a king that ruled as he thought fit
> The universal monarchy of wit.

Shakespeare was living, remember, and it was Elizabethan poetry that Donne set himself to correct. He began with metre, and invented a system of prosody which has many merits, and would have had more in less arbitrary hands. 'Donne, for not keeping of accent, deserved hanging,' said Ben Jonson, who was nevertheless his friend and admirer. And yet, if one will but read him always for the sense, for the natural emphasis of what he has to say, there are few lines which will not come out in at all events the way that he meant them to be delivered. The way he meant them to be delivered is not always as beautiful as it is expressive. Donne would be original at all costs, preferring himself to his art. He treated poetry as Æsop's master treated his slave, and broke what he could not bend.

But Donne's novelty of metre is only a part of his too deliberate novelty as a poet. As Mr. Gosse has pointed out, with a self-evident truth which has apparently waited for him to say it, Donne's real position in regard to the poetry of his time was that of a realistic writer, who makes a clean sweep of tradition, and puts everything down in the most modern words and with the help of the most trivial actual images.

To what a cumbersome unwieldiness,
And burdensome corpulence my love hath grown,

he will begin a poem on *Love's Diet*. Of love, as the master of
hearts, he declares seriously:

He swallows us and never chaws;
By him, as by chain'd shot, whole ranks do die;
He is the tyrant pike, our hearts the fry.

And, in his unwise insistence that every metaphor shall be
absolutely new, he drags medical and alchemical and legal
properties into verse really full of personal passion, producing at
times poetry which is a kind of disease of the intellect, a sick
offshoot of science. Like most poets of powerful individuality,
Donne lost precisely where he gained. That cumulative and
crowding and sweeping intellect which builds up his greatest
poems into miniature Escurials of poetry, mountainous and four-
square to all the winds of the world, 'purges' too often the flowers
as well as the weeds out of 'the Muses' garden.' To write poetry as
if it had never been written before is to attempt what the greatest
poets never attempted. There are only two poets in English
literature who thus stand out of the tradition, who are without
ancestors, Donne and Browning. Each seems to have certain
qualities almost greater than the qualities of the greatest; and yet
in each some precipitation of arrogant egoism remains in the
crucible, in which the draught has all but run immortally clear.

Donne's quality of passion is unique in English poetry. It is a
rapture in which the mind is supreme, a reasonable rapture, and
yet carried to a pitch of actual violence. The words themselves
rarely count for much, as they do in Crashaw, for instance, where
words turn giddy at the height of their ascension. The words
mean things, and it is the things that matter. They can be brutal:
'For God's sake, hold your tongue, and let me love!' as if a long,
pre-supposed self-repression gave way suddenly, in an outburst.
'Love, any devil else but you,' he begins, in his abrupt leap to

the heart of the matter. Or else his exaltation will be grave, tranquil, measureless in assurance.

> All kings, and all their favourites,
> All glory of honours, beauties, wits,
> The sun itself, which makes time, as they pass,
> Is elder by a year now than it was
> When thou and I first one another saw.
> All other things to their destruction draw,
> Only our love hath no decay;
> This no to-morrow hath, no yesterday;
> Running, it never runs from us away,
> But truly keeps his first, last, everlasting day.

This lover loves with his whole nature, and so collectedly because reason, in him, is not in conflict with passion, but passion's ally. His senses speak with unparalleled directness, as in those elegies which must remain the model in English of masculine sensual sobriety. He distinguishes the true end of such loving in a forcible, characteristically prosaic image:

> Whoever loves, if he do not propose
> The right true end of love, he's one that goes
> To sea for nothing but to make him sick.

And he exemplifies every motion and the whole pilgrim's progress of physical love, with a deliberate, triumphant, unluxurious explicitness which 'leaves no doubt,' as we say 'of his intentions,' and can be no more than referred to passingly in modern pages. In a series of hate poems, of which I will quote the finest, he gives expression to a whole region of profound human sentiment which has never been expressed, out of Catullus, with such intolerable truth.

> When by thy scorn, O murderess, I am dead,
> And that thou think'st thee free
> From all solicitation from me,
> Then shall my ghost come to thy bed,
> And thee, feign'd vestal, in worse arms shall see:

Then thy sick taper will begin to wink,
And he, whose thou art then, being tired before,
Will, if thou stir, or pinch to wake him, think
Thou call'st for more,
And, in false sleep, will from thee shrink;
And then, poor aspen wretch, neglected thou
Bathed in a cold quicksilver sweat wilt lie
A verier ghost than I.
What I will say, I will not tell thee now,
Lest that preserve thee; and since my love is spent,
I'd rather thou should'st painfully repent,
Than by my threatenings rest still innocent.

Yet it is the same lover, and very evidently the same, who winnows all this earthly passion to a fine, fruitful dust, fit to make bread for angels. Ecstatic reason, passion justifying its intoxication by revealing the mysteries that it has come thus to apprehend, speak in the quintessence of Donne's verse with an exalted simplicity which seems to make a new language for love. It is the simplicity of a perfectly abstract geometrical problem, solved by one to whom the rapture of solution is the blossoming of pure reason. Read the poem called *The Ecstasy*, which seems to anticipate a metaphysical Blake; it is all close reasoning, step by step, and yet is what its title claims for it.

It may be, though I doubt it, that other poets who have written personal verse in English, have known as much of women's hearts and the senses of men, and the interchanges of passionate intercourse between man and woman; but, partly by reason of this very method of saying things, no one has ever rendered so exactly, and with such elaborate subtlety, every mood of the actual passion. It has been done in prose; may one not think of Stendhal, for a certain way he has of turning the whole forces of the mind upon those emotions and sensations which are mostly left to the heat of an unreflective excitement? Donne, as he suffers all the colds and fevers of love, is as much the sufferer and the physician of his disease as we have seen him to be in cases of actual physical sickness. Always detached from himself, even when he is most helplessly the slave of circumstances, he has that frightful faculty of seeing through his own illusions; of having no illusions to the mind, only to the senses. Other poets, with more wisdom towards poetry, give us the beautiful or pathetic results of no matter what creeping or soaring passions. Donne, making a new thing certainly, if not always a thing of beauty, tells us exactly what a man really feels as he makes love to a woman, as he sits beside her husband at table, as he dreams of her in absence, as he scorns himself for loving her, as he hates or despises her for loving him, as he realises all that is stupid in her devotion, and all that is animal in his. 'Nature's lay idiot, I taught thee to love,' he tells her, in a burst of angry contempt, priding himself on his superior craft in the art. And his devotions to her are exquisite, appealing to what is most responsive in woman, beyond those of tenderer poets. A woman cares most for the lover who understands her best, and is least taken in by what it is the method of her tradition to feign. So wearily conscious that she is not the abstract angel of her pretence and of her adorers, she will go far in sheer thankfulness to the man who can see so straight into her heart as to have

> found something like a heart,
> But colours it and corners had;
> It was not good, it was not bad,
> It was entire to none, and few had part.

Donne shows women themselves, in delight, anger, or despair; they know that he finds nothing in the world more interesting, and they much more than forgive him for all the ill he says of them. If women most conscious of their sex were ever to read Donne, they would say, He was a great lover; he understood.

And, in the poems of divine love, there is the same quality of mental emotion as in the poems of human love. Donne adores God reasonably, knowing why he adores Him. He renders thanks point by point, celebrates the heavenly perfections with metaphysical precision, and is no vaguer with God than with woman.

Donne knew what he believed and why he believed, and is carried into no heat or mist as he tells over the recording rosary of his devotions. His *Holy Sonnets* are a kind of argument with God; they tell over, and discuss, and resolve, such perplexities of faith and reason as would really occur to a speculative brain like his. Thought crowds in upon thought, in these tightly packed lines, which but rarely admit a splendour of this kind:

> At the round earth's imagined corners blow
> Your trumpets, angels, and arise, arise
> From death, you numberless infinities
> Of souls, and to your scattered bodies go.

More typical is this too knotted beginning of another sonnet:

> Batter my heart, three-person'd God; for you
> As yet but knock; breathe, shine, and seek to mend;
> That I may rise, and stand, o'erthrow me, and bend
> Your force, to break, blow, burn, and make me new.

Having something very minute and very exact to say, he hates to leave anything out; dreading diffuseness, as he dreads the tame sweetness of an easy melody, he will use only the smallest possible number of words to render his thought; and so, as here, he is too often ingenious rather than felicitous, forgetting that to the poet poetry comes first, and all the rest afterwards.

For the writing of great poetry something more is needed than to be a poet and to have great occasions. Donne was a poet, and he had the passions and the passionate adventures, in body and mind, which make the material for poetry; he was sincere to himself in expressing what he really felt under the burden of strong emotion and sharp sensation. Almost every poem that he wrote is written on a genuine inspiration, a genuine personal inspiration, but most of his poems seem to have been written before that personal inspiration has had time to fuse itself with the poetic inspiration. It is always useful to remember Wordsworth's phrase of 'emotion recollected in tranquillity,' for nothing so well defines that moment of crystallisation in which direct emotion or sensation deviates exquisitely into art. Donne is intent on the passion itself, the thought, the reality; so intent that he is not at the same time, in that half-unconscious way which is the way of the really great poet, equally intent on the form, that both may come to ripeness together. Again it is the heresy of the realist. Just as he drags into his verse words that have had no time to take colour from men's association of them with beauty, so he puts his 'naked thinking heart' into verse as if he were setting forth an argument. He gives us the real thing, as he would have been proud to assure us. But poetry will have nothing to do with real things, until it has translated them into a diviner world. That world may be as closely the pattern of ours as the worlds which Dante saw in hell and purgatory; the language of the poet may be as close to the language of daily speech as the supreme poetic language of Dante. But the personal or human reality and the imaginative or divine reality must be perfectly interfused, or the art will be at fault. Donne is too proud to abandon himself to his own inspiration, to his inspiration as a poet; he would be something more than a voice for deeper yet speechless powers; he would make poetry speak straight. Well, poetry will not speak straight, in the way Donne wished it to, and under the goading that his restless intellect gave it.

He forgot beauty, preferring to it every form of truth, and beauty has revenged itself upon him, glittering miraculously out of many lines in which he wrote humbly, and leaving the darkness of a retreating shadow upon great spaces in which a confident intellect was conscious of shining.

> For, though mind be the heaven, where love may sit,
> Beauty a convenient type may be to figure it,

he writes, in the *Valediction to his Book*, thus giving formal expression to his heresy. 'The greatest wit, though not the best poet of our nation,' Dryden called him; the greatest intellect, that is, which had expressed itself in poetry. Dryden himself was not always careful to distinguish between what material was fit and what unfit for verse; so that we can now enjoy his masterly prose with more equable pleasure than his verse. But he saw clearly enough the distinction in Donne between intellect and the poetical spirit; that fatal division of two forces, which, had they pulled together instead of apart, might have achieved a result wholly splendid. Without a great intellect no man was ever a great poet; but to possess a great intellect is not even a first step in the direction of becoming a poet at all.

Compare Donne, for instance, with Herrick. Herrick has little enough of the intellect, the passion, the weight and the magnificence of Donne; but, setting out with so much less to carry, he certainly gets first to the goal, and partly by running always in the right direction. The most limited poet in the language, he is the surest. He knows the airs that weave themselves into songs, as he knows the flowers that twine best into garlands. Words come to him in an order which no one will ever alter, and no one will ever forget. Whether they come easily or not is no matter; he knows when they have come right, and they always come right before he lets them go. But Donne is only occasionally sure of his words as airs; he sets them doggedly to the work of saying something, whether or no they step to the beat of the music. Conscious writer though he was, I suppose he was more or less unconscious of his extraordinary felicities, more conscious probably of how they came than of what they were doing. And they come chiefly through a sudden heightening of mood, which brings with it a clearer and a more exalted mode of speech, in its merely accurate expression of itself. Even then I cannot imagine him quite reconciled to beauty, at least actually doing homage to it, but rather as one who receives a gift by the way.

1899.

EMILY BRONTË

This was a woman young and passionate,
Loving the Earth, and loving most to be
Where she might be alone with liberty;
Loving the beasts, who are compassionate;
The homeless moors, her home; the bright elate
Winds of the cold dawn; rock and stone and tree;
Night, bringing dreams out of eternity;
And memory of Death's unforgetting date.
She too was unforgetting: has she yet
Forgotten that long agony when her breath
Too fierce for living fanned the flame of death?
Earth for her heather, does she now forget
What pity knew not in her love from scorn,
And that it was an unjust thing to be born?

The Stoic in woman has been seen once only, and that in the only
woman in whom there has been seen the paradox of passion
without sensuousness. Emily Brontë lived with an unparalleled
energy a life of outward quiet, in a loneliness which she shared
only with the moors and with the animals whom she loved. She
required no passion-experience to endow her with more than a
memory of passion. Passion was alive in her as flame is alive in
the earth. And the vehemence of that inner fire fed on itself, and
wore out her body before its time, because it had no respite and
no outlet. We see her condemned to self-imprisonment, and dying
of too much life.

Her poems are few and brief, and nothing more personal has ever been written. A few are as masterly in execution as in conception, and almost all have a direct truth of utterance, which rarely lacks at least the bare beauty of muscle and sinew, of a kind of naked strength and alertness. They are without heat or daylight, the sun is rarely in them, and then 'blood-red'; light comes as starshine, or comes as

> hostile light
> That does not warm but burn.

At times the landscape in this bare, grey, craggy verse, always a landscape of Yorkshire moors, with its touches of stern and tender memory, 'The mute bird sitting on the stone,' 'A little and a lone green lane,' has a quality more thrilling than that of Wordsworth. There is none of his observation, and none of his sense of a benignant 'presence far more deeply interfused'; but there is the voice of the heart's roots, crying out to its home in the earth.

At first this unornamented verse may seem forbidding, may seem even to be ordinary, as an actual moorland may, to those for whom it has no special attraction. But in the verse, as on the moors, there is space, wind, and the smell of the earth; and there is room to be alone, that liberty which this woman cried for when she cried:

> Leave the heart that now I bear,
> And give me liberty.

To be alone was for her to be alone with 'a chainless soul,' which asked of whatever powers might be only 'courage to endure,' constancy not to forget, and the right to leave the door wide open to those visions that came to her out of mere fixed contemplation: 'the God of Visions,' as she called her imagination, 'my slave, my comrade, and my king.' And we know that her courage was flawless, heroic, beyond praise; that she forgot nothing, not even that love for her unspeakable brother, for whom she has expressed in two of her poems a more than masculine magnanimity of pity and contempt; and that at all times she could turn inward to that world within, where her imagination waited for her,

Where thou, and I, and Liberty
Have undisputed sovereignty.

Yet even imagination, though 'benignant,' is to her a form of 'phantom bliss' to which she will not trust herself wholly. 'So hopeless is the world without': but is the world within ever quite frankly accepted as a substitute, as a truer reality? She is always on her guard against imagination as against the outer world, whose 'lies' she is resolved shall not 'beguile' her. She has accepted reason as the final arbiter, and desires only to see clearly, to see things as they are. She really believed that

Earth reserves no blessing
For the unblest of heaven;

and she had an almost Calvinistic sense of her own condemnation to unhappiness. That being so, she was suspicious of those opportunities of joy which did come to her, or at least resolute not to believe too implicitly in the good messages of the stars, which might be mere dreams, or of the earth, which was only certainly kind in preparing for her that often-thought-of grave. 'No coward soul is mine' is one of her true sayings; but it was with difficulty that she trusted even that message of life which she seemed to discover in death. She has to assure herself of it, again and again: 'Who once lives, never dies!' And that sense of personal identity which aches throughout all her poems is a sense, not of the delight, but of the pain and ineradicable sting of personal identity.

Her poems are all outcries, as her great novel, *Wuthering Heights*, is one long outcry. A soul on the rack seems to make itself heard at moments, when suffering has grown too acute for silence. Every poem is as if torn from her. Even when she does not write seemingly in her own person, the subjects are such disguises as 'The Prisoner,' 'Honour's Martyr,' 'The Outcast Mother,' echoes of all the miseries and useless rebellions of the earth. She spells over the fading characters in dying faces, unflinchingly, with an austere curiosity; and looks closely into the eyes of shame, not dreading what she may find there. She is always arguing with herself, and the answers are inflexible, the answers of a clear intellect which rebels but accepts defeat. Her doubt is itself an affirmation, her defiance would be an entreaty but for the 'quenchless will' of her pride. She faces every terror, and to her pained apprehension birth and death and life are alike terrible. Only Webster's dirge might have been said over her coffin.

> What my soul bore my soul alone
> Within itself may tell,

she says truthfully; but some of that long endurance of her life, in which exile, the body's weakness, and a sense of some 'divinest anguish' which clung about the world and all things living, had their share, she was able to put into ascetic and passionate verse. It is sad-coloured and desolate, but when gleams of sunlight or of starlight pierce the clouds that hang generally above it, a rare and stormy beauty comes into the bare outlines, quickening them with living splendour.

1906.

EDGAR ALLAN POE

The poems of Edgar Allan Poe are the work of a poet who thought persistently about poetry as an art, and would have reduced inspiration to a method. At their best they are perfectly defined by Baudelaire, when he says of Poe's poetry that it is a thing 'deep and shimmering as dreams, mysterious and perfect as crystal.' Not all the poems, few as they are, are flawless. In a few unequal poems we have the only essential poetry which has yet come from America, Walt Whitman's vast poetical nature having remained a nature only, not come to be an art. Because Poe was fantastically inhuman, a conscious artist doing strange things with strange materials, not every one has realised how fine, how rare, was that beauty which this artist brought into the world. It is true that there was in the genius of Poe something meretricious; it is the flaw in his genius; but then he had genius, and Whittier and Bryant and Longfellow and Lowell had only varying degrees of talent. Let us admit, by all means, that a diamond is flawed; but need we compare it with this and that fine specimen of quartz?

Poetry Poe defined as 'the rhythmical creation of beauty'; and the first element of poetry he found in 'the thirst for supernal beauty.' 'It is not,' he repeats, 'the mere appreciation of the beauty before us. It is a wild effort to reach the beauty above... Inspired with a prescient ecstasy of the beauty beyond the grave, it struggles by multiform novelty of combination among the things and thoughts of time, to anticipate some portions of that loveliness whose very elements, perhaps, appertain solely to eternity.' The poet, then, 'should limit his endeavours to the creation of novel moods of beauty, in form, in colour, in sound, in sentiment.' Note the emphasis upon novel: to Poe there was no beauty without strangeness. He makes his favourite quotation: '"But," says Lord Bacon (how justly!) "there is no exquisite beauty without some strangeness in the proportions." Take away this element of strangeness – of unexpectedness – of novelty – of originality – call it what we will – and all that is ethereal in loveliness is lost at once... We lose, in short, all that assimilates the beauty of earth with what we dream of the beauty of heaven!' And, as another of the elements of this creation of beauty, there must be indefiniteness. 'I *know*,' he says, 'that indefiniteness is an element of the true music – I mean of the true musical expression. Give to it any undue decision – imbue it with any very determinate tone – and you deprive it at once of its ethereal, its ideal, its intrinsic and essential character.' Do we not seem to find here an anticipation of Verlaine's 'Art Poétique': '*Pas la couleur, rien que la nuance*'? And is not the essential part of the poetical theory of Mallarmé and of the French Symbolists enunciated in this definition and commendation of 'that class of composition in which there lies beneath the transparent upper current of meaning an under or *suggestive* one'? To this 'mystic or secondary impression' he attributes 'the vast force of an accompaniment in music... With each note of the lyre is heard a ghostly, and not always a distinct, but an august soul-exalting *echo*.' Has anything that has been said since on that conception of poetry without which no writer of verse would, I suppose, venture to write verse, been said more subtly or more precisely?

And Poe does not end here, with what may seem generalities. 'Beyond the limits of beauty,' he says of poetry, 'its province does not extend. Its sole arbiter is Taste. With the Intellect or with the Conscience it has only collateral relations. It has no dependence, unless incidentally, upon either Duty or Truth.' And of the poet who said, not meaning anything very different from what Poe meant, 'Beauty is truth, truth beauty,' he says: 'He is the sole British poet who has never erred in his themes.' And, as if still thinking of Keats, he says: 'It is chiefly amid forms of physical loveliness (we use the word *forms* in its widest sense as embracing modifications of sound and colour) that the soul seeks the realisation of its dreams of Beauty.' And, with more earnest insistence on those limits which he knew to be so much more necessary to guard in poetry than its so-called freedom ('the true artist will avail himself of no "license" whatever'), he states, with categorical precision: 'A poem, in my opinion, is opposed to a work of science by having, for its *immediate* object, pleasure, not truth; to romance, by having, for its object, an *indefinite* instead of a *definite* pleasure, being a poem only so far as this object is attained; romance presenting perceptible images with definite, poetry with *in*definite sensations, to which end music is an *essential*, since comprehension of sweet sound is our most indefinite conception. Music, when combined with a pleasurable idea, is poetry; music, without the idea, is simply music; the idea, without the music, is prose, from its very definiteness.'

And he would set these careful limits, not only to the province of poetic pleasure, but to the form and length of actual poetry. 'A long poem,' he says, with more truth than most people are quite willing to see, 'is a paradox.' 'I hold,' he says elsewhere, 'that a long poem does not exist. I maintain that the phrase, "a long poem," is simply a flat contradiction in terms.' And, after defining his ideal, 'a rhymed poem, not to exceed in length what might be perused in an hour,' he says, very justly, that 'within this limit alone can the highest order of true poetry exist.' In another essay he narrows the duration to 'half an hour, at the very utmost'; and wisely. In yet another essay he suggests 'a length of about one hundred lines' as the length most likely to convey that unity of impression, with that intensity of true poetical effect, in which he found the highest merit of poetry. Remember, that of true poetry we have already had his definition; and concede, that a loftier conception of poetry as poetry, poetry as lyric essence, cannot easily be imagined. We are too ready to accept, under the general name of poetry, whatever is written eloquently in metre; to call even Wordsworth's *Excursion* a poem, and to accept *Paradise Lost* as throughout a poem. But there are not thirty consecutive lines of essential poetry in the whole of *The Excursion*, and, while *Paradise Lost* is crammed with essential poetry, that poetry is not consecutive; but the splendid workmanship comes in to fill up the gaps, and to hold our attention until the poetry returns. Essential poetry is an essence too strong for the general sense; diluted, it can be endured; and, for the most part, the poets dilute it. Poe could conceive of it only in the absolute; and his is the counsel of perfection, if of a perfection almost beyond mortal powers. He sought for it in the verse of all poets; he sought, as few have ever sought, to concentrate it in his own verse; and he has left us at least a few poems, '*ciascun distinto e di fulgore e d'arte,*' in which he has found, within his own limits, the absolute.

1906.

THOMAS LOVELL BEDDOES

With the strange fortune that always accompanied him, in life and in death, Beddoes has not merely escaped the indiscriminate applause which he would never have valued, but he has remained a bibliographical rather than a literary rarity. Few except the people who collect first editions – not, as a rule, the public for a poet – have had the chance of possessing *Death's Jest-Book* (1850) and the *Poems* (1851). At last Beddoes has been made accessible, the real story of his death, that suicide so much in the casual and determined manner of one of his own characters.

'The power of the man is immense and irresistible.' Browning's emphatic phrase comes first to the memory, and remains always the most appropriate word of eulogy. Beddoes has been rashly called a great poet. I do not think he was a great poet, but he was, in every sense of the word, an astonishing one. Read these lines, and remember that they were written just at that stagnant period (1821-1826) which comes between the period of Keats, Shelley, and Byron, and the period of Browning and Tennyson. It is a murderer who speaks:

> I am unsouled, dishumanised, uncreated;
> My passions swell and grow like brutes conceived;
> My feet are fixing roots, and every limb
> Is billowy and gigantic, till I seem
> A wild, old, wicked mountain in the air:
> And the abhorred conscience of this murder,

It will grow up a lion, all alone,
A mighty-maned, grave-mouthed prodigy,
And lair him in my caves: and other thoughts,
Some will be snakes, and bears, and savage wolves,
And when I lie tremendous in the desert,
Or abandoned sea, murderers and idiot men
Will come to live upon my rugged sides,
Die, and be buried in me. Now it comes;
I break, and magnify, and lose my form,
And yet I shall be taken for a man,
And never be discovered till I die.

How much this has of the old, splendid audacity of the Elizabethans! How unlike timid modern verse! Beddoes is always large, impressive; the greatness of his aim gives him a certain claim on respectful consideration. That his talent achieved itself, or ever could have achieved itself, he himself would have been the last to affirm. But he is a monumental failure, more interesting than many facile triumphs.

The one important work which Beddoes actually completed, *Death's Jest-Book*, is nominally a drama in five acts. All the rest of his work, except a few lyrics and occasional poems, is also nominally dramatic. But there never was anything less dramatic in substance than this mass of admirable poetry in dialogue. Beddoes' genius was essentially lyrical: he had imagination, the gift of style, the mastery of rhythm, a strange choiceness and curiosity of phrase. But of really dramatic power he had nothing. He could neither conceive a coherent plot, nor develop a credible situation. He had no grasp on human nature, he had no conception of what character might be in men and women, he had no faculty of expressing emotion convincingly. Constantly you find the most beautiful poetry where it is absolutely inappropriate, but never do you find one of those brief and memorable phrases, words from the heart, for which one would give much beautiful poetry. To take one instance: an Arab slave wishes to say that he has caught sight of a sail nearing the coast. And this is how he says it:

I looked abroad upon the wide old world,
And in the sky and sea, through the same clouds,
The same stars saw I glistening, and nought else,
And as my soul sighed unto the world's soul,
Far in the north a wind blackened the waters,
And, after that creating breath was still,
A dark speck sat on the sky's edge: as watching
Upon the heaven-girt border of my mind
The first faint thought of a great deed arise,
With force and fascination I drew on
The wished sight, and my hope seemed to stamp
Its shade upon it. Not yet is it clear
What, or from whom, the vessel.

In scenes which aim at being passionate one sees the same inability to be natural. What we get is always literature; it is never less than that, nor more than that. It is never frank, uncompromising nature. The fact is, that Beddoes wrote from the head, collectively, and without emotion, or without inspiration, save in literature. All Beddoes' characters speak precisely the same language, express the same desires; all in the same way startle us by their ghostly remoteness from flesh and blood. 'Man is tired of being merely human,' Siegfried says, in *Death's Jest-Book*, and Beddoes may be said to have grown tired of humanity before he ever came to understand it.

Looked at from the normal standpoint, Beddoes' idea of the drama was something wildly amateurish. As a practical playwright he would be beneath contempt; but what he aimed at was something peculiar to himself, a sort of spectral dramatic fantasia. He would have admitted his obligations to Webster and Tourneur, to all the *macabre* Elizabethan work; he would have admitted that his foundations were based on literature, not on life; but he would have claimed, and claimed justly, that he had produced, out of many strange elements, something which has a place apart in English poetry. *Death's Jest-Book* is perhaps the most morbid poem in our literature. There is not a page without its sad, grotesque, gay, or abhorrent imagery of the tomb. A slave cannot say that a lady is asleep without turning it into a parable of death:

> Sleeping, or feigning sleep,
> Well done of her: 'tis trying on a garb
> Which she must wear, sooner or later, long:
> 'Tis but a warmer, lighter death.

Not Baudelaire was more amorous of corruption; not Poe was more spellbound by the scent of graveyard earth. So Beddoes has written a new Dance of Death, in poetry; has become the chronicler of the praise and ridicule of Death. 'Tired of being merely human,' he has peopled a play with confessed phantoms. It is natural that these eloquent speakers should pass us by with their words, that they should fail to move us by their sorrows or their hates: they are not intended to be human, except, indeed, in the wizard humanity of Death.

I have said already that the genius of Beddoes is not dramatic, but lyrical. What was really most spontaneous in him (nothing was quite spontaneous) was the impulse of song-writing. And it seems to me that he is really most successful in sweet and graceful lyrics like this *Dirge*, so much more than 'half in love with easeful death.'

If thou wilt ease thine heart
Of love and all its smart,
    Then sleep, dear, sleep;
And not a sorrow
    Hang any tear on your eyelashes;
      Lie still and deep,
    Sad soul, until the sea-wave washes
The rim o' the sun to-morrow,
    In eastern sky.

But wilt thou cure thine heart
Of love and all its smart,
    Then die, dear, die;
'Tis deeper, sweeter,
    Than on a rose-bank to lie dreaming
      With folded eye;

> And then alone, amid the beaming
> Of love's stars, thou'lt meet her
> In eastern sky.

A beautiful lyrist, a writer of charming, morbid, and magnificent poetry in dramatic form, Beddoes will survive to students, not to readers, of English poetry, somewhere in the neighbourhood of Ebenezer Jones and Charles Wells. Charles Wells was certainly more of a dramatist, a writer of more sustained and Shakespearean blank verse; Ebenezer Jones had certainly a more personal passion to express in his rough and tumultuous way; but Beddoes, not less certainly, had more of actual poetical genius than either. And in the end only one thing counts: actual poetical genius.

1891.

GUSTAVE FLAUBERT

Salammbô is an attempt, as Flaubert, himself his best critic, has told us, to 'perpetuate a mirage by applying to antiquity the methods of the modern novel.' By the modern novel he means the novel as he had reconstructed it; he means *Madame Bovary*. That perfect book is perfect because Flaubert had, for once, found exactly the subject suited to his method, had made his method and his subject one. On his scientific side Flaubert is a realist, but there is another, perhaps a more intimately personal side, on which he is lyrical, lyrical in a large, sweeping way. The lyric poet in him made *La Tentation de Saint-Antoine*, the analyst made *L'Education Sentimentale*; but in *Madame Bovary* we find the analyst and the lyric poet in equilibrium. It is the history of a woman, as carefully observed as any story that has ever been written, and observed in surroundings of the most ordinary kind. But Flaubert finds the romantic material which he loved, the materials of beauty, in precisely that temperament which he studies so patiently and so cruelly. Madame Bovary is a little woman, half vulgar and half hysterical, incapable of a fine passion; but her trivial desires, her futile aspirations after second-rate pleasures and second-hand ideals, give to Flaubert all that he wants: the opportunity to create beauty out of reality. What is common in the imagination of Madame Bovary becomes exquisite in Flaubert's rendering of it, and by that counterpoise of a commonness in the subject he is saved from any vague ascents of rhetoric in his rendering of it.

In writing *Salammbô* Flaubert set himself to renew the historical novel, as he had renewed the novel of manners. He would have admitted, doubtless, that perfect success in the historical novel is impossible, by the nature of the case. We are at best only half conscious of the reality of the things about us, only able to translate them approximately into any form of art. How much is left over, in the closest transcription of a mere line of houses in a street, of a passing steamer, of one's next-door neighbour, of the point of view of a foreigner looking along Piccadilly, of one's own state of mind, moment by moment, as one walks from Oxford Circus to the Marble Arch? Think, then, of the attempt to reconstruct no matter what period of the past, to distinguish the difference in the aspect of a world perhaps bossed with castles and ridged with ramparts, to two individualities encased within chain-armour! Flaubert chose his antiquity wisely: a period of which we know too little to confuse us, a city of which no stone is left on another, the minds of Barbarians who have left us no psychological documents. 'Be sure I have made no fantastic Carthage,' he says proudly, pointing to his documents; Ammianus Marcellinus, who has furnished him with 'the *exact* form of a door'; the Bible and Theophrastus, from which he obtains his perfumes and his precious stones; Gresenius, from whom he gets his Punic names; the *Mémoires de l'Académie des Inscriptions*. 'As for the temple of Tanit, I am sure of having reconstructed it as it was, with the treatise of the Syrian Goddess, with the medals of the Duc de Luynes, with what is known of the temple at Jerusalem, with a passage of St. Jerome, quoted by Seldon (*De Diis Syriis*), with the plan of the temple of Gozzo, which is quite Carthaginian, and best of all, with the ruins of the temple of Thugga, which I have seen myself, with my own eyes, and of which no traveller or antiquarian, so far as I know, has ever spoken.' But that, after all, as he admits (when, that is, he has proved point by point his minute accuracy to all that is known of ancient Carthage, his faithfulness to every indication which can serve for his guidance, his patience in grouping rather than his daring in the invention of action and details), that is not the question. 'I care little enough for archæology! If the colour is not uniform, if the details are out of keeping, if the manners do not spring from the religion and the actions from the passions, if the characters are not consistent, if the costumes are not appropriate to the habits and the architecture to the climate, if, in a word, there is not harmony, I am in error. If not, no.'

And there, precisely, is the definition of the one merit which can give a historical novel the right to exist, and at the same time a definition of the merit which sets *Salammbô* above all other historical novels. Everything in the book is strange, some of it might easily be bewildering, some revolting; but all is in harmony. The harmony is like that of Eastern music, not immediately conveying its charm, or even the secret of its measure, to Western ears; but a monotony coiling perpetually upon itself, after a severe law of its own. Or rather, it is like a fresco, painted gravely in hard, definite colours, firmly detached from a background of burning sky; a procession of Barbarians, each in the costume of his country, passes across the wall; there are battles, in which elephants fight with men; an army besieges a great city, or rots to death in a defile between mountains; the ground is paved with dead men; crosses, each bearing its living burden, stand against the sky; a few figures of men and women appear again and again, expressing by their gestures the soul of the story.

Flaubert himself has pointed, with his unerring self-criticism, to the main defect of his book: 'The pedestal is too large for the statue.' There should have been, as he says, a hundred pages more about Salammbô. He declares: 'There is not in my book an isolated or gratuitous description; all are useful to my characters, and have an influence, near or remote, on the action.' This is true, and yet, all the same, the pedestal is too large for the statue. Salammbô, 'always surrounded with grave and exquisite things,' has something of the somnambulism which enters into the heroism of Judith; she has a hieratic beauty, and a consciousness as pale and vague as the moon whom she worships. She passes before us, 'her body saturated with perfumes,' encrusted with jewels like an idol, her head turreted with violet hair, the gold chain tinkling between her ankles; and is hardly more than an attitude, a fixed gesture, like the Eastern women whom one sees passing, with oblique eyes and mouths painted into smiles, their faces curiously traced into a work of art, in the languid movements of a pantomimic dance. The soul behind those eyes? the temperament under that at times almost terrifying mask? Salammbô is as inarticulate for us as the serpent, to whose drowsy beauty, capable of such sudden awakenings, hers seems half akin; they move before us in a kind of hieratic pantomime, a coloured, expressive thing, signifying nothing. Mâtho, maddened with love, 'in an invincible stupor, like those who have drunk some draught of which they are to die,' has the same somnambulistic life; the prey of Venus, he has an almost literal insanity, which, as Flaubert reminds us, is true to the ancient view of that passion. He is the only quite vivid person in the book, and he lives with the intensity of a wild beast, a life 'blinded alike' from every inner and outer interruption to one or two fixed ideas. The others have their places in the picture, fall into their attitudes naturally, remain so many coloured outlines for us. The illusion is perfect; these people may not be the real people of history, but at least they have no self-consciousness, no Christian tinge in their minds.

'The metaphors are few, the epithets definite,' Flaubert tells us, of his style in this book, where, as he says, he has sacrificed less 'to the amplitude of the phrase and to the period,' than in *Madame Bovary*. The movement here is in briefer steps, with a more earnest gravity, without any of the engaging weakness of adjectives. The style is never archaic, it is absolutely simple, the precise word being put always for the precise thing; but it obtains a dignity, a historical remoteness, by the large seriousness of its manner, the absence of modern ways of thought, which, in *Madame Bovary*, bring with them an instinctively modern cadence.

Salammbô is written with the severity of history, but Flaubert notes every detail visually, as a painter notes the details of natural things. A slave is being flogged under a tree: Flaubert notes the movement of the thong as it flies, and tells us: 'The thongs, as they whistled through the air, sent the bark of the plane trees flying.' Before the battle of the Macar, the Barbarians are awaiting the approach of the Carthaginian army. First 'the Barbarians were surprised to see the ground undulate in the distance.' Clouds of dust rise and whirl over the desert, through which are seen glimpses of horns, and, as it seems, wings. Are they bulls or birds, or a mirage of the desert? The Barbarians watch intently. 'At last they made out several transverse bars, bristling with uniform points. The bars became denser, larger; dark mounds swayed from side to side; suddenly square bushes came into view; they were elephants and lances. A single shout, "The Carthaginians!" arose.' Observe how all that is seen, as if the eyes, unaided by the intelligence, had found out everything for themselves, taking in one indication after another, instinctively. Flaubert puts himself in the place of his characters, not so much to think for them as to see for them.

Compare the style of Flaubert in each of his books, and you will find that each book has its own rhythm, perfectly appropriate to its subject-matter. That style, which has almost every merit and hardly a fault, becomes what it is by a process very different from that of most writers careful of form. Read Chateaubriand, Gautier, even Baudelaire, and you will find that the aim of these writers has been to construct a style which shall be adaptable to every occasion, but without structural change; the cadence is always the same. The most exquisite word-painting of Gautier can be translated rhythm for rhythm into English, without difficulty; once you have mastered the tune, you have merely to go on; every verse will be the same. But Flaubert is so difficult to translate because he has no fixed rhythm; his prose keeps step with no regular march-music. He invents the rhythm of every sentence, he changes his cadence with every mood or for the convenience of every fact. He has no theory of beauty in form apart from what it expresses. For him form is a living thing, the physical body of thought, which it clothes and interprets. 'If I call stones blue, it is because blue is the precise word, believe me,' he replies to Sainte-Beuve's criticism. Beauty comes into his words from the precision with which they express definite things, definite ideas, definite sensations. And in his book, where the material is so hard, apparently so unmalleable, it is a beauty of sheer exactitude which fills it from end to end, a beauty of measure and order, seen equally in the departure of the doves of Carthage, at the time of their flight into Sicily, and in the lions feasting on the corpses of the Barbarians, in the defile between the mountains.

1901.

John Donne

The Brontë sisters, by their brother Bramwell, c. 1834

Edgar Allan Poe, 1898

Gustave Flaubert by Félix Nadar.

Dante Gabriel Rossetti, Self-Portrait, 1847,
National Portrait Gallery, London

Thomas Hardy

J.-K. Huysmans

Stéphane Mallarmé by Félix Nadar

Count Philippe Auguste Mathias de Villiers de L'Isle-Adam

Charles Baudelaire by Etienne Carjat, 1863

GEORGE MEREDITH AS A POET

Meredith has always suffered from the curse of too much ability. He has both genius and talent, but the talent, instead of acting as a counterpoise to the genius, blows it yet more windily about the air. He has almost all the qualities of a great writer, but some perverse spirit in his blood has mixed them to their mutual undoing. When he writes prose, the prose seems always about to burst into poetry; when he writes verse, the verse seems always about to sink into prose. He thinks in flashes, and writes in shorthand. He has an intellectual passion for words, but he has never been able to accustom his mind to the slowness of their service; he tosses them about the page in his anger, tearing them open and gutting them with a savage pleasure. He has so fastidious a fear of dirtying his hands with what other hands have touched that he makes the language over again, so as to avoid writing a sentence or a line as any one else could have written it. His hatred of the commonplace becomes a mania, and it is by his head-long hunt after the best that he has lost by the way its useful enemy, good. In prose he would have every sentence shine, in verse he would have every line sparkle; like a lady who puts on all her jewellery at once, immediately after breakfast. As his own brain never rests, he does not realise that there are other brains which feel fatigue; and as his own taste is for what is hard, ringing, showy, drenched with light, he does not leave any cool shadows to be a home for gentle sounds, in the whole of his work. His books are like picture galleries, in which every inch of wall is covered, and picture screams at picture across its narrow division of frame. Almost every picture is good, but each suffers from its context. As time goes on, Meredith's mannerisms have grown rigid, like old bones. Exceptions have become rules, experiments have been accepted for solutions.

In Meredith's earliest verse there is a certain harshness, which seems to come from a too urgent desire to be at once concise and explicit. *Modern Love*, published in 1862, remains Meredith's masterpiece in poetry, and it will always remain, beside certain things of Donne and of Browning, an astonishing feat in the vivisection of the heart in verse. It is packed with imagination, but with imagination of so nakedly human a kind that there is hardly an ornament, hardly an image, in the verse: it is like scraps of broken, of heart-broken, talk, overheard and jotted down at random, hardly suggesting a story, but burning into one like the touch of a corroding acid. These cruel and self-torturing lovers have no illusions, and their 'tragic hints' are like a fine, pained mockery of love itself, as they struggle open-eyed against the blindness of passion. The poem laughs while it cries, with a double-mindedness more constant than that of Heine; with, at times, an acuteness of sensation carried to the point of agony at which Othello sweats words like these:

> O thou weed,
> Who art so lovely fair, and smell'st so sweet
> That the sense aches at thee, would thou hadst ne'er been born!

Meredith has written nothing more like *Modern Love*, and for twenty years after the publication of the volume containing it he published no other volume of verse. In 1883 appeared *Poems and Lyrics of the Joy of Earth*; in 1887 *Poems and Ballads of Tragic Life*; and, in 1888, *A Reading of Earth*, to which *A Reading of Life* is a sort of companion volume. The main part of this work is a kind of nature-poetry unlike any other nature-poetry; but there are several groups which must be distinguished from it. One group contains *Cassandra*, from the volume of 1862, *The Nuptials of Attila, The Song of Theodolinda*, from the volume of 1887. There is something fierce, savage, convulsive, in the passion which informs these poems; a note sounded in our days by no other poet. The words rush rattling on one another, like the clashing of spears or the ring of iron on iron in a day of old-world battle. The lines are javelins, consonanted lines full of force and fury, as if sung or played by a northern skald harping on a field of slain. There is another group of romantic ballads, containing the early *Margaret's Bridal Eve*, and the later *Arch-duchess Anne* and *The Young Princess*. There are also the humorous and pathetic studies in *Roadside Philosophers* and the like, in which, forty years ago, Meredith anticipated, with the dignity of a poet, the vernacular studies of others. And, finally, there is a section containing poems of impassioned meditation, beginning with the lofty and sustained ode to *France, December* 1870, and ending with the volcanic volume of *Odes in Contribution to the Song of French History*, published in 1900.

But it is in the poems of nature that Meredith is most consistent to an attitude, most himself as he would have himself. There is in them an almost pagan sense of the nearness and intimacy of the awful and benignant powers of nature; but this sense, once sufficient for the making of poetry, is interpenetrated, in this modern poet, by an almost scientific consciousness of the processes of evolution. Earth seen through a brain, not a tempera-ment, it might be defined; and it would be possible to gather a complete philosophy of life from these poems, in which, though 'the joy of earth' is sung, it is sung with the wise, collected ecstasy of Melampus, not with the irresponsible ecstasy of the Mænads. It is not what Browning calls 'the wild joy of living,' but the strenuous joy of living in perfect accordance with nature, with the sanity of animals who have climbed to reason, and are content to be guided by it. It is a philosophy which may well be contrasted with the transcendental theories of one with whom Meredith may otherwise be compared, Emerson. Both, in different ways, have tried to make poetry out of the brain, forgetting that poetry draws nourishment from other soil, and dies in the brain as in a vacuum. Both have taken the abstract, not the concrete, for their province; both have tortured words in the cause of ideas, both have had so much to say that they have had little time left over for singing.

Meredith has never been a clear writer in verse; *Modern Love* requires reading and re-reading; but at one time he had a somewhat exasperating semblance of lucidity, which still lurks mockingly about his work. A freshman who heard Mallarmé lecture at Oxford said when he came away: 'I understood every word, but not a single sentence.' Meredith is sometimes equally tantalising. The meaning seems to be there, just beyond one, clearly visible on the other side of some hard transparency through which there is no passage. Have you ever seen a cat pawing at the glass from the other side of a window? It paws and paws, turns its head to the right, turns its head to the left, walks to and fro, sniffing at the corner of every pane; its claws screech on the glass, in a helpless endeavour to get through to what it sees before it; it gives up at last, in an evident bewilderment. That is how one figures the reader of Meredith's later verse. It is not merely that Meredith's meaning is not obvious at a glance, it is, when obscure, ugly in its obscurity, not beautiful. There is not an uglier line in the English language than:

Or is't the widowed's dream of her new mate.

It is almost impossible to say it at all. Often Meredith wishes to be too concise, and squeezes his thoughts together like this:

and the totterer Earth detests,
Love shuns, grim logic screws in grasp, is he.

In his desire to cram a separate sentence into every line, he writes such lines as:

Look I once back, a broken pinion I,

He thinks differently from other people, and not only more quickly; and his mind works in a kind of double process. Take, for instance, this phrase:

Ravenous all the line for speed.

An image occurs to him, the image of a runner, who, as we say, 'devours' the ground. Thereupon he translates this image into his own dialect, where it becomes intensely vivid if it can be caught in passing; only, to catch it in passing, you must go through two mental processes at once. That is why he cannot be read aloud. In a poem where every line is on the pattern of the line I have quoted, every line has to be unriddled; and no brain works fast enough to catch so many separate meanings, and to translate as it goes.

Meredith has half the making of a great artist in verse. He has harmony without melody; he invents and executes marvellous variations upon verse; he has footed the tight-rope of the galliambic measure and the swaying planks of various trochaic experiments; but his resolve to astonish is stronger than his desire to charm, and he lets technical skill carry him into such excesses of ugliness in verse as technical skill carried Liszt, and sometimes Berlioz, in music. Meredith has written lines which any poet who ever wrote in English would be proud of; he has also written lines as tuneless as a deal table and as rasping as a file. His ear for the sweep and texture of harmonies, for the building up of rhythmical structure, is not seconded by an ear for the delicacies of sound in words or in tunes. In one of the finest of his poems, the *Hymn to Colour*, he can begin one stanza with this ample magnificence:

Look now where Colour, the soul's bridegroom, makes
The house of heaven splendid for the bride;

and can end another stanza thus lumpishly:

With thee, O fount of the Untimed! to lead,
Drink they of thee, thee eyeing, they unaged
   Shall on through brave wars waged.

Meredith is not satisfied with English verse as it is; he persists in trying to make it into something wholly different, and these eccentricities come partly from certain theories. He speaks in one place of

A soft compulsion on terrene
By heavenly,

which is not English, but a misapplication of the jargon of science. In another place he speaks of

The posts that named the swallowed mile,

which is a kind of pedantry. He chooses harsh words by preference, liking unusual or insoluble rhymes, like 'haps' and 'yaps,' 'thick' and 'sick,' 'skin' and 'kin,' 'banks' and 'thanks,' 'skims' and 'limbs.' Two lines from *The Woods of Westermain*, published in 1883 in the *Poems and Lyrics of the Joy of Earth*, sum up in themselves the whole theory:

Life, the small self-dragon ramped,
Thrill for service to be stamped.

Here every word is harsh, prickly, hard of sense; the rhymes come like buffets in the face. It is possible that Meredith has more or less consciously imitated the French practice in the matter of rhymes, for in France rarity of rhyme is sought as eagerly as in England it is avoided. Rhyme in French poetry is an important part of the art of verse; in English poetry, except to some extent at the time of Pope, it has been accepted as a thing rather to be disguised than accentuated. There is something a little barbarous in rhyme itself, with its mnemonic click of emphasis, and the skill of the most skilful English poets has always been shown in the softening of that click, in reducing it to the inarticulate answer of an echo. Meredith hammers out his rhymes on the anvil on which he has forged his clanging and rigid-jointed words. His verse moves in plate-armour, 'terrible as an army with banners.'

To Meredith poetry has come to be a kind of imaginative logic, and almost the whole of his later work is a reasoning in verse. He reasons, not always clearly to the eye, and never satisfyingly to the ear, but with a fiery intelligence which has more passion than most other poets put into frankly emotional verse. He reasons in pictures, every line having its imagery, and he uses pictorial words to express abstract ideas. Disdaining the common subjects of poetry, as he disdains common rhythms, common rhymes, and common language, he does much by his enormous vitality to give human warmth to arguments concerning humanity. He does much, though he attempts the impossible. His poetry is always what Rossetti called 'amusing'; it has, in other words, what Baudelaire called 'the supreme literary grace, energy'; but with what relief does one not lay down this *Reading of Life* and take up the *Modern Love* of forty years ago, in which life speaks! Meredith has always been in wholesome revolt against convention, against every deadening limitation of art, but he sometimes carries revolt to the point of anarchy. In finding new subjects and new forms for verse he is often throwing away the gold and gathering up the ore. In taking for his foundation the stone which the builders rejected he is sometimes only giving a proof of their wisdom in rejecting it.

1901.

ALGERNON CHARLES SWINBURNE

I

It is forty-four years since the publication of Swinburne's first volume, and it is scarcely to the credit of the English public that we should have had to wait so long for a collected edition of the poems of one of the greatest poets of this or any country. 'It is nothing to me,' Swinburne tells us, with a delicate precision in his pride, 'that what I write should find immediate or general acceptance.' And indeed 'immediate' it can scarcely be said to have been; 'general' it is hardly likely ever to be. Swinburne has always been a poet writing for poets, or for those rare lovers of poetry who ask for poetry, and nothing more or less, in a poet. Such writers can never be really popular, any more than gold without alloy can ever really be turned to practical uses. Think of how extremely little the poetical merit of his poetry had to do with the immense success of Byron; think how very much besides poetical merit contributed to the surprising reputation of Tennyson. There was a time when the first series of *Poems and Ballads* was read for what seemed startling in its subject-matter; but that time has long since passed, and it is not probable that any reviewer of the new edition now reprinted verbatim from the edition of 1866 will so much as allude to the timid shrieks which went up from the reviewers of that year, except perhaps as one of the curiosities of literature.

A poet is always interesting and instructive when he talks about himself, and Swinburne, in his dedicatory epistle to his 'best and dearest friend,' Mr. Watts-Dunton, who has been the finest, the surest, and the subtlest critic of poetry now living, talks about himself, or rather about his work, with a proud and simple frankness. It is not only interesting, but of considerable critical significance, to know that, among his plays, Swinburne prefers *Mary Stuart*, and, among his lyrical poems, the ode on Athens and the ode on the Armada. 'By the test of these two poems,' he tells us, 'I am content that my claims should be decided and my station determined as a lyric poet in the higher sense of the term; a craftsman in the most ambitious line of his art that ever aroused or can arouse the emulous aspiration of his kind.'

In one sense a poet is always the most valuable critic of his own work; in another sense his opinion is almost valueless. He knows, better than any one else, what he wanted to do, and he knows, better than any one else, how nearly he has done it. In judging his own technical skill in the accomplishment of his aim, it is easy for him to be absolutely unbiased, technique being a thing wholly apart from one's self, an acquirement. But, in a poem, the way it is done is by no means everything; something else, the vital element in it, the quality of inspiration, as we rightly call it, has to be determined. Of this the poet is rarely a judge. To him it is a part of himself, and he is scarcely more capable of questioning its validity than he is of questioning his own intentions. To him it is enough that it is his. Conscious, as he may rightly be, of genius, how can he discriminate, in his own work, between the presence or the absence of that genius, which, though it means everything, may be absent in a production technically faultless, or present in a production less strictly achieved according to rule? Swinburne, it is evident, grudges some of the fame which has set *Atalanta in Calydon* higher in general favour than *Erechtheus*, and, though he is perfectly right in every reason which he gives for setting *Erechtheus* above *Atalanta in Calydon*, the fact remains that there is something in the latter which is not, in anything like the same degree, in the former: a certain spontaneity, a prodigal wealth of inspiration. In exactly the same way, while the ode on Athens and the ode on the Armada are alike magnificent as achievements, there is no more likelihood of Swinburne going down to posterity as the writer of those two splendid poems than there is of Coleridge, to take Swinburne's own instance, being remembered as the writer of the ode to France rather than as the writer of the ode on Dejection. The ode to France is a product of the finest poetical rhetoric; the ode on Dejection is a growth of the profoundest poetical genius.

Another point on which Swinburne takes for granted what is perhaps his highest endowment as a poet, while dwelling with fine enthusiasm on the 'entire and absolute sincerity' of a whole section of poems in which the sincerity itself might well have been taken for granted, is that marvellous metrical inventiveness which is without parallel in English or perhaps in any other literature. 'A writer conscious of any natural command over the musical resources of his language,' says Swinburne, 'can hardly fail to take such pleasure in the enjoyment of this gift or instinct as the greatest writer and the greatest versifier of our age must have felt at its highest possible degree when composing a musical exercise of such incomparable scope and fulness as *Les Djinns*.' In metrical inventiveness Swinburne is as much Victor Hugo's superior as the English language is superior to the French in metrical capability. His music has never the sudden bird's flight, the thrill, pause, and unaccountable ecstasy of the very finest lyrics of Blake or of Coleridge; one never wholly forgets the artist in the utterance. But where he is incomparable is in an 'arduous fulness' of intricate harmony, around which the waves of melody flow, foam and scatter like the waves of the sea about a rock. No poet has ever loved or praised the sea as Swinburne has loved and praised it; and to no poet has it been given to create music with words in so literal an analogy with the inflexible and vital rhythmical science of the sea.

In his reference to the 'clatter aroused' by the first publication of the wonderful volume now reprinted, the first series of *Poems and Ballads*, Swinburne has said with tact, precision, and finality all that need ever be said on the subject. He records, with a touch of not unkindly humour, his own 'deep diversion of collating and comparing the variously inaccurate verdicts of the scornful or mournful censors who insisted on regarding all the studies of passion or sensation attempted or achieved in it as either confessions of positive fact or excursions of absolute fancy.' And, admitting that there was work in it of both kinds, he claims, with perfect justice, that 'if the two kinds cannot be distinguished, it is surely rather a credit than a discredit to an artist whose medium or material has more in common with a musician's than with a sculptor's.' Rarely has the prying ignorance of ordinary criticism been more absurdly evident than in the criticisms on *Poems and Ballads*, in which the question as to whether these poems were or were not the record of personal experience was debated with as much solemn fury as if it really mattered in the very least. When a poem has once been written, of what consequence is it to anybody whether it was inspired by a line of Sappho or by a lady living round the corner? There may be theoretical preferences, and these may be rationally enough argued, as to whether one should work from life or from memory or from imagination. But, the poem once written, only one question remains: is it a good or a bad poem? A poem of Coleridge or of Wordsworth is neither better nor worse because it came to the one in a dream and to the other in 'a storm, worse if possible, in which the pony could (or would) only make his way slantwise.' The knowledge of the circumstances or the antecedents of composition is, no doubt, as gratifying to human curiosity as the personal paragraphs in the newspapers; it can hardly be of much greater importance.

A passage in Swinburne's dedicatory epistle which was well worth saying, a passage which comes with doubled force from a poet who is also a scholar, is that on books which are living things: 'Marlowe and Shakespeare, Æschylus and Sappho, do not for us live only on the dusty shelves of libraries.' To Swinburne, as he says, the distinction between books and life is but a 'dullard's distinction,' and it may justly be said of him that it is with an equal instinct and an equal enthusiasm that he is drawn to whatever in nature, in men, in books, or in ideas is great, noble, and heroic. The old name of *Laudi*, which has lately been revived by d'Annunzio, might be given to the larger part of Swinburne's lyric verse: it is filled by a great praising of the universe. To the prose-minded reader who reads verse in the intervals of newspaper and business there must be an actual fatigue in merely listening to so unintermittent a hymn of thanksgiving. Here is a poet, he must say, who is without any moderation at all; birds at dawn, praising light, are not more troublesome to a sleeper.

Reading the earlier and the later Swinburne on a high rock around which the sea is washing, one is struck by the way in which these cadences, in their unending, ever-varying flow, seem to harmonise with the rhythm of the sea. Here one finds, at least, and it is a great thing to find, a rhythm inherent in nature. A mean, or merely bookish, rhythm is rebuked by the sea, as a trivial or insincere thought is rebuked by the stars. 'We are what suns and winds and waters make us,' as Landor knew: the whole essence of Swinburne seems to be made by the rush and soft flowing impetus of the sea. The sea has passed into his blood like a passion and into his verse like a transfiguring element. It is actually the last word of many of his poems, and it is the first and last word of his poetry.

He does not make pictures, for he does not see the visible world without an emotion which troubles his sight. He sees as through a cloud of rapture. Sight is to him a transfiguring thrill, and his record of things seen is clouded over with shining words and broken into little separate shafts and splinters of light. He has still, undimmed, the child's awakenings to wonder, love, reverence, the sense of beauty in every sensation. He has the essentially lyric quality, joy, in almost unparalleled abundance. There is for him no tedium in things, because, to his sense, books catch up and continue the delights of nature, and with books and nature he has all that he needs for a continual inner communing.

In this new book there are poems of nature, poems of the sea, the lake, the high oaks, the hawthorn, a rosary, Northumberland; and there are poems of books, poems about Burns, Christina Rossetti, Rabelais, Dumas, and about Shakespeare and his circle. In all the poems about books in this volume there is excellent characterisation, excellent criticism, and in the ode to Burns a very notable discrimination of the greater Burns, not the Burns of the love-poems but the fighter, the satirist, the poet of strenuous laughter.

> But love and wine were moon and sun
> For many a fame long since undone,
> And sorrow and joy have lost and won
>   By stormy turns
> As many a singer's soul, if none
>   More bright than Burns.
>
> And sweeter far in grief and mirth
> Have songs as glad and sad of birth
> Found voice to speak of wealth or dearth
>   In joy of life:
> But never song took fire from earth
>   More strong for strife.
> • • •
> Above the storms of praise and blame
> That blur with mist his lustrous name,
> His thunderous laughter went and came,
>   And lives and flies;
> The war that follows on the flame
>   When lightning dies.

Here the homage is given with splendid energy, but with fine justice. There are other poems of homage in this book, along with denunciations, as there are on so many pages of the *Songs before Sunrise* and the *Songs of Two Nations*, in which the effect is far less convincing, as it is far less clear. Whether Mazzini or Nelson be praised, Napoleon III. or Gladstone be buffeted, little distinction, save of degree, can be discerned between the one and the other. The hate poems, it must be admitted, are more interesting, partly because they are more distinguishable, than the poems of adoration; for hate seizes upon the lineaments which love glorifies willingly out of recognition. There was a finely ferocious energy in the *Dirae* ending with *The Descent into Hell* of 9th January 1873, and there is a good swinging and slashing vigour in *The Commonweal* of 1886. Why is it that this deeply felt political verse, like so much of the political verse of the *Songs before Sunrise*, does not satisfy the ear or the mind like the early love poetry or the later nature poetry? Is it not that one distinguishes only a voice, not a personality behind the voice? Speech needs weight, though song only needs wings.

I set the trumpet to my lips and blow,

said Swinburne in the *Songs before Sunrise*, when he was the trumpeter of Mazzini.

And yet, it must be remembered, Swinburne has always meant exactly what he has said, and this fact points an amusing contrast between the attitude of the critics thirty years ago towards work which was then new and their attitude now towards the same work when it is thirty years old. There is, in the *Songs before Sunrise*, an arraignment of Christianity as deliberate as Leconte de Lisle's, as wholesale as Nietzsche's; in the *Poems and Ballads*, a learned sensuality without parallel in English poetry; and the critics, or the descendants of the critics, who, when these poems first appeared, could see nothing but these accidental qualities of substance, are now, thanks merely to the triumph of time, to the ease with which time forgets and forgives, able to take all such things for granted, and to acknowledge the genuine and essential qualities of lyric exaltation and generous love of liberty by which the poems exist, and have a right to exist, as poems. But when we are told that *Before a Crucifix* is a poem fundamentally reverent towards Christianity, and that *Anactoria* is an ascetic experiment in scholarship, a learned attempt at the reconstruction of the order of Sappho, it is difficult not to wonder with what kind of smile the writer of these poems reflects anew over the curiosities of criticism. I have taken the new book and the old book together, because there is surprisingly little difference between the form and manner of the old poems and the new. The contents of *A Channel Passage* are unusually varied in subject, and the longest poem, *The Altar of Righteousness*, a marvellous piece of rhythmical architecture, is unusually varied in form. Technically the whole book shows Swinburne at his best; if, indeed, he may ever be said not to be at his best, technically. Is there any other instance in our literature of a perfection of technique so unerring, so uniform, that it becomes actually fatiguing? It has often foolishly been said that the dazzling brilliance of Swinburne's form is apt to disguise a certain thinness or poverty of substance. It seems to me, on the contrary, that we are often in danger of overlooking the imaginative subtlety of phrases and epithets which are presented to us and withdrawn from us in a flash, on the turn of a wave. Most poets present us with their best effects deliberately, giving them as weighty an accent as they can; Swinburne scatters them by the way. Take, for instance, the line:

The might of the night subsided: the tyranny kindled in darkness fell.

The line comes rearing like a wave, and has fallen and raced past us before we have properly grasped what is imaginatively fine in the latter clause. Presented to us in the manner of slower poets, thus:

The tyranny
Kindled in darkness fell,

how much more easily do we realise the quality of the speech which goes to make this song.

And yet there is no doubt that Swinburne has made his own moulds of language, as he has made his own moulds of rhythm, and that he is apt, when a thought or a sensation which he has already expressed recurs to him, to use the mould which stands ready made in his memory, instead of creating language over again, to fit a hair's-breadth of difference in the form of thought or sensation. That is why, in this book, in translating a 'roundel' of Villon which Rossetti had already translated, he misses the naïve quality of the French which Rossetti, in a version not in all points so faithful as this, had been able, in some subtle way, to retain. His own moulds of language recur to him, and he will not stop to think that 'wife,' though a good word for his rhyme scheme, is not a word that Villon could have used, and that

Deux estions et n'avions qu'ung cueur,

though it is perfectly rendered by Rossetti in

Two we were and the heart was one,

is turned into a wholly different, a Swinburnian thing, by

Twain we were, and our hearts one song,
One heart.

Nor is 'Dead as the carver's figured throng' (for 'Comme les images, par cueur') either clear in meaning, or characteristic of Villon in form. Is it not one of the penalties of extreme technical ability that the hand at times works, as it were, blindly, without the delicate vigilance or direction of the brain?

Of the poems contained in this new volume, the title-poem, *A Channel Passage*, is perhaps the finest. It is the record of a memory, fifty years old, and it is filled with a passionate ecstasy in the recollection of

Three glad hours, and it seemed not an hour of supreme and supernal joy,

Filled full with delight that revives in remembrance a sea-bird's
heart   in a boy.

It may be that Swinburne has praised the sea more
eloquently, or sung of it more melodiously, but not in the whole
of his works is there a poem fuller of personal rapture in the
communion of body and soul with the very soul of the sea in
storm. *The Lake of Gaube* is remarkable for an exultant and very
definite and direct rendering of the sensation of a dive through
deep water. There are other sea-poems in the two brief and
concentrated poems in honour of Nelson; the most delicate of the
poems of flowers in *A Rosary*; the most passionate and memorable
of the political poems in *Russia: an Ode*; the Elizabethan
prologues. These poems, so varied in subject and manner, are the
work of many years; to those who love Swinburne most as a lyric
poet they will come with special delight, for they represent, in
almost absolute equality, almost every side of his dazzling and
unique lyric genius.

The final volume of the greatest lyrical poet since Shelley
contains three books, each published at an interval of ten years:
the *Midsummer Holiday* of 1884, the *Astrophel* of 1894, and the
Channel Passage of 1904. Choice among them is as difficult as it is
unnecessary. They are alike in their ecstatic singing of the sea, of
great poets and great men, of England and liberty, and of
children. One contains the finest poems about the sea from on
shore, another the finest poem about the sea from at sea, and the
other the finest poem about the earth from the heart of the woods.
Even in Swinburne's work the series of nine ballades in long lines
which bears the name of *A Midsummer Holiday* stands out as a
masterpiece of its kind, and of a unique kind. A form of French
verse, which up to then had been used, since the time when
Villon used it as no man has used it before or since, and almost
exclusively in iambic measures, is suddenly transported from the
hothouse into the open air, is stretched and moulded beyond all

known limits, and becomes, it may almost be said, a new lyric form. After *A Midsummer Holiday* no one can contend any longer that the ballade is a structure necessarily any more artificial than the sonnet. But then in the hands of Swinburne an acrostic would cease to be artificial.

In this last volume the technique which is seen apparently perfected in the *Poems and Ballads* of 1866 has reached a point from which that relative perfection looks easy and almost accidental. Something is lost, no doubt, and much has changed. But to compare the metrical qualities of *Dolores* or even of *The Triumph of Time* with the metrical qualities of *On the Verge* is almost like comparing the art of Thomas Moore with the art of Coleridge. In Swinburne's development as a poet the metrical development is significant of every change through which the poet has passed. Subtlety and nobility, the appeal of ever homelier and loftier things, are seen more and more clearly in his work, as the metrical qualities of it become purified and intensified, with always more of subtlety and distinction, an energy at last tamed to the needs and paces of every kind of beauty.

II

'Charles Lamb, as I need not remind you,' says Swinburne in his dedicatory epistle to the collected edition of his poems, 'wrote for antiquity: nor need you be assured that when I write plays it is with a view to their being acted at the Globe, the Red Bull, or the Black Friars.' In another part of the same epistle, he says: 'My first if not my strongest ambition was to do something worth doing, and not utterly unworthy of a young countryman of Marlowe the teacher and Webster the pupil of Shakespeare, in the line of work which those three poets had left as a possibly unattainable example for ambitious Englishmen. And my first book, written while yet under academic or tutoral authority, bore evidence of that ambition in every line.' And indeed we need not turn four pages to come upon a mimicry of the style of Shakespeare so close as this:

We are so more than poor,
The dear'st of all our spoil would profit you
Less than mere losing; so most more than weak
It were but shame for one to smite us, who
Could but weep louder.

A Shakespearean trick is copied in such lines as:

All other women's praise
Makes part of my blame, and things of least account
In them are all my praises.

And there is a jester who talks in a metre that might have come straight out of Beaumont and Fletcher, as here:

I am considering of that apple still;
It hangs in the mouth yet sorely; I would fain know too
Why nettles are not good to eat raw. Come, children,
Come, my sweet scraps; come, painted pieces; come.

Touches of the early Browning come into this Elizabethan work, come and go there, as in these lines:

What are you made God's friend for but to have
His hand over your head to keep it well
And warm the rainy weather through, when snow
Spoils half the world's work?

And does one not hear Beddoes in the grim line, spoken of the earth:

Naked as brown feet of unburied men?

An influence still more closely contemporary seems to be felt in *Fair Rosamond*, the influence of that extraordinarily individual blank verse which William Morris had made his first and last experiment in, two years earlier, in *Sir Peter Harpdon's End*.

So many influences, then, are seen at work on the form at least of these two plays, published at the age of twenty-three. *Fair Rosamond*, though it has beautiful lines here and there, and shows some anticipation of that luxurious heat and subtle rendering of physical sensation which was to be so evident in the *Poems and Ballads*, is altogether a less mature piece of work, less satisfactory in every way, than the longer and more regular drama of *The Queen-Mother*. Swinburne speaks of the two pieces without distinction, and finds all that there is in them of promise or of merit 'in the language and the style of such better passages as may perhaps be found in single and separable speeches of Catherine and of Rosamond.' But the difference between these speeches is very considerable. Those of Rosamond are wholly elegiac, lamentations and meditations recited, without or against occasion. In the best speeches of Catherine there is not only a more masculine splendour of language, a firmer cadence, there is also some indication of that 'power to grapple with the realities and subtleties of character and of motive' which Swinburne finds largely lacking in them. A newspaper critic, reviewing the book in 1861, said: 'We should have conceived it hardly possible to make the crimes of Catherine de' Medici dull, however they were presented. Swinburne, however, has done so.' It seems to me, on the contrary, that the whole action, undramatic as it is in the strict sense of the theatre, is breathlessly interesting. The two great speeches of the play, the one beginning 'That God that made high things,' and the one beginning 'I would fain see rain,' are indeed more splendid in execution than significant as drama, but they have their dramatic significance, none the less. There is a Shakespearean echo, but is there not also a preparation of the finest Swinburnian harmonies, in such lines as these?

> I should be mad,
> I talk as one filled through with wine; thou God,
> Whose thunder is confusion of the hills,
> And with wrath sown abolishes the fields,
> I pray thee if thy hand would ruin us,
> Make witness of it even this night that is
> The last for many cradles, and the grave
> Of many reverend seats; even at this turn,
> This edge of season, this keen joint of time,
> Finish and spare not.

The verse is harder, tighter, more closely packed with figurative meaning than perhaps any of Swinburne's later verse. It is less fluid, less 'exuberant and effusive' (to accept two epithets of his own in reference to the verse of *Atalanta in Calydon*). He is ready to be harsh when harshness is required, abrupt for some sharp effect; he holds out against the enervating allurements of alliteration; he can stop when he has said the essential thing.

In the first book of most poets there is something which will be found in no other book; some virginity of youth, lost with the first intercourse with print. In *The Queen-Mother* and *Rosamond* Swinburne is certainly not yet himself, he has not yet settled down within his own limits. But what happy strayings beyond those limits! What foreign fruits and flowers, brought back from far countries! In these two plays there is no evidence, certainly, of a playwright; but there is no evidence that their writer could never become one. And there is evidence already of a poet of original genius and immense accomplishment, a poet with an incomparable gift of speech. That this technical quality, at least, the sound of these new harmonies in English verse, awakened no ears to attention, would be more surprising if one did not remember that two years earlier the first and best of William Morris's books was saluted as 'a Manchester mystery, not a real vision,' and that two years later the best though not the first of George Meredith's books of verse, *Modern Love*, was noticed only to be hooted at. Rossetti waited, and was wise.

The plays of Swinburne, full as they are of splendid poetry,

and even of splendid dramatic poetry, suffer from a lack of that
'continual slight novelty' which great drama, more than any other
poetical form, requires. There is, in the writing, a monotony of
excellence, which becomes an actual burden upon the reader.
Here is a poet who touches nothing that he does not transform,
who can, as in *Mary Stuart*, fill scores of pages with talk of
lawyers, conspirators, and statesmen, versifying history as closely
as Shakespeare versified it, and leaving in the result less prose
deposit than Shakespeare left. It is perhaps because in this play he
has done a more difficult thing than in any other that the writer
has come to prefer this to any other of his plays; as men in
general prefer a triumph over difficulties to a triumph. A similar
satisfaction, not in success but in the overcoming of difficulties,
leads him to say of the modern play, *The Sisters*, that it is the only
modern English play 'in which realism in the reproduction of
natural dialogue and accuracy in the representation of natural
intercourse between men and women of gentle birth and
breeding have been found or made compatible with expression in
genuine if simple blank verse.' This may be as true as that, in the
astounding experiment of *Locrine*, none of 'the life of human
character or the life-likeness of dramatic dialogue has suffered
from the bondage of rhyme or has been sacrificed to the exigences
of metre.' But when all is said, when an unparalleled skill in
language, versification, and everything that is verbal in form, has
been admitted, and with unqualified admiration; when, in
addition, one has admitted, with not less admiration, noble
qualities of substance, superb qualities of poetic imagination,
there still remains the question: is either substance or form
consistently dramatic? and the further question: can work
professedly dramatic which is not consistently dramatic in
substance and form be accepted as wholly satisfactory from any
other point of view?

The trilogy on Mary Queen of Scots must remain the largest
and most ambitious attempt which Swinburne has made. The first
part, *Chastelard*, was published in 1865; the last, *Mary Stuart*, in

1881. And what Swinburne says in speaking of the intermediate play, *Bothwell*, may be said of them all: 'I will add that I took as much care and pains as though I had been writing or compiling a history of the period to do loyal justice to all the historic figures which came within the scope of my dramatic or poetic design.' Of *Bothwell*, the longest of the three plays – indeed, the longest play in existence, Swinburne says: 'That ambitious, conscientious, and comprehensive piece of work is of course less properly definable as a tragedy than by the old Shakespearean term of a chronicle history.' Definition is not defence, and it has yet to be shown that the 'chronicle' form is in itself a legitimate or satisfactory dramatic form. Shakespeare's use of it proves only that he found his way through chronicle to drama, and to take his work in the chronicle play as a model is hardly more reasonable than to take *Venus and Adonis* as a model for narrative poetry. But, further, there is no play of Shakespeare's, chronicle or other, which might not at least be conceived of, if not on the stage of our time, at least on that of his, or on that of any time when drama was allowed to live its own life according to its own nature. Can we conceive of *Bothwell* even on the stage which has seen *Les Burgraves*? The Chinese theatre, which goes on from morning to night without a pause, might perhaps grapple with it; but no other. Nor would cutting be of any use, for what the stage-manager would cut away would be largely just such parts as are finest in the printed play.

There is, in most of Swinburne's plays, some scene or passage of vital dramatic quality, and in *Bothwell* there is one scene, the scene leading to the death of Darnley, which is among the great single scenes in drama. But there is not even any such scene in the whole of the lovely and luxurious song of *Chastelard* or in the severe and strenuous study of *Mary Stuart*. There are moments, in all, where speech is as simple, as explicit, as expressive as speech in verse can be; and no one will ever speak in verse more naturally than this:

> Well, all is one to me: and for my part
> I thank God I shall die without regret
> Of anything that I have done alive.

These simple beginnings are apt indeed to lead to their end by ways as tortuous as this:

> Indeed I have done all this if aught I have,
> And loved at all or loathed, save what mine eye
> Hath ever loathed or loved since first it saw
> That face which taught it faith and made it first
> Think scorn to turn and look on change, or see
> How hateful in my love's sight are their eyes
> That give love's light to others.

But, even when speech is undiluted, and expresses with due fire or calmness the necessary feeling of the moment, it is nearly always mere speech, a talking about action or emotion, not itself action or emotion. And every scene, even the finest, is thought of as a scene of talk, not as visible action; the writer hears his people speak, but does not see their faces or where or how they stand or move. It is this power of visualisation that is the first requirement of the dramatist; by itself it can go no further than the ordering of dumb show; but all drama must begin with the ordering of dumb show, and should be playable without words.

It was once said by William Morris that Swinburne's poems did not make pictures. The criticism was just, but mattered little; because they make harmonies. No English poet has ever shown so great and various a mastery over harmony in speech, and it is this lyrical quality which has given him a place among the great lyrical poets of England. In drama the lyrical gift is essential to the making of great poetic drama, but to the dramatist it should be an addition rather than a substitute. Throughout all these plays it is first and last and all but everything. It is for this reason that a play like *Locrine*, which is confessedly, by its very form, a sequence of lyrics, comes more nearly to being satisfactory as a whole than any of the more 'ambitious, conscientious, and

▶ 132

comprehensive' plays. *Marino Faliero*, though an episode of history, comes into somewhat the same category, and repeats with nobler energy the song-like character of *Chastelard*. The action is brief and concentrated, tragic and heroic. Its 'magnificent monotony,' its 'fervent and inexhaustible declamation,' have a height and heat in them which turn the whole play into a poem rather than a play, but a poem comparable with the 'succession of dramatic scenes or pictures' which makes the vast lyric of *Tristram of Lyonesse*. To think of Byron's play on the same subject, to compare the actual scenes which can be paralleled in both plays, is to realise how much more can be done, in poetry and even in drama, by a great lyric poet with a passion for what is heroic in human nature and for what is ardent and unlimited in human speech, than by a poet who saw in Faliero only the politician, and in the opportunities of verse only the opportunity for thin and shrewish rhetoric pulled and lopped into an intermittent resemblance to metre.

The form of *Locrine* has something in common with the form of *Atalanta in Calydon*, with a kind of sombre savagery in the subject which recurs only once, and less lyrically, in *Rosamund, Queen of the Lombards*. It is written throughout in rhyme, and the dialogue twists and twines, without effort, through rhyme arrangements which change in every scene, beginning and ending with couplets, and passing through the sonnet, Petrarchan and Shakespearean, ottava rima, terza rima, the six-line stanza of crossed rhymes and couplet, the seven-line stanza used by Shakespeare in the *Rape of Lucrece*, a nine-line stanza of two rhymes, and a scene composed of seven stanzas of chained octaves in which a third rhyme comes forward in the last line but one (after the manner of terza rima) and starts a new octave, which closes at the end in a stanza of two rhymes only, the last line but one turning back instead of forward, to lock the chain's circle. No other English poet who ever lived could have written dialogue under such conditions, and it is not less true than strange that these fetters act as no more than a beating of time to the feet that dance in them. The emotion is throughout at white heat; there is lyrical splendour even in the arguments: and a child's prattle, in nine-line stanzas of two rhymes apiece, goes as merrily as this:

> That song is hardly even as wise as I –
> Nay, very foolishness it is. To die
> In March before its life were well on wing,
> Before its time and kindly season – why
> Should spring be sad – before the swallows fly –
> Enough to dream of such a wintry thing?
> Such foolish words were more unmeet for spring
> Than snow for summer when his heart is high:
> And why should words be foolish when they sing?

Swinburne is a great master of blank verse; there is nothing that can be done with blank verse that he cannot do with it. Listen to these lines from *Mary Stuart*:

> She shall be a world's wonder to all time,
> A deadly glory watched of marvelling men
> Not without praise, not without noble tears,
> And if without what she would never have
> Who had it never, pity – yet from none
> Quite without reverence and some kind of love
> For that which was so royal.

There is in them something of the cadence of Milton and something of the cadence of Shakespeare, and they are very Swinburne. Yet, after reading *Locrine*, and with *Atalanta* and *Erechtheus* in memory, it is difficult not to wish that Swinburne had written all his plays in rhyme, and that they had all been romantic plays and not histories. *Locrine* has been acted, and might well be acted again. Its rhyme would sound on the stage with another splendour than the excellent and well-sounding rhymes into which Mr. Gilbert Murray has translated Euripides. And there would be none of that difficulty which seems to be insuperable on the modern stage: the chorus, which, whether it speaks, or chants, or sings, seems alike out of place and out of key.

The tragic anecdote which Swinburne has told in *Rosamund,*
Queen of the Lombards, is told with a directness and conciseness
unusual in his dramatic or lyric work. The story, simple,
barbarous, and cruel – a story of the year 573 – acts itself out
before us in large clear outlines, with surprisingly little of modern
self-consciousness. The book is a small one, the speeches are short,
and the words for the most part short too; every speech tells like
an action in words; there is scarcely a single merely decorative
passage from beginning to end. Here and there the lines become
lyric, as in

Thou rose,

Why did God give thee more than all thy kin,
Whose pride is perfume only and colour, this?
Music? No rose but mine sings, and the birds
Hush all their hearts to hearken. Dost thou hear not
How heavy sounds her note now?

But even here the lyrical touch marks a point of 'business.'
And for the most part the speeches are as straightforward as
prose; are indeed written with a deliberate aim at a sort of prose
effect. For instance:

Almachildes.
God must be

Dead. Such a thing as thou could never else
Live.

Rosamund.
That concerns not thee nor me. Be thou

Sure that my will and power to serve it live.
Lift now thine eyes to look upon thy lord.

Compare these lines with the lines which end the fourth act:

Almachildes.
I cannot slay him

Thus.

> Rosamund.
> Canst thou slay thy bride by fire? He dies,
> Or she dies, bound against the stake. His death
> Were the easier. Follow him: save her: strike but once.

> Almachildes.
> I cannot. God requite thee this! I will.

> *[Exit.*

> Rosamund.
> And I will see it. And, father, thou shalt see.

> *[Exit.*

In both these instances one sees the quality which is most conspicuous in this play – a naked strength, which is the same kind of strength that has always been present in Swinburne's plays, but hitherto draped elaborately, and often more than half concealed in the draperies. The outline of every play has been hard, sharp, firmly drawn; the characters always forthright and unwavering; there has always been a real precision in the main drift of the speeches; but this is the first time in which the outlines have been left to show themselves in all their sharpness. Development or experiment, whichever it may be, this resolute simplicity brings a new quality into Swinburne's work, and a quality full of dramatic possibilities. All the luxuriousness of his verse has gone, and the lines ring like sword clashing against sword. These savage and simple people of the sixth century do not turn over their thoughts before concentrating them into words, and they do not speak except to tell their thoughts. Imagine what even Murray, in *Chastelard*, a somewhat curt speaker, would have said in place of Almachildes's one line, a whole conflict of love, hate, honour, and shame in eight words:

I cannot. God requite thee this! I will.

Dramatic realism can go no further than such lines. The question remains whether dramatic realism is in itself an altogether desirable thing, and whether Swinburne in particular does not lose more than he gains by such self-restraint.

The poetic drama is in itself a compromise. That people should speak in verse is itself a violation of probability; and so strongly is this felt by most actors that they endeavour, in acting a play in verse, to make the verse sound as much like prose as possible. But, as it seems to me, the aim of the poetic drama is to create a new world in a new atmosphere, where the laws of human existence are no longer recognised. The aim of the poetic drama is beauty, not truth; and Shakespeare, to take the supreme example, is great, not because he makes Othello probable as a jealous husband, or gives him exactly the words that a jealous husband might have used, but because he creates in him an image of more than human energy, and puts into his mouth words of a more splendid poetry than any one but Shakespeare himself could have found to say. Fetter the poetic drama to an imitation of actual speech, and you rob it of the convention which is its chief glory and best opportunity. A new colour may certainly be given to that convention, by which a certain directness, rather of Dante than of Shakespeare, may be employed for its novel kind of beauty, convention being still recognised as convention. No doubt that is really Swinburne's aim, and to have succeeded in it is to show that he can master every form, and do as he pleases with language. And there are passages in the play, like this one, which have a fervid colour of their own, fully characteristic of the writer who has put more Southern colouring into English verse than any other English poet:

This sun – no sun like ours – burns out my soul.
I would, when June takes hold on us like fire,
The wind could waft and whirl us northward: here
The splendour and the sweetness of the world

Eat out all joy of life or manhood. Earth
Is here too hard on heaven – the Italian air
Too bright to breathe, as fire, its next of kin,
Too keen to handle. God, whoe'er God be,
Keep us from withering as the lords of Rome –
Slackening and sickening toward the imperious end
That wiped them out of empire! Yea, he shall.

The atmosphere of the play is that of June at Verona, and the sun's heat seems to beat upon us all through its brief and fevered action. Swinburne's words never make pictures, but they are unparalleled in their power of conveying atmosphere. He sees with a certain generalised vision – it might almost be said that he sees musically; but no English poet has ever presented bodily sensation with such curious and subtle intensity. And just as he renders bodily sensation carried to the point of agony, so he is at his best when dealing, as here, with emotion tortured to the last limit of endurance. Albovine, the king, sets bare his heart, confessing:

The devil and God are crying in either ear
One murderous word for ever, night and day,
Dark day and deadly night and deadly day,
Can she love thee who slewest her father? I
Love her.

Rosamund, his wife, meditating her monstrous revenge, confesses:

I am yet alive to question if I live
And wonder what may ever bid me die.
. . . .   There is nought
Left in the range and record of the world
For me that is not poisoned: even my heart
Is all envenomed in me.

And she recognises that

No healing and no help for life on earth
Hath God or man found out save death and sleep.

The two young lovers, caught innocently in a net of intolerable shame, can but question and answer one another thus:

> Hildegard.
> Hast thou forgiven me?
>
> Almachildes.
> I have not forgiven
> God.

And at the end Narsetes, the old councillor, the only one of the persons of the drama who is not the actor or the sufferer of some subtle horror, sums up all that has happened in a reflection which casts the responsibility of things further off than to the edge of the world:

> Let none make moan. This doom is none of man's.

As in the time of the great first volume of *Poems and Ballads*, Swinburne is still drawn to

> see
> What fools God's anger makes of men.

He has never been a philosophical thinker; but he has acquired the equivalent of a philosophy through his faithfulness to a single outlook upon human life and destiny. And in this brief and burning play, more than in much of his later writing, I find the reflection of that unique temperament, to which real things are so abstract, and abstract things so coloured and tangible; a temperament in which there is almost too much poetry for a poet – as pure gold, to be worked in, needs to be mingled with alloy.

There is, perhaps, no more terrible story in the later history of the world, no actual tragedy more made to the hand of the dramatist, than the story of the Borgias. In its entirety it would make another *Cenci*, in the hands of another Shelley, and another

Censor would prohibit the one as he prohibits the other. We are not permitted to deal with some form of evil on the stage. Yet what has Shelley said?

> There must be nothing attempted to make the exhibition subservient to what is vulgarly termed a moral purpose. The highest moral purpose aimed at in the highest species of the drama is the teaching the human heart, through its sympathies and antipathies, the knowledge of itself.

A great drama on the story of the Borgias could certainly have much to teach the human heart in the knowledge of itself. It would be moral in its presentation of the most ignobly splendid vices that have swayed the world; of the pride and defiance which rise like a strangling serpent, coiling about the momentary weakness of good; of that pageant in which the pagan gods came back, drunk and debauched with their long exile under the earth, and the garden-god assumed the throne of the Holy of Holies. Alexander, Cæsar, Lucrezia, the threefold divinity, might be shown as a painter has shown one of them on the wall of one of his own chapels: a swinish portent in papal garments, kneeling, bloated, thinking of Lucrezia, with fingers folded over the purple of his rings. Or the family might have been shown as Rossetti, in one of the loveliest, most cruel, and most significant of his pictures, has shown it: a light, laughing masquerade of innocence, the boy and girl dancing before the cushioned idol and her two worshippers.

Swinburne in *The Duke of Gandia* has not dealt with the whole matter of the story – only, in a single act of four scenes, with the heart or essence of it. The piece is not drama for the stage, nor intended to be seen or heard outside the pages of a book; but it is meant to be, and is, a great, brief, dramatic poem, a lyric almost, of hate, ambition, fear, desire, and the conquest of ironic evil. Swinburne has written nothing like it before. The manner of it is new, or anticipated only in the far less effectual *Rosamund, Queen of the Lombards*; the style, speech, and cadence are tightened, restrained, full of sullen fierceness. Lucrezia, strangely, is no more than a pale image passing without consciousness through some hot feast-room; she is there, she is hidden under their speech, but we scarcely see her, and, like her historians, wonder if she was so evil, or only a scholar to whom learned men wrote letters, as if to a pattern of virtue. But in the father and son live a flame and a cloud, the flame rising steadily to beat back and consume the cloud.

It is Cæsar Borgia who is the flame, and Alexander the Pope who fills the Vatican and the world with his contagious clouds. The father, up to this moment, has held all his vices well in hand; he has no rival; his sons and his daughter he has made, and they live about him for their own pleasure, and he watches them, and is content. Now one steps out, the circle is broken; there is no longer a younger son, a cardinal, but the Duke of Gandia, eldest son and on the highest step of the Pope's chair. It is, in this brief, almost speechless moment of action, as if the door of a furnace had suddenly been thrown open and then shut. One scene stands out, only surpassed by the terrible and magnificent scene leading up to the death of Darnley – a scene itself only surpassed, in its own pitiful and pitiless kind, by that death of Marlowe's king in the dungeons of Berkeley Castle, which, to all who can endure to read it, 'moves pity and terror,' as to Lamb, 'beyond any scene ancient or modern.' And only in *Bothwell*, in the whole of Swinburne's drama, is there speech so adequate, so human, so full of fear and suspense. Take, for instance, the opening of the great final scene. The youngest son has had his elder brother drowned in the Tiber, and after seven days he appears calmly before his father.

> Alex. Thou hast done this deed.
> Cæsar. Thou hast said it.
> Alex. Dost thou think
> To live, and look upon me?
> Cæsar. Some while yet.
> Alex. I would there were a God – that he might hear.
> Cæsar. 'Tis pity there should be – for thy sake – none.
> Alex. Wilt thou slay me?
> Cæsar. Why?

Alex. Am I not thy sire?
Cæsar. And Christendom's to boot.
Alex. I pray thee, man,
Slay me.
Cæsar. And then myself? Thou art crazed, but I
Sane.
Alex. Art thou very flesh and blood?
Cæsar. They say,
Thine.
Alex. If the heaven stand still and smite thee not,
There is no God indeed.
Cæsar. Nor thou nor I
Know.
Alex. I could pray to God that God might be,
Were I but mad. Thou sayest I am mad: thou liest:
I do not pray.

There, surely, is great dramatic speech, and the two men who speak face to face are seen clearly before us, naked to the sight. Yet even these lines do not make drama that would hold the stage. How is it that only one of our greater poets since the last of Shakespeare's contemporaries, and that one Shelley, has understood the complete art of the playwright, and achieved it? Byron, Coleridge, Browning, Tennyson, all wrote plays for the stage; all had their chance of being acted; Tennyson only made even a temporary success, and *Becket* is likely to have gone out with Irving. Landor wrote plays full of sublime poetry, but not meant for the stage; and now we have Swinburne following his example, but with an unexampled lyrical quality. Why, without capacity to deal with it, are our poets so insistent on using the only form for which a special faculty, outside the pure poetic gift, is inexorably required?

A poet so great as Swinburne, possessed by an ecstasy which turns into song as instinctively as the flawless inspiration of Mozart turned into divine melody, cannot be questioned. Mozart, without a special genius for dramatic music, wrote *Die Zauberflöte* to a bad libretto with as great a perfection as the music to *Don Giovanni*, which had a good one. The same inspiration was there, always apt to the occasion. Swinburne is ready to write in any known form of verse, with an equal facility and (this is the all-important point) the same inspiration. Loving the form of the drama, and capable of turning it to his uses, not of bending it to its own, he has filled play after play with music, noble feeling, brave eloquence. Here in this briefest and most actual of his plays – an act, an episode – he has concentrated much of this floating beauty, this overflowing imagination, into a few stern and adequate words, and made a new thing, as always, in his own image. It is the irony that has given its precise form to this representation of a twofold Satan, as Blake might have seen him in vision, parodying God with unbreakable pride. The conflict between father and son ends in a kind of unholy litany. 'And now,' cries Cæsar, fresh from murder,

> Behoves thee rise again as Christ our God,
> Vicarious Christ, and cast as flesh away
> This grief from off thy godhead.

And the old man, temporising with his grief, answers:

> Thou art subtle and strong.
> I would thou hadst spared him – couldst have spared him.

And the son replies:

> Sire,
> I would so too. Our sire, his sire and mine,
> I slew him not for lust of slaying, or hate,
> Or aught less like thy wiser spirit and mine.

But Cæsar-Satan has already said the epilogue to the whole representation, when, speaking to his mother, he bids her leave the responsibility of things:

> And God, who made me and my sire and thee,
> May take the charge upon him.

1899-1908.

DANTE GABRIEL ROSSETTI

Rossetti's phrase about poetry, that it must be 'amusing'; his 'commandment' about verse translation, 'that a good poem shall not be turned into a bad one'; his roughest and most random criticisms about poets, are as direct and inevitable as his finest verse. Only Coleridge among English poets has anything like the same definite grasp upon whatever is essential in poetry. And it is this intellectual sanity partly, this complete knowledge of the medium in which he worked, that has given Rossetti a position of his own, a kind of leadership in art.

And, technically, Rossetti has done much for English poetry. Such a line as

And when the night-vigil was done,

is a perfectly good metrical line if read without any dis-placement of the normal accent in speaking, and the rhyme of 'of' to 'enough' is as satisfying to the ear as the more commonly accepted rhyme of 'love' and 'move.' Rossetti did nothing but good by his troubling of many rhythms which had become stagnant, and it is in his extraordinary subtlety of rhythm, most accomplished where it seems most hesitating, that he has produced his finest emotional effects, effects before his time found but rarely, and for the most part accidentally, in English poetry.

Like Baudelaire and like Mallarmé in France, Rossetti was not only a wholly original poet, but a new personal force in literature. That he stimulated the sense of beauty is true in a way it is not true of Tennyson, for instance, as it is true of Baudelaire in a way it is not true of Victor Hugo. In Rossetti's work, perhaps because it is not the greatest, there is an actually hypnotic quality which exerts itself on those who come within his circle at all; a quality like that of an unconscious medium, or like that of a woman against whose attraction one is without defence. It is the sound of a voice, rather than anything said; and, when Rossetti speaks, no other voice, for the moment, seems worth listening to. Even after one has listened, not very much seems to have been said; but the world is not quite the same. He has stimulated a new sense, by which a new mood of beauty can be apprehended.

Dreams are precise; it is only when we awake, when we go outside, that they become vague. In a certain sense Rossetti, with all his keen practical intelligence, was never wholly awake, had never gone outside that house of dreams in which the only real things were the things of the imagination. In the poetry of most poets there is a double kind of existence, of which each half is generally quite distinct; a real world, and a world of the imagination. But the poetry of Rossetti knows but one world, and it inhabits a corner there, like a perfectly contented prisoner, or like a prisoner to whom the sense of imprisonment is a joy. The love of beauty, the love of love, because love is the supreme energy of beauty, suffices for an existence in which every moment is a crisis; for to him, as Pater has said, 'life is a crisis at every moment': life, that is to say, the inner life, the life of imagination, in which the senses are messengers from the outer world, from which they can but bring disquieting tidings.

The whole of this poetry is tragic, though without pathos or even self-pity. Every human attempt to maintain happiness is foredoomed to be a failure, and this is an attempt to maintain ecstasy in a region where everything which is not ecstasy is pain. In reading every other poet who has written of love one is conscious of compensations: the happiness of loving or of being loved, the honour of defeat, the help and comfort of nature or of action. But here all energy is concentrated on the one ecstasy, and this exists for its own sake, and the desire of it is like thirst, which returns after every partial satisfaction. The desire of beauty, the love of love, can but be a form of martyrdom when, as with Rossetti, there is also the desire of possession.

Circumstances have very little to do with the making of a poet's temperament or vision, and it would be enough to point to Christina Rossetti, who was hardly more in the country than her brother, but to whom a blade of grass was enough to summon the whole country about her, and whose poetry is full of the sense of growing things. Rossetti instinctively saw faces, and only faces, and he would have seen them if he had lived in the loneliest countryside, and he would never have learned to distinguish between oats and barley if he had had fields of them about his door from childhood. It was in the beauty of women, and chiefly in the mysterious beauty of faces, that Rossetti found the supreme embodiment of beauty; and it was in the love of women, and not in any more abstract love, of God, of nature, or of ideas, that he found the supreme revelation of love.

With this narrowness, with this intensity, he has rendered in his painting as in his poetry one ideal, one obsession. He calls what is really the House of Love *The House of Life*, and this is because the house of love was literally to him the house of life. There is no mystic to whom love has not seemed to be the essence or ultimate expression of the soul. Rossetti's whole work is a parable of this belief, and it is a parable written with his life-blood. Of beauty he has said, 'I drew it in as simply as my breath,' but, as the desire of beauty possessed him, as he laboured to create it over again, with rebellious words or colours, always too vague for him when they were most precise, never the precise embodiment of a dream, the pursuit turned to a labour and the labour to a pain. Part of what hypnotises us in this work is, no doubt, that sense of personal tragedy which comes to us out of its elaborate beauty: the eternal tragedy of those who have loved the absolute in beauty too well, and with too mortal a thirst.

1904.

A NOTE ON THE GENIUS OF THOMAS HARDY

He has a kind of naked face, in which you see the brain always working, with an almost painful simplicity – just saved from being painful by a humorous sense of external things, which becomes also a kind of intellectual criticism. He is a fatalist, and he studies the workings of fate in the chief vivifying and disturbing influence in life, women. His view of women is more French than English; it is subtle, a little cruel, not as tolerant as it seems, thoroughly a man's point of view, and not, as with Meredith, man's and woman's at once. He sees all that is irresponsible for good and evil in a woman's character, all that is unreliable in her brain and will, all that is alluring in her variability. He is her apologist, but always with a certain reserve of private judgment. No one has created more attractive women, women whom a man would have been more likely to love, or more likely to regret loving. *Jude the Obscure* is perhaps the most unbiased consideration of the more complicated questions of sex which we can find in English fiction. At the same time, there is almost no passion in his work, neither the author nor any of his characters ever seeming able to pass beyond the state of curiosity, the most intellectually interesting of limitations, under the influence of any emotion. In his feeling for nature, curiosity sometimes seems to broaden into a more intimate kind of communion. The heath, the village with its peasants, the change of every hour among the fields and on the roads, mean more to him, in a sense, than even the spectacle of man and woman in their blind, and painful, and absorbing struggle for existence. His knowledge of woman confirms him in a suspension of judgment; his knowledge of nature brings him nearer to the unchanging and consoling element in the world. All the quite happy entertainment which he gets out of life comes to him from his contemplation of the peasant, as himself a rooted part of the earth, translating the dumbness of the fields into humour. His peasants have been compared with Shakespeare's; that is, because he has the Shakespearean sense of their placid vegetation by the side of hurrying animal life, to which they act the part of chorus, with an unconscious wisdom in their close, narrow, and undistracted view of things.

In his verse there is something brooding, obscure, tremulous, half-inarticulate, as he meditates over man, nature, and destiny: Nature, 'waking by touch alone,' and Fate, who sees and feels. In *The Mother Mourns*, a strange, dreary, ironical song of science, Nature laments that her best achievement, man, has become discontented with her in his ungrateful discontent with himself. It is like the whimpering of a hurt animal, and the queer, ingenious metre, with its one rhyme set at wide but distinct and heavily recurrent intervals, beats on the ear like a knell. Blind and dumb forces speak, conjecture, half awakening out of sleep, turning back heavily to sleep again. Many poets have been sorry for man, angry with Nature on man's behalf. Here is a poet who is sorry for Nature, who feels the earth and its roots, as if he had sap in his veins instead of blood, and could get closer than any other man to the things of the earth.

Who else could have written this crabbed, subtle, strangely impressive poem?

AN AUGUST MIDNIGHT

A shaded lamp and a waving blind,
And the beat of a clock from a distant floor;
On this scene enter – winged, horned, and spined –
A longlegs, a moth, and a dumbledore;
While 'mid my page there idly stands
A sleepy fly, that rubs its hands.

Thus meet we five, in this still place,
At this point of time, at this point in space.
 – My guests parade my new-penned ink,
Or bang at the lamp-glass, whirl, and sink.
'God's humblest, they!' I muse. Yet why?
They know Earth-secrets that know not I.

No such drama has been written in verse since Browning, and the people of the drama are condensed to almost as pregnant an utterance as *Adam, Lilith, and Eve*.

Why is it that there are so few novels which can be read twice, while all good poetry can be read over and over? Is it something inherent in the form, one of the reasons in nature why a novel cannot be of the same supreme imaginative substance as a poem? I think it is, and that it will never be otherwise. But, among novels, why is it that one here and there calls us back to its shelf with almost the insistence of a lyric, while for the most part a story read is a story done with? Balzac is always good to re-read, but not Tolstoi: and I couple two of the giants. To take lesser artists, I would say that we can re-read *Lavengro* but not *Romola*. But what seems puzzling is that Hardy, who is above all a story-teller, and whose stories are of the kind that rouse suspense and satisfy it, can be read more than once, and never be quite without novelty. There is often, in his books, too much story, as in *The Mayor of Casterbridge*, where the plot extends into almost inextricable entanglements; and yet that is precisely one of the books that can be re-read. Is it on account of that concealed poetry, never absent though often unseen, which gives to these fantastic or real histories a meaning beyond the meaning of the facts, beneath it like an under-current, around it like an atmosphere? Facts, once known, are done with; stories of mere action gallop through the brain and are gone; but in Hardy there is a vision or interpretation, a sense of life as a growth out of the earth, and as much a mystery between soil and sky as the corn is, which will draw men back to the stories with an interest which outlasts their interest in the story.

It is a little difficult to get accustomed to Hardy, or to do him justice without doing him more than justice. He is always right, always a seer, when he is writing about 'the seasons in their moods, morning and evening, night and noon, winds in their different tempers, trees, waters and mists, shades and silences, and the voices of inanimate things.' (What gravity and intimacy in his numbering of them!) He is always right, always faultless in matter and style, when he is showing that 'the impressionable peasant leads a larger, fuller, more dramatic life than the pachydermatous king.' But he requires a certain amount of emotion to shake off the lethargy natural to his style, and when he has merely a dull fact to mention he says it like this: 'He reclined on his couch in the sitting-room, and extinguished the light.' In the next sentence, where he is interested in expressing the impalpable emotion of the situation, we get this faultless and uncommon use of words: 'The night came in, and took up its place there, unconcerned and indifferent; the night which had already swallowed up his happiness, and was now digesting it listlessly; and was ready to swallow up the happiness of a thousand other people with as little disturbance or change of mien.'

No one has ever studied so scrupulously as Hardy the effect of emotion on inanimate things, or has ever seen emotion so visually in people. For instance: 'Terror was upon her white face as she saw it; her cheek was flaccid, and her mouth had almost the aspect of a round little hole.' But so intense is his preoccupation with these visual effects that he sometimes cannot resist noting a minute appearance, though in the very moment of assuring us

▶ 151

that the person looking on did not see it. 'She hardly observed that a tear descended slowly upon his cheek, a tear so large that it magnified the pores of the skin over which it rolled, like the object lens of a microscope.' And it is this power of seeing to excess, and being limited to sight which is often strangely revealing, that leaves him at times helpless before the naked words that a situation supremely seen demands for its completion. The one failure in what is perhaps his masterpiece, *The Return of the Native*, is in the words put into the mouth of Eustacia and Yeobright in the perfectly imagined scene before the mirror, a scene which should be the culminating scene of the book; and it is, all but the words: the words are crackle and tinsel.

What is it, then, that makes up the main part of the value and fascination of Hardy, and how is it that what at first seem, and may well be, defects, uncouthnesses, bits of formal preaching, grotesque ironies of event and idea, come at last to seem either good in themselves or good where they are, a part of the man if not of the artist? One begins by reading for the story, and the story is of an attaching interest. Here is a story-teller of the good old kind, a story-teller whose plot is enough to hold his readers. With this point no doubt many readers stop and are content. But go on, and next after the story-teller one comes on the philosopher. He is dejected and a little sinister, and may check your pleasure in his narrative if you are too attentive to his criticism of it. But a new meaning comes into the facts as you observe his attitude towards them, and you may be well content to stop and be fed with thoughts by the philosopher. But if you go further still you will find, at the very last, the poet, and you need look for nothing beyond. I am inclined to question if any novelist has been more truly a poet without ceasing to be in the true sense a novelist. The poetry of Hardy's novels is a poetry of roots, and it is a voice of the earth. He seems often to be closer to the earth (which is at times, as in *The Return of the Native*, the chief person, or the chorus, of the story) than to men and women, and to see men and women out of the eyes of wild creatures, and out of the weeds and stones of the heath. How often, and for how profound a reason, does he not show us to ourselves, not as we or our fellows see us, but out of the continual observation of humanity which goes on in the wary and inquiring eyes of birds, the meditative and indifferent regard of cattle, and the deprecating aloofness and inspection of sheep?

1907.

LÉON CLADEL

I hope that the life of Léon Cladel by his daughter Judith, which Lemerre has brought out in a pleasant volume, will do something for the fame of one of the most original writers of our time. Cladel had the good fortune to be recognised in his lifetime by those whose approval mattered most, beginning with Baudelaire, who discovered him before he had printed his first book, and helped to teach him the craft of letters. But so exceptional an artist could never be popular, though he worked in living stuff and put the whole savour of his countryside into his tragic and passionate stories. A peasant, who writes about peasants and poor people, with a curiosity of style which not only packs his vocabulary with difficult words, old or local, and with unheard of rhythms, chosen to give voice to some never yet articulated emotion, but which drives him into oddities of printing, of punctuation, of the very shape of his accents! A page of Cladel has a certain visible uncouthness, and at first this seems in keeping with his matter; but the uncouthness, when you look into it, turns out to be itself a refinement, and what has seemed a confused whirl, an improvisation, to be the result really of reiterated labour, whose whole aim has been to bring the spontaneity of the first impulse back into the laboriously finished work.

In this just, sensitive, and admirable book, written by one who has inherited a not less passionate curiosity about life, but with more patience in waiting upon it, watching it, noting its surprises, we have a simple and sufficient commentary upon the books and upon the man. The narrative has warmth and reserve, and is at once tender and clear-sighted. *J'entrevois nettement*, she says with truth, *combien seront précieux pour les futurs historiens de la littérature du xixe siècle, les mémoires tracés au contact immédiat de l'artiste, exposés de ses faits et gestes particuliers, de ses origines, de la germination de ses croyances et de son talent; ses critiques à venir y trouveront de ateurs un aliment à leur piété et les philosophes un des aspects de l'Âme française.* The man is shown to us, *les élans de cette âme toujours grondante et fulgurante comme une forge, et les nuances de ce fiévreux visage d'apôtre, brun, fin et sinueux,* and we see the inevitable growth, out of the hard soil of Quercy and out of the fertilising contact of Paris and Baudelaire, of this whole literature, these books no less astonishing than their titles: *Ompdrailles-le-Tombeau-des-Lutteurs*, *Celui de la Croix-aux-Bœufs*, *La Fête Votive de Saint-Bartholomée-Porte-Glaive.* The very titles are an excitement. I can remember how mysterious and alluring they used to seem to me when I first saw them on the cover of what was perhaps his best book, *Les Va-Nu-Pieds*.

It is by one of the stories, and the shortest, in *Les Va-Nu-Pieds*, that I remember Cladel. I read it when I was a boy, and I cannot think of it now without a shiver. It is called *L'Hercule*, and it is about a Sandow of the streets, a professional strong man, who kills himself by an over-strain; it is not a story at all, it is the record of an incident, and there is only the strong man in it and his friend the zany, who makes the jokes while the strong man juggles with bars and cannon-balls. It is all told in a breath, without a pause, as if some one who had just seen it poured it out in a flood of hot words. Such vehemence, such pity, such a sense of the cruelty of the spectacle of a man driven to death like a beast, for a few pence and the pleasure of a few children; such an evocation of the sun and the streets and this sordid tragic thing happening to the sound of drum and cymbals; such a vision in sunlight of a barbarous and ridiculous and horrible accident, lifted by the telling of it into a new and unforgettable beauty, I have never felt or seen in any other story of a like grotesque tragedy. It realises an ideal, it does for once what many artists have tried and failed to do; it wrings the last drop of agony out of that subject which it is so easy to make pathetic and effective. Dickens could not have done it, Bret Harte could not have done it, Kipling could not do it: Cladel did it only once, with this perfection.

Something like it he did over and over again, with unflagging vehemence, with splendid variations, in stories of peasants and wrestlers and thieves and prostitutes. They are all, as his daughter says, epic; she calls them Homeric, but there is none of the Homeric simplicity in this tumult of coloured and clotted speech, in which the language is tortured to make it speak. The comparison with Rabelais is nearer. *La recherche du terme vivant, sa mise en valeur et en saveur, la surabondance des vocables puisés à toutes sources ... la condensation de l'action autour de ces quelques motifs éternels de l'épopée: combat, ripaille, palabre et luxure*, there, as she sees justly, are links with Rabelais. Goncourt, himself always aiming at an impossible closeness of written to spoken speech, noted with admiration *la vraie photographie de la parole avec ses tours, ses abbréviations ses ellipses, son essoufflement presque*. Speech out of breath, that is what Cladel's is always; his words, never the likely ones, do not so much speak as cry, gesticulate, overtake one another. *L'âme de Léon Cladel*, says his daughter, *était dans un constant et flamboyant automne*. Something of the colour and fever of autumn is in all he wrote. Another writer since Cladel, who has probably never heard of him, has made heroes of peasants and vagabonds. But Maxim Gorki makes heroes of them, consciously, with a mental self-assertion, giving them ideas which he has found in Nietzsche. Cladel put into all his people some of his own passionate way of seeing 'scarlet,' to use Barbey d'Aurevilly's epithet: *un rural écarlate*. Vehement and voluminous, he overflowed: his whole aim as an artist, as a pupil of Baudelaire, was to concentrate, to hold himself back; and the effort added impetus to the checked overflow. To the realists he seemed merely extravagant; he saw certainly what they could not see; and his romance was always a fruit of the soil. The artist in him, seeming to be in conflict with the peasant, fortified, clarified the peasant, extracted from that hard soil a rare fruit. You see in his face an extraordinary mingling of the peasant, the visionary, and the dandy: the long hair and beard, the sensitive mouth and nose, the fierce brooding eyes, in which wildness and delicacy, strength and a kind of stealthiness, seem to be grafted on an inflexible peasant stock.

1906.

HENRIK IBSEN

'Everything which I have created as a poet,' Ibsen said in a letter, 'has had its origin in a frame of mind and a situation in life; I never wrote because I had, as they say, found a good subject.' Yet his chief aim as a dramatist has been to set character in independent action, and to stand aside, reserving his judgment. 'The method, the technique of the construction,' he says, speaking of what is probably his masterpiece, *Ghosts*, 'in itself entirely precludes the author's appearing in the speeches. My intention was to produce the impression in the mind of the reader that he was witnessing something real.' That, at his moment of most perfect balance, was his intention; that was what he achieved in an astonishing way. But his whole life was a development; and we see him moving from point to point, deliberately, and yet inevitably; reaching the goal which it was his triumph to reach, then going beyond the goal, because movement in any direction was a necessity of his nature.

In Ibsen's letters we shall find invaluable help in the study of this character and this development. The man shows himself in them with none the less disguise because he shows himself unwillingly. In these hard, crabbed, formal, painfully truthful letters we see the whole narrow, precise, and fanatical soul of this Puritan of art, who sacrificed himself, his family, his friends, and his country to an artistic sense of duty only to be paralleled among those religious people whom he hated and resembled.

His creed, as man and as artist, was the cultivation, the realisation of self. In quite another sense that, too, was the creed of Nietzsche; but what in Nietzsche was pride, the pride of individual energy, in Ibsen was a kind of humility, or a practical deduction from the fact that only by giving complete expression to oneself can one produce the finest work. Duty to oneself: that was how he looked upon it; and though, in a letter to Björnson, he affirmed, as the highest praise, 'his life was his best work,' to himself it was the building-up of the artist in him that he chiefly cared for. And to this he set himself with a moral fervour and a scientific tenacity. There was in Ibsen none of the abundance of great natures, none of the ease of strength. He nursed his force, as a miser hoards his gold; and does he not give you at times an uneasy feeling that he is making the most of himself, as the miser makes the most of his gold by scraping up every farthing?

'The great thing,' he says in a letter of advice, 'is to hedge about what is one's own, to keep it free and clear from everything outside that has no connexion with it.' He bids Brandes cultivate 'a genuine, full-blooded egoism, which shall force you for a time to regard what concerns you as the only thing of any consequence, and everything else as non-existent.' Yet he goes on to talk about 'benefiting society,' is conscious of the weight which such a conviction or compromise lays upon him, and yet cannot get rid of the burden, as Nietzsche does. He has less courage than Nietzsche, though no less logic, and is held back from a complete realisation of his own doctrine because he has so much worldly wisdom and is so anxious to make the best of all worlds.

'In every new poem or play,' he writes, 'I have aimed at my own personal spiritual emancipation and purification, for a man shares the responsibility and the guilt of the society to which he belongs.' This queer entanglement in social bonds on the part of one whose main endeavour had always been to free the individual from the conventions and restrictions of society is one of those signs of parochialism which peep out in Ibsen again and again. 'The strongest man,' he says in a letter, anticipating the epilogue of one of his plays, 'is he who stands alone.' But Ibsen did not find it easy to stand alone, though he found pleasure in standing aloof. The influence of his environment upon him is marked from the first. He breaks with his father and mother, never writes to them or goes back to see them; partly because he feels it necessary to avoid contact with 'certain tendencies prevailing there.' 'Friends are an expensive luxury,' he finds, because they keep him from doing what he wishes to do, out of consideration for them. Is not this intellectual sensitiveness the corollary of a practical cold-heartedness? He cannot live in Norway because, he says, 'I could never lead a consistent spiritual life there.' In Norway he finds that 'the accumulation of small details makes the soul small.' How curious an admission for an individualist, for an artist! He goes to Rome, and feels that he has discovered a new mental world. 'After I had been in Italy I could not understand how I had been able to exist before I had been there.' Yet before long he must go on to Munich, because 'here one is too entirely out of touch with the movements of the day.'

He insists, again and again: 'Environment has a great influence upon the forms in which the imagination creates'; and, in a tone of half-burlesque, but with something serious in his meaning, he declares that wine had something to do with the exaltation of *Brand* and *Peer Gynt*, and sausages and beer with the satirical analysis of *The League of Youth*. And he adds: 'I do not intend by this to place the last-mentioned play on a lower level. I only mean that my point of view has changed, because here I am in a community well ordered even to weariness.' He says elsewhere that he could only have written *Peer Gynt* where he wrote it, at Ischia and Sorrento, because it is 'written without regard to consequences – as I only dare to write far away from home.' If we trace him through his work we shall see him, with a strange docility, allowing not only 'frame of mind and situation in life,' but his actual surroundings, to mould his work, alike in form and in substance. If he had never left Norway he might have written verse to the end of his life; if he had not lived in Germany, where there is 'up-to-date civilisation to study,' he would certainly never have written the social dramas; if he had not returned to Norway at the end of his life, the last plays would not have been what they were. I am taking him at his word; but Ibsen is a man who must be taken at his word.

What is perhaps most individual in the point of view of Ibsen in his dramas is his sense of the vast importance trifles, of the natural human tendency to invent or magnify misunderstandings. A misunderstanding is his main lever of the tragic mischief; and he has studied and diagnosed this unconscious agent of destiny more minutely and persistently than any other dramatist. He found it in himself. We see just this brooding over trifles, this sensitiveness to wrongs, imaginary or insignificant, in the revealing pages of his letters. It made the satirist of his earlier years; it made him a satirist of non-essentials. A criticism of one of his books sets him talking of wide vengeance; and he admitted in later life that he said to himself, 'I am ruined,' because a newspaper had attacked him overnight.

With all his desire to 'undermine the idea of the state,' he besieges king and government with petitions for money; and he will confess in a letter, 'I should very much like to write publicly about the mean behaviour of the government,' which, however, he refrains from doing. He gets sore and angry over party and parochial rights and wrongs, even when he is far away from them, and has congratulated himself on the calming and enlightening effect of distance. A Norwegian bookseller threatens to pirate one of his books, and he makes a national matter of it. 'If,' he says, 'this dishonest speculation really obtains sympathy and support at home, it is my intention, come what may, to sever all ties with Norway and never set foot on her soil again.' How petty, how like a hysterical woman that is! How, in its way of taking a possible trifling personal injustice as if it were a thing of vital and even national moment, he betrays what was always to remain narrow, as well as bitter, in the centre of his being! He has recorded it against himself (for he spared himself, as he proudly and truthfully said, no more than others) in an anecdote which is a profound symbol.

> During the time I was writing *Brand*, I had on my desk a glass with a scorpion in it. From time to time the little animal was ill. Then I used to give it a piece of soft fruit, upon which it fell furiously and emptied its poison into it – after which it was well again. Does not something of the kind happen with us poets?

Poets, no; but in Ibsen there is always some likeness of the sick scorpion in the glass.

In one of his early letters to Björnson, he had written: 'When I read the news from home, when I gaze upon all that respectable, estimable narrow-mindedness and worldliness, it is with the feeling of an insane man staring at one single, hopelessly dark spot.' All his life Ibsen gazed until he found the black spot somewhere; but it was with less and less of this angry, reforming feeling of the insane man. He saw the black spot at the core of the earth's fruit, of the whole apple of the earth; and as he became more hopeless, he became less angry; he learned something of the supreme indifference of art. He had learned much when he came to realise that, in the struggle for liberty, it was chiefly the energy of the struggle that mattered. 'He who possesses liberty,' he said, 'otherwise than as a thing to be striven for, possesses it dead and soulless... So that a man who stops in the midst of the struggle and says, "Now I have it," thereby shows that he has lost it.' He had learned still more when he could add to his saying, 'The minority is always right,' this subtle corollary, that a fighter in the intellectual vanguard can never collect a majority around him. 'At the point where I stood when I wrote each of my books, there now stands a tolerably compact crowd; but I myself am no longer there; I am elsewhere; farther ahead, I hope.' 'That man is right,' he thought, 'who has allied himself most closely with the future.' The future, to Ibsen, was a palpable thing, not concerned merely with himself as an individual, but a constantly removing, continually occupied promised land, into which he was not content to go alone. Yet he would always have asked of a follower, with Zarathustra: 'This is my road; which is yours?' His future was to be peopled by great individuals.

It was in seeking to find himself that Ibsen sought to find truth; and truth he knew was to be found only within him. The truth which he sought for himself was not at all truth in the abstract, but a truth literally 'efficacious,' and able to work out the purpose of his existence. That purpose he never doubted. The work he had to do was the work of an artist, and to this everything must be subservient. 'The great thing is to become honest and truthful in dealing with oneself – not to determine to do this or determine to do that, but to do what one *must* do because one is oneself. All the rest simply leads to falsehood.' He conceives of truth as being above all clear-sighted, and the approach to truth as a matter largely of will. No preacher of God and of righteousness and the kingdom to come was ever more centred, more convinced, more impregnably minded every time that he has absorbed a new idea or is constructing a new work of art. His conception of art often changes; but he never deviates at any one time from any one conception. There is something narrow as well as something intense in this certainty, this calmness, this moral attitude towards art. Nowhere has he expressed more of himself than in a letter to a woman who had written some kind of religious sequel to *Brand*. He tells her:

> *Brand* is an æsthetic work, pure and simple. What it may have demo-lished or built up is a matter of absolute indifference to me. It came into being as the result of something which I had not observed, but experienced; it was a necessity for me to free myself from something which my inner man had done with, by giving poetic form to it; and, when by this means I had got rid of it, my book had no longer any interest for me.

It is in the same positive, dogmatic way that he assures us that *Peer Gynt* is a poem, not a satire; *The League of Youth* a 'simple comedy and nothing more'; *Emperor and Galilean* an 'entirely realistic work'; that in *Ghosts* 'there is not a single opinion, a single utterance which can be laid to the account of the author... My intention was to produce the impression in the mind of the reader that he was witnessing something real... It preaches nothing at all.' Of *Hedda Gabler* he says: 'It was not really my desire to deal in this play with so-called problems. What I principally wanted to do was to depict human beings, human emotions, and human destinies, upon a groundwork of the social conditions and principles of the present day.' 'My chief life-task,' he defines: 'to depict human characters and human destinies.'

•

Ibsen's development has always lain chiefly in the perfecting of his tools. From the beginning he has had certain ideas, certain tendencies, a certain consciousness of things to express; he has been haunted, as only creative artists are haunted, by a world waiting to be born; and, from the beginning, he has built on a basis of criticism, a criticism of life. Part of his strength has gone out in fighting: he has had the sense of a mission. Part of his strength has gone out in the attempt to fly: he has had the impulse, without the wings, of the poet. And when he has been content to leave fighting and flying alone, and to build solidly on a solid foundation, it is then that he has achieved his great work. But he has never been satisfied, or never been able, to go on doing just that work, his own work; and the poet in him, the impotent poet who is full of a sense of what poetry is, but is never able, for more than a moment, to create poetry, has come whispering in the ear of the man of science, who is the new, unerring artist, the maker of a wonderful new art of prose, and has made him uneasy, and given uncertainty to his hand. The master-builder has altered his design, he has set up a tower here, 'too high for a dwelling-house,' and added a window there, with the stained glass of a church window, and fastened on ornaments in stucco, breaking the severe line of the original design.

In Ibsen science has made its great stand against poetry; and the Germans have come worshipping, saying, 'Here, in our era of marvellously realistic politics, we have come upon correspondingly realistic poetry... We received from it the first idea of a possible new poetic world... We were adherents of this new school of realistic art: we had found our æsthetic creed.' But the maker of this creed, the creator of this school of realistic art, was not able to be content with what he had done, though this was the greatest thing he was able to do. It is with true insight that he boasts, in one of his letters, of what he can do 'if I am only careful to do what I am quite capable of, namely, combine this relentlessness of mind with deliberateness in the choice of means.' There lay his success: deliberateness in the choice of means for the doing of a given thing, the thing for which his best energies best fitted him. Yet it took him forty years to discover exactly what those means to that end were; and then the experimenting impulse, the sense of what poetry is, was soon to begin its disintegrating work. Science, which seemed to have conquered poetry, was to pay homage to poetry.

Ibsen comes before us as a man of science who would have liked to be a poet; or who, half-equipped as a poet, is halved or hampered by the scientific spirit until he realises that he is essentially a man of science. From the first his aim was to express himself; and it was a long time before he realised that verse was not his native language. His first three plays were in verse, the fourth in verse alternating with prose; then came two plays, historic and legendary, written in more or less archaic prose; then a satire in verse, *Love's Comedy*, in which there is the first hint of the social dramas; then another prose play, the nearest approach that he ever made to poetry, but written in prose, *The Pretenders*; and then the two latest and most famous of the poems, *Brand* and *Peer Gynt*. After this, verse is laid aside, and at last we find him condemning it, and declaring 'it is improbable that verse will be employed to any extent worth mentioning in the drama of the immediate future... It is therefore doomed.' But the doom was Ibsen's: to be a great prose dramatist, and only the segment of a poet.

Nothing is more interesting than to study Ibsen's verse in the making. His sincerity to his innermost aim, the aim at the expression of himself, is seen in his refusal from the beginning to accept any poetic convention, to limit himself in poetic subject, to sift his material or clarify his metre. He has always insisted on producing something personal, thoughtful, fantastic, and essentially prosaic; and it is in a vain protest against the nature of things that he writes of *Peer Gynt*, 'My book *is* poetry; and if it is not, then it will be. The conception of poetry in our country, in Norway, shall be made to conform to the book.' His verse was the assertion of his individuality at all costs; it was a costly tool, which he cast aside only when he found that it would not carve every material.

Ibsen's earliest work in verse has not been translated. Dr. Brandes tells us that it followed Danish models, the sagas, and the national ballads. In the prose play, *Lady Inger of Östraat*, we see the dramatist, the clever playwright, still holding on to the skirts of romance, and ready with rhetoric enough on occasion, but more concerned with plot and stage effect than with even what is interesting in the psychology of the characters. *The Vikings*, also in prose, is a piece of strong grappling with a heroic subject, with better rhetoric, and some good poetry taken straight out of the sagas, with fervour in it, and gravity; yet an experiment only, a thing not made wholly personal, nor wholly achieved. It shows how well Ibsen could do work which was not his work. In *Love's Comedy*, a modern play in verse, he is already himself. Point of view is there; materials are there; the man of science has already laid his hand upon the poet. We are told that Ibsen tried to write it in prose, failed, and fell back upon verse. It is quite likely; he has already an accomplished technique, and can put his thoughts into verse with admirable skill. But the thoughts are not born in verse, and, brilliantly rhymed as they are, they do not make poetry.

Dr. Brandes admits everything that can be said against Ibsen as a poet when he says, speaking of this play and of *Brand*:

> Even if the ideas they express have not previously found utterance in
> poetry, they have done so in prose literature. In other words, these
> poems do not set forth new thoughts, but translate into metre and
> rhyme thoughts already expressed.

Love's Comedy is a criticism of life; it is full of hard, scientific,
prose thought about conduct, which has its own quality as long as
it sticks to fact and remains satire; but when the prose curvets and
tries to lift, when criticism turns constructive, we find no more
than bubbles and children's balloons, empty and coloured, that
soar and evaporate. There is, in this farce of the intellect, a
beginning of social drama; realism peeps through the artificial
point and polish of a verse which has some of the qualities of Pope
and some of the qualities of Swift; but the dramatist is still content
that his puppets shall have the air of puppets; he stands in the
arena of his circus and cracks his whip; they gallop round
grimacing, and with labels on their backs. The verse comes
between him and nature, as the satire comes between him and
poetry. Cynicism has gone to the making of poetry more than
once, but only under certain conditions: that the poet should be a
lyric poet, like Heine, or a great personality in action, like Byron,
to whom cynicism should be but one of the tones of his speech,
the gestures of his attitude. With Ibsen it is a petty anger, an
anger against nature, and it leads to a transcendentalism which is
empty and outside nature.

The criticism of love, so far as it goes beyond what is amusing
and Gilbertian, is the statement of a kind of arid soul-culture more
sterile than that of any cloister, the soul-culture of the scientist who
thinks he has found out, and can master, the soul. It is a new
asceticism, a denial of nature, a suicide of the senses which may
lead to some literal suicide such as that in *Rosmersholm*, or may
feed the brain on some air unbreathable by the body, as in *When
we Dead Awaken*. It is the old idea of self-sacrifice creeping back
under cover of a new idea of self-intensification; and it comes, like

asceticism, from a contempt of nature, a distrust of nature, an abstract intellectual criticism of nature.

Out of such material no poetry will ever come; and none has come in *Love's Comedy*. In the prose play which followed, *The Pretenders*, which is the dramatisation of an inner problem in the form of a historical drama, there is a much nearer approach to poetry. The stagecraft is still too obvious; effect follows effect like thunder-claps; there is melodrama in the tragedy; but the play is, above all, the working-out of a few deep ideas, and in these ideas there is both beauty and wisdom.

It was with the publication of *Brand* that Ibsen became famous, not only in his own country, but throughout Europe. The poem has been seriously compared, even in England, with *Hamlet*; even in Germany with *Faust*. A better comparison is that which Mr. Gosse has made with Sidney Dobell's *Balder*. It is full of satire and common-sense, of which there is little enough in *Balder*: but not *Balder* is more abstract, or more inhuman in its action. Types, not people, move in it; their speech is doctrine, not utterance; it is rather a tract than a poem. The technique of the verse, if we can judge it from the brilliant translation of Professor Herford, which reads almost everywhere like an original, is more than sufficient for its purpose; all this argumentative and abstract and realistic material finds adequate expression in a verse which has aptly been compared with the verse of Browning's *Christmas-eve and Easter-day*. The comparison may be carried further, and it is disastrous to Ibsen. Browning deals with hard matter, and can be boisterous; but he is never, as Ibsen is always, pedestrian. The poet, though, like St. Michael, he carry a sword, must, like St. Michael, have wings. Ibsen has no wings.

But there is another comparison by which I think we can determine more precisely the station and quality of *Brand* as poetry. Take any one of the vigorous and vivid statements of dogma, which are the very kernel of the poem, and compare them with a few lines from Blake's *Everlasting Gospel*. There every line, with all its fighting force, is pure poetry; it was conceived as poetry, born as poetry, and can be changed into no other substance. Here we find a vigorous technique fitting striking thought into good swinging verse, with abundance of apt metaphor; but where is the vision, the essence, which distinguishes it from what, written in prose, would have lost nothing? Ibsen writes out of the intellect, adding fancy and emotion as he goes; but in Blake every line leaps forth like lightning from a cloud.

The motto of *Brand* was 'all or nothing'; that of *Peer Gynt* 'to be master of the situation.' Both are studies of egoism, in the finding and losing of self; both are personal studies and national lessons. Of *Peer Gynt* Ibsen said, 'I meant it to be a caprice.' It is Ibsen in high spirits; and it is like a mute dancing at a funeral. It is a harlequin of a poem, a thing of threads and patches; and there are gold threads in it and tattered clouts. It is an experiment which has hardly succeeded, because it is not one but a score of experiments. It is made up of two elements, an element of folklore and an element of satire. The first comes and goes for the most part with Peer and his mother; and all this brings Norwegian soil with it, and is alive. The satire is fierce, local, and fantastic. Out of the two comes a clashing thing which may itself suggest, as has been said, the immense contrast between Norwegian summer, which is day, and winter, which is night. Grieg's music, childish, mumbling, singing, leaping, and sombre, has aptly illustrated it. It was a thing done on a holiday, for a holiday. It was of this that Ibsen said he could not have written it any nearer home than Ischia and Sorrento. But is it, for all its splendid scraps and patches, a single masterpiece? is it, above all, a poem? The idea, certainly, is one and coherent; every scene is an illustration of that idea; but is it born of that idea? Is it, more than once or twice, inevitable? What touches at times upon poetry is the folk element; the irony at times has poetic substance in it; but this glimmer of poetic substance, which comes and goes, is lost for the most part among mists and vapours, and under artificial light. That poet which exists somewhere in Ibsen, rarely quite out of sight, never wholly at liberty, comes into this queer dance of ideas and humours, and gives it, certainly, the main value it has. But the 'state satirist' is always on the heels of the poet; and imagination, whenever it appears for a moment, is led away into bondage by the spirit of the fantastic, which is its prose equivalent or makeshift. It is the fantastic that Ibsen generally gives us in the place of imagination; and the fantastic is a kind of rhetoric, manufactured by the will, and has no place in poetry.

In *The League of Youth* Ibsen takes finally the step which he had half taken in *Loves Comedy*. 'In my new comedy,' he writes to Dr. Brandes, 'you will find the common order of things – no strong emotions, no deep feelings, and, more particularly, no isolated thoughts.' He adds: 'It is written in prose, which gives it a strong realistic colouring. I have paid particular attention to form, and, among other things, I have accomplished the feat of doing without a single monologue, in fact without a single "aside." 'The play is hardly more than a good farce; the form is no more than the slightest of advances towards probability on the strict lines of the Scribe tradition; the 'common order of things' is there, in subject, language, and in everything but the satirical intention which underlies the whole trivial, stupid, and no doubt lifelike talk and action. Two elements are still in conflict, the photographic and the satirical; and the satirical is the only relief from the photographic. The stage mechanism is still obvious; but the intention, one sees clearly, is towards realism; and the play helps to get the mechanism in order.

After *The League of Youth* Ibsen tells us that he tried to 'seek salvation in remoteness of subject'; so he returned to his old scheme for a play on Julian the Apostate, and wrote the two five-act plays which make up *Emperor and Galilean*. He tells us that it is the first work which he wrote under German intellectual influences, and that it contains 'that positive theory of life which the critics have demanded of me so long.' In one letter he affirms that it is 'an entirely realistic work,' and in another, 'It is a part of my own spiritual life which I am putting into this book ... and the historical subject chosen has a much more intimate connexion with the movements of our own time than one might at first imagine.' How great a relief it must have been, after the beer and sausages of *The League of Youth*, to go back to an old cool wine, no one can read *Emperor and Galilean* and doubt. It is a relief and an escape; and the sense of the stage has been put wholly on one side in both of these plays, of which the second reads almost like a parody of the first: the first so heated, so needlessly colloquial, the second so full of argumentative rhetoric. Ibsen has turned against his hero in the space between writing the one and the other; and the Julian of the second is more harshly satirised from within than ever *Peer Gynt* was. In a letter to Dr. Brandes, Ibsen says: 'What the book is or is not, I have no desire to enquire. I only know that I saw a fragment of humanity plainly before my eyes, and that I tried to reproduce what I saw.' But in the play itself this intention comes and goes; and, while some of it reminds one of *Salammbô* in its attempt to treat remote ages realistically, other parts are given up wholly to the exposition of theories, and yet others to a kind of spectacular romance, after the cheap method of George Ebers and the German writers of historical fiction. The satire is more serious, the criticism of ideas more fundamental than anything in *The League of Youth*; but, as in almost the whole of Ibsen's more characteristic work up to this point, satire strives with realism; it is still satire, not irony, and is not yet, as the later irony is to be, a deepening, and thus a justification, of the realism.

Eight years passed between *The League of Youth* and *The Pillars of Society*; but they are both woven of the same texture. Realism has made for itself a firmer footing; the satire has more significance; the mechanism of the stage goes much more smoothly, though indeed to a more conventionally happy ending; melodrama has taken some of the place of satire. Yet the 'state satirist' is still at his work, still concerned with society and bringing only a new detail of the old accusation against society. Like every play of this period, it is the unveiling of a lie. See yourselves as you are, the man of science seems to be saying to us. Here are your 'pillars of society'; they are the tools of society. Here is your happy marriage, and it is a doll's house. Here is your respected family, here is the precept of 'honour your father and your mother' in practice; and here is the little voice of heredity whispering 'ghosts!' There is the lie of respectability, the lie hidden behind marriage, the lie which saps the very roots of the world.

Ibsen is no preacher, and he has told us expressly that *Ghosts* 'preaches nothing at all.' This pursuit of truth to its most secret hiding-place is not a sermon against sin; it sets a scientific dogma visibly to work, and watches the effect of the hypothesis. As the dogma is terrible and plausible, and the logic of its working-out faultless, we get one of the deeper thrills that modern art has to give us. I would take *A Doll's House*, *Ghosts*, and *The Wild Duck* as Ibsen's three central plays, the plays in which his method completely attained its end, in which his whole capacities are seen at their finest balance; and this work, this reality in which every word, meaningless in itself, is alive with suggestion, is the finest scientific work which has been done in literature. Into this period comes his one buoyant play, *An Enemy of the People*, his rebound against the traditional hypocrisy which had attacked *Ghosts* for its telling of unseasonable truths; it is an allegory, in the form of journalism, or journalism in the form of allegory, and is the 'apology' of the man of science for his mission. Every play is a dissection, or a vivisection rather; for these people who suffer so helplessly, and are shown us so calmly in their agonies, are terribly alive. *A Doll's House* is the first of Ibsen's plays in which the puppets have no visible wires. The playwright has perfected his art of illusion; beyond *A Doll's House* and *Ghosts* dramatic illusion has never gone. And the irony of the ideas that work these living puppets has now become their life-blood. It is the tragic irony of a playwright who is the greatest master of technique since Sophocles, but who is only the playwright in Sophocles, not the poet.

For this moment, the moment of his finest achievement, that fantastic element which was Ibsen's resource against the prose of fact is so sternly repressed that it seems to have left no trace behind. With *The Wild Duck* fantasy comes back, but with a more precise and explicit symbolism, not yet disturbing the reality of things. Here the irony is more disinterested than even in *Ghosts*, for it turns back on the reformer and shows us how tragic a muddle we may bring about in the pursuit of truth and in the name of our ideals. In each of the plays which follows we see the return and encroachment of symbolism, the poetic impulse crying for satisfaction and offering us ever new forms of the fantastic in place of any simple and sufficing gift of imagination. The man of science has had his way, has fulfilled his aim, and is discontented with the limits within which he has fulfilled it. He would extend those limits; and at first it seems as if those limits are to be extended. But the exquisite pathos which humanises what is fantastic in *The Wild Duck* passes, in *Rosmersholm*, in which the problems of *Love's Comedy* are worked out to their logical conclusion, into a form, not of genuine tragedy, but of mental melodrama. In *The Lady from the Sea*, how far is the symbol which has eaten up reality really symbol? Is it not rather the work of the intelligence than of the imagination? Is it not allegory intruding into reality, disturbing that reality and giving us no spiritual reality in its place?

Hedda Gabler is closer to life; and Ibsen said about it in a letter:

> It was not really my desire to deal in this play with so-called problems. What I principally wanted to do was to depict human beings, human emotions, and human destinies, upon a groundwork of certain of the social conditions and principles of the present day.'

The play might be taken for a study in that particular kind of 'decadence' which has come to its perfection in uncivilised and overcivilised Russia; and the woman whom Ibsen studied as his model was actually half-Russian. Eleonora Duse has created Hedda over again, as a poet would have created her, and has made a wonderful creature whom Ibsen never conceived, or at least never rendered. Ibsen has tried to add his poetry by way of ornament, and gives us a trivial and inarticulate poet about whom float certain catchwords. Here the chief catchword is 'vine-leaves in the hair'; in *The Master-builder* it is 'harps in the air'; in *Little Eyolf* it takes human form and becomes the Rat-wife; in *John Gabriel Borkman* it drops to the tag of 'a dead man and two shadows'; in *When we Dead Awaken* there is nothing but icy allegory. All that queer excitement of *The Master-builder*, that 'ideal' awake again, is it not really a desire to open one's door to the younger generation? But is it the younger generation that finds itself at home there? is it not rather *Peer Gynt* back again, and the ride through the air on the back of the reindeer?

In his earlier plays Ibsen had studied the diseases of society, and he had considered the individual only in his relation to society. Now he turns to study the diseases of the individual conscience. Only life interests him now, and only life feverishly alive; and the judicial irony has gone out of his scheme of things. The fantastic, experimental artist returns, now no longer external, but become morbidly curious. The man of science, groping after something outside science, reaches back, though with a certain uneasiness, to the nursery legend of the Rat-wife in *Little Eyolf*; and the Rat-wife is neither reality nor imagination, neither Mother Bombie nor Macbeth's witches, but the offspring of a supernaturalism that does not believe in itself. In *John Gabriel Borkman*, which is the culmination of Ibsen's skill in construction, a play in four acts with only the pause of a minute between each, he is no longer content to concern himself with the old material, lies or misunderstandings, the irony of things happening as they do; but will have fierce hatreds, and a kind of incipient madness in things. In *When we Dead Awaken* all the people are quite consciously insane, and act a kind of charade with perfectly solemn faces and a visible effort to look their parts.

In these last plays, with their many splendid qualities, not bound together and concentrated as in *Ghosts*, we see the revenge of the imagination upon the realist, who has come to be no longer interested in the action of society upon the individual, but in the individual as a soul to be lost or saved. The man of science has discovered the soul, and does not altogether know what to do with it. He has settled its limits, set it to work in space and time, laid bare some of its secrets, shown its 'physical basis.' And now certain eccentricities in it begin to beckon to him; he would follow the soul into the darkness, but it is dark to him; he can but strain after it as it flutters. In the preface to the collected edition of his plays, published in 1901, Maeterlinck has pointed out, as one still standing at the cross-roads might point out to those who have followed him so far on his way, the great uncertainty in which the poet, the dramatist of to-day, finds himself, as what seems to be known or conjectured of 'the laws of nature' is forced upon him, making the old, magnificently dramatic opportunities of the ideas of fate, of eternal justice, no longer possible for him to use.

> *Le poète dramatique est obligé de faire descendre dans la vie réelle, dans la vie de tous les jours, l'idée qu'il se fait de l'inconnu. Il faut qu'il nous montre de quelle façon, sous quelle forme, dans quelles conditions, d'après quelles lois, à quelle fin, agissent sur nos destinées les puissances supérieures, les influences inintelligibles, les principes infinis, dont, en tant que poète, il est persuadé que l'univers est plein. Et comme il est arrivé à une heure où loyalement il lui est à peu près impossible d'admettre les anciennes, et où celles qui les doivent remplacer ne sont pas encore déterminées, n'ont pas encore de nom, il hésite, tâtonne, et s'il veut rester absolument sincère, il n'ose plus se risquer hors de la réalité immédiate. Il se borne à étudier les sentiments humains dans leurs effets matériels et psychologiques.*

So long as Ibsen does this, he achieves great and solid things; and in *Ghosts* a scientific dogma, the law or theory of heredity, has for once taken the place of fate, and almost persuaded us that science, if it takes poetry from us, can restore to us a kind of poetry. But, as Maeterlinck has seen, as it is impossible not to see,

> *quand Ibsen, dans d'autres drames, essaie de relier à d'autres mystères les gestes de ses hommes en mal de conscience exceptionelle ou de ses*

femmes hallucinées, il faut convenir que, si l'atmosphère qu'il parvient à créer est étrange et troublante, elle est rarement saine et respirable, parce qu'elle est rarement raisonnable et réele.

From the time when, in *A Doll's House*, Ibsen's puppets came to life, they have refused ever since to be put back into their boxes. The manager may play what tricks with them he pleases, but he cannot get them back into their boxes. They are alive, and they live with a weird, spectacular, but irrevocable life. But, after the last play of all, the dramatic epilogue, *When we Dead Awaken*, the puppets have gone back into their boxes. Now they have come to obey the manager, and to make mysterious gestures which they do not understand, and to speak in images and take them for literal truths. Even their spectral life has gone out of them; they are rigid now, and only the strings set them dancing. The puppets had come to life, they had lived the actual life of the earth; and then a desire of the impossible, the desire of a life rarefied beyond human limits, took their human life from them, and they were puppets again. The epilogue to the plays is the apostasy of the man of science, and, as with all apostates, his new faith is not a vital thing; the poet was not really there to reawaken.

•

Before Ibsen the drama was a part of poetry; Ibsen has made it prose. All drama up to Ibsen had been romantic; Ibsen made it science. Until Ibsen no playwright had ever tried to imitate life on the stage, or even, as Ibsen does, to interpret it critically. The desire of every dramatist had been to create over again a more abundant life, and to create it through poetry or through humour; through some form, that is, of the imagination. There was a time when Ibsen too would have made poetry of the drama; there was a time when verse seemed to him the only adequate form in which drama could be written. But his power to work in poetry was not equal to his desire to be a poet; and, when he revolted against verse and deliberately adopted as his material 'the common order of things,' when he set himself, for the first time in the history of the drama, to produce an illusion of reality rather than a translation or transfiguration of reality, he discovered his own strength, the special gift which he had brought into the world; but at the same time he set, for himself and for his age, his own limits to drama.

It is quite possible to write poetic drama in prose, though to use prose rather than verse is to write with the left hand rather than with the right. Before Ibsen, prose had been but a serving-maid to verse; and no great dramatist had ever put forward the prose conception of the drama. Shakespeare and the Elizabethans had used prose as an escape or a side-issue, for variety, or for the heightening of verse. Molière had used prose as the best makeshift for verse, because he was not himself a good craftsman in the art. And, along with the verse, and necessarily dependent upon it, there was the poetic, the romantic quality in drama. Think of those dramatists who seem to have least kinship with poetry; think, I will not say of Molière, but of Congreve. What is more romantic than *The Way of the World*? But Ibsen extracts the romantic quality from drama as if it were a poison; and, in deciding to write realistically in prose, he gives up every aim but that which he defines, so early as 1874, as the wish 'to produce the impression on the reader that what he was reading was something that had really happened.' He is not even speaking of the effect in a theatre; he is defining his aim inside the covers of a book, his whole conception of drama.

The art of imitation has never been carried further than it has been carried by Ibsen in his central plays; and with him, at his best, it is no mere imitation but a critical interpretation of life. How greatly this can be done, how greatly Ibsen has done it, there is *Ghosts* to show us. Yet at what point this supreme criticism may stop, what remains beyond it in the treatment of the vilest contemporary material, we shall see if we turn to a play which seems at first sight more grossly realistic than the most realistic play of Ibsen – Tolstoi's *Powers of Darkness*. Though, as one reads and sees it, the pity and fear seem to weigh almost intolerably upon one, the impression left upon the mind when the reading or the performance is over, is that left by the hearing of noble and tragic music. How, out of such human discords, such a divine harmony can be woven I do not know; that is the secret of Tolstoi's genius, as it is the secret of the musician's. Here, achieved in terms of naked horror, we find some of the things which Maeterlinck has aimed at and never quite rendered through an atmosphere and through forms of vague beauty. And we find also another kind of achievement, by the side of which Ibsen's cunning adjustments of reality seem a little trivial or a little unreal. Here, for once, human life is islanded on the stage, a pin-point of light in an immense darkness; and the sense of that surrounding darkness is conveyed to us, as in no other modern play, by an awful sincerity and an unparalleled simplicity. Whether Tolstoi has learned by instinct some stagecraft which playwrights have been toiling after in vain, or by what conscious and deliberate art he has supplemented instinct, I do not know. But, out of horror and humour, out of some creative abundance which has taken the dregs of human life up into itself and transfigured them by that pity which is understanding, by that faith which is creation, Tolstoi has in this play done what Ibsen has never done – given us an interpretation of life which owes nothing to science, nothing to the prose conception of life, but which, in spite of its form, is essential poetry.

Ibsen's concern is with character; and no playwright has created a more probable gallery of characters with whom we can become so easily and so completely familiar. They live before us, and with apparently so unconscious a self-revelation that we speculate about them as we would about real people, and sometimes take sides with them against their creator. Nora would, would not, have left her children! We know all their tricks of mind, their little differences from other people, their habits, the things that a novelist spends so much of his time in bringing laboriously before us. Ibsen, in a single stage direction, gives you more than you would find in a chapter of a novel. His characters, when they are most themselves, are modern, of the day or moment; they are average, and represent nothing which we have not met with, nothing which astonishes us because it is of a nobility, a heroism, a wildness beyond our acquaintance. It is for this that he has been most praised; and there is something marvellous in the precision of his measurements of just so much and no more of the soul.

Yet there are no great characters in Ibsen; and do not great characters still exist? Ibsen's exceptional people never authenticate themselves as being greatly exceptional; their genius is vouched for on a report which they are themselves unable to confirm, as in the inarticulate poet Lövborg, or on their own assertion, as with John Gabriel Borkman, of whom even Dr. Brandes admits, 'His own words do not convince me, for one, that he has ever possessed true genius.' When he is most himself, when he has the firmest hold on his material, Ibsen limits himself to that part of the soul which he and science know. By taking the average man as his hero, by having no hero, no villain, only probable levels, by limiting human nature to the bounds within which he can clinically examine it, he shirks, for the most part, the greatest crisis of the soul. Can the greatest drama be concerned with less than the ultimate issues of nature, the ultimate types of energy? with Lear and with Œdipus? The world of Shakespeare and of the Greeks is the world; it is universal, whether Falstaff blubbers in the tavern or Philoctetes cries in the cave. But the world which Ibsen really knows is that little segment of the world which we call society; its laws are not those of nature, its requirements are not the requirements of God or of man; it is a business association for the capture and division of profits; it is, in short, a fit subject for scientific study, but no longer a part of the material of poetry. The characteristic plays of Ibsen are rightly known as 'social dramas.' Their problem, for the main part, is no longer man in the world, but man in society. That is why they have no atmosphere, no background, but are carefully localised.

The rhythm of prose is physiological; the rhythm of poetry is musical. There is in every play of Ibsen a rhythm perfect of its kind, but it is the physiological rhythm of prose. The rhythm of a play of Shakespeare speaks to the blood like wine or music; it is with exultation, with intoxication, that we see or read *Antony and Cleopatra*, or even *Richard II*. But the rhythm of a play of Ibsen is like that of a diagram in Euclid; it is the rhythm of logic, and it produces in us the purely mental exaltation of a problem solved. These people who are seen so clearly, moving about in a well-realised world, using probable words and doing necessary things, may owe some of their manner at least to the modern French stage, and to the pamphleteer's prose world of Dumas *fils*; yet, though they may illustrate problems, they no longer recite them. They are seen, not as the poet sees his people, naked against a great darkness, but clothed and contemporary, from the level of an ironical observer who sits in a corner of the same room. It is the doctor who sits there, watching his patients, and smiling ambiguously as he infers from his knowledge of their bodies what pranks their souls are likely to play.

If Ibsen gets no other kind of beauty, does he not get beauty of emotion? Or can there be beauty in an intensity of emotion which can be at least approached, in the power of thrilling, by an Adelphi melodrama? Is the speech of his people, when it is most nearly a revelation of the obscure forces outside us or within us, more than a stammering of those to whom unconsciousness does not lend distinction but intensifies idiosyncrasy? Drama, in its essence, requires no speech; it can be played by marionettes, or in dumb show, and be enthralling. But, speech once admitted, must not that speech, if it is to collaborate in supreme drama, be filled with imagination, be itself a beautiful thing? To Ibsen beauty has always been of the nature of an ornament, not an end. He would concentrate it into a catchword, repeated until it has lost all emotional significance. For the rest, his speech is the language of the newspaper, recorded with the fidelity of the phonograph. Its whole aim is at economy, as if economy were an end rather than a means.

Has not Ibsen, in the social dramas, tried to make poems without words? There is to be beauty of motive and beauty of emotion; but the words are to be the plainest of all the plain words which we use in talking with one another, and nothing in them is to speak greatly when great occasions arise. Men's speech in great drama is as much higher than the words they would use in real life as their thoughts are higher than those words. It says the unuttered part of our speech. Ibsen would suppress all this heightening as he has suppressed the soliloquy and the aside. But here what he suppresses is not a convention but a means of interpretation. It is suppressing the essence for the sake of the accident.

Ibsen's genius for the invention of a situation has never been surpassed. More living characters than the characters of Ibsen have never moved on the stage. His women are at work now in the world, interpreting women to themselves, helping to make the women of the future. He has peopled a new world. But the inhabitants of this new world, before they begin to transgress its laws and so lose their own citizenship there, are so faithfully copied from the people about us that they share their dumbness, that dumbness to which it is the power and privilege of poetry to give speech. Given the character and the situation, what Ibsen asks at the moment of crisis is: What would this man be most likely to say? not, What would be the finest, the most deeply revealing thing that he could say? In that difference lies all the difference between prose and poetry.

1906.

JORIS-KARL HUYSMANS

The novels of Huysmans, however we may regard them as novels, are, at all events, the sincere and complete expression of a very remarkable personality. From *Marthe* to *Là-Bas* every story, every volume, disengages the same atmosphere – the atmosphere of a London November, when mere existence is a sufficient burden, and the little miseries of life loom up through the fog into a vague and formidable grotesqueness. Here, for once, is a pessimist whose philosophy is mere sensation – and sensation, after all, is the one certainty in a world which may be well or ill arranged, for ultimate purposes, but which is certainly, for each of us, what each of us feels it to be. To Huysmans the world appears to be a profoundly uncomfortable, unpleasant, ridiculous place, with a certain solace in various forms of art, and certain possibilities of at least temporary escape. Part of his work presents to us a picture of ordinary life as he conceives it, in its uniform trivial wretchedness; in another part he has made experiment in directions which have seemed to promise escape, relief; in yet other portions he has allowed himself the delight of his sole enthusiasm, the enthusiasm of art. He himself would be the first to acknowledge – indeed, practically, he has acknowledged – that the particular way in which he sees life is a matter of personal temperament and constitution, a matter of nerves. The Goncourts have never tired of insisting on the fact of their *névrose*, of pointing out its importance in connection with the form and structure of their work, their touch on style, even. To them the *maladie fin de siècle* has come delicately, as to the chlorotic fine ladies of the Faubourg Saint-Germain: it has sharpened their senses to a point of morbid acuteness, it has given their work a certain feverish beauty. To Huysmans it has given the exaggerated horror of whatever is ugly and unpleasant, with the fatal instinct of discovering, the fatal necessity of contemplating, every flaw and every discomfort that a somewhat imperfect world can offer for inspection. It is the transposition of the ideal. Relative values are lost, for it is the sense of the disagreeable only that is heightened; and the world, in this strange disorder of vision, assumes an aspect which can only be compared with that of a drop of impure water under the microscope. 'Nature seen through a temperament' is Zola's definition of all art. Nothing, certainly, could be more exact and expressive as a definition of the art of Huysmans.

To realise how faithfully and how completely Huysmans has revealed himself in all he has written, it is necessary to know the man. 'He gave me the impression of a cat,' some interviewer once wrote of him; 'courteous, perfectly polite, almost amiable, but all nerves, ready to shoot out his claws at the least word.' And, indeed, there is something of his favourite animal about him. The face is grey, wearily alert, with a look of benevolent malice. At first sight it is commonplace, the features are ordinary, one seems to have seen it at the Bourse or the Stock Exchange. But gradually that strange, unvarying expression, that look of benevolent malice, grows upon you as the influence of the man makes itself felt. I have seen Huysmans in his office – he is an employé in the Ministry of Foreign Affairs, and a model employé; I have seen him in a café, in various houses; but I always see him in memory as I used to see him at the house of the bizarre Madame X. He leans back on the sofa, rolling a cigarette between his thin, expressive fingers, looking at no one and at nothing, while Madame X. moves about with solid vivacity in the midst of her

extraordinary menagerie of *bric-à-brac*. The spoils of all the world
are there, in that incredibly tiny *salon*; they lie underfoot, they
climb up walls, they cling to screens, brackets, and tables; one of
your elbows menaces a Japanese toy, the other a Dresden china
shepherdess; all the colours of the rainbow clash in a barbaric
discord of notes. And in a corner of this fantastic room, Huysmans
lies back indifferently on the sofa, with the air of one perfectly
resigned to the boredom of life. Something is said by my learned
friend who is to write for the new periodical, or perhaps it is the
young editor of the new periodical who speaks, or (if that were
not impossible) the taciturn Englishman who accompanies me;
and Huysmans, without looking up, and without taking the
trouble to speak very distinctly, picks up the phrase, transforms
it, more likely transpierces it, in a perfectly turned sentence, a
phrase of impromptu elaboration. Perhaps it is only a stupid book
that some one has mentioned, or a stupid woman; as he speaks,
the book looms up before one, becomes monstrous in its dulness,
a masterpiece and miracle of imbecility; the unimportant little
woman grows into a slow horror before your eyes. It is always the
unpleasant aspect of things that he seizes, but the intensity of his
revolt from that unpleasantness brings a touch of the sublime into
the very expression of his disgust. Every sentence is an epigram,
and every epigram slaughters a reputation or an idea. He speaks
with an accent as of pained surprise, an amused look of contempt,
so profound that it becomes almost pity, for human imbecility.

Yes, that is the true Huysmans, the Huysmans of *A Rebours*,
and it is just such surroundings that seem to bring out his peculiar
quality. With this contempt for humanity, this hatred of
mediocrity, this passion for a somewhat exotic kind of modernity,
an artist who is so exclusively an artist was sure, one day or
another, to produce a work which, being produced to please
himself, and being entirely typical of himself, would be, in a
way, the quintessence of contemporary Decadence. And it is
precisely such a book that Huysmans has written, in the
extravagant, astonishing *A Rebours*. All his other books are a sort

of unconscious preparation for this one book, a sort of inevitable and scarcely necessary sequel to it. They range themselves along the line of a somewhat erratic development, from Baudelaire, through Goncourt, by way of Zola, to the surprising originality of so disconcerting an exception to any and every order of things.

The descendant of a long line of Dutch painters – one of whom, Cornelius Huysmans, has a certain fame among the lesser landscape men of the great period – Joris-Karl Huysmans was born at Paris, February 5, 1848. His first book, *Le Drageoir á Epices*, published at the age of twenty-six, is a *pasticcio* of prose poems, done after Baudelaire, of little sketches, done after Dutch artists, together with a few studies of Parisian landscape, done after nature. It shows us the careful, laboured work of a really artistic temperament; it betrays, here and there, the spirit of acrimonious observation which is to count for so much with Huysmans – in the crude malice of 'L'Extase,' for example, in the notation of the 'richness of tone,' the 'superb colouring,' of an old drunkard. And one sees already something of the novelty and the precision of his description, the novelty and the unpleasantness of the subjects which he chooses to describe, in this vividly exact picture of the carcass of a cow hung up outside a butcher's shop: 'As in a hothouse, a marvellous vegetation flourished in the carcass. Veins shot out on every side like trails of bind-weed; dishevelled branch-work extended itself along the body, an efflorescence of entrails unfurled their violet-tinted corollas, and big clusters of fat stood out, a sharp white, against the red medley of quivering flesh.'

In *Marthe: histoire d'une fille*, which followed in 1876, two years later, Huysmans is almost as far from actual achievement as in *Le Drageoir à Epices*, but the book, in its crude attempt to deal realistically, and somewhat after the manner of Goncourt, with the life of a prostitute of the lowest depths, marks a considerable advance upon the somewhat casual experiments of his earlier manner. It is important to remember that *Marthe* preceded *La Fille Elisa* and *Nana*. 'I write what I see, what I feel, and what I have experienced,' says the brief and defiant preface, 'and I write it as well as I can: that is all. This explanation is not an excuse, it is simply the statement of the aim that I pursue in art.' Explanation or excuse notwithstanding, the book was forbidden to be sold in France. It is Naturalism in its earliest and most pitiless stage – Naturalism which commits the error of evoking no sort of interest in this unhappy creature who rises a little from her native gutter, only to fall back more woefully into the gutter again. Goncourt's Elisa at least interests us; Zola's Nana at all events appeals to our senses. But Marthe is a mere document, like her story. Notes have been taken – no doubt *sur le vif* – they have been strung together, and here they are, with only an interesting brutality, a curious sordidness to note, in these descriptions that do duty for psychology and incident alike, in the general flatness of character, the general dislocation of episode.

Les Sœurs Vatard, published in 1879, and the short story *Sac au Dos*, which appeared in 1880 in the famous Zolaist manifesto, *Les Soirées de Médan*, show the influence of *Les Rougon-Macquart* rather than of *Germinie Lacerteux*. For the time the 'formula' of Zola has been accepted: the result is, a remarkable piece of work, but a story without a story, a frame without a picture. With Zola, there is at all events a beginning and an end, a chain of events, a play of character upon incident. But in *Les Sœurs Vatard* there is no reason for the narrative ever beginning or ending; there are miracles of description – the workroom, the rue de Sèvres, the locomotives, the *Foire du pain d'épice* – which lead to nothing; there are interiors, there are interviews, there are the two work-girls, Céline and Désirée, and their lovers; there is what Zola himself described as *tout ce milieu ouvrier, ce coin de misère et d'ignorance, de tranquille ordure et d'air naturellement empesté*. And with it all there is a heavy sense of stagnancy, a dreary lifelessness. All that is good in the book reappears, in vastly better company, in *En Ménage* (1881), a novel which is, perhaps, more in the direct line of heritage from *L'Education Sentimentale* – the starting-point of the Naturalistic novel – than any other novel of the Naturalists.

En Ménage is the story of '*Monsieur Tout-le-monde*, an insignificant personality, one of those poor creatures who have not even the supreme consolation of being able to complain of any injustice in their fate, for an injustice supposes at all events a misunderstood merit, a force.' André is the reduction to the bourgeois formula of the invariable hero of Huysmans. He is just enough removed from the commonplace to suffer from it with acuteness. He cannot get on either with or without a woman in his establishment. Betrayed by his wife, he consoles himself with a mistress, and finally goes back to the wife. And the moral of it all is: 'Let us be stupidly comfortable, if we can, in any way we can: but it is almost certain that we cannot.' In *A Vau-l'Eau*, a less interesting story which followed *En Ménage*, the daily misery of the respectable M. Folantin, the government employé, consists in the impossible search for a decent restaurant, a satisfactory dinner: for M. Folantin, too, there is only the same counsel of a desperate, an inevitable resignation. Never has the intolerable monotony of small inconveniences been so scrupulously, so unsparingly chronicled, as in these two studies in the heroic degree of the commonplace. It happens to André, at a certain epoch in his life, to take back an old servant who had left him many years before. He finds that she has exactly the same defects as before, and 'to find them there again,' comments the author, 'did not displease him. He had been expecting them all the time, he saluted them as old acquaintances, yet with a certain surprise, notwithstanding, to see them neither grown nor diminished. He noted for himself with satisfaction that the stupidity of his servant had remained stationary.' On another page, referring to the inventor of cards, Huysmans defines him as one who 'did something towards suppressing the free exchange of human imbecility.' Having to say in passing that a girl has returned from a ball, 'she was at home again,' he observes, 'after the half-dried sweat of the waltzes.' In this invariably sarcastic turn of the phrase, this absoluteness of contempt, this insistence on the disagreeable, we find the note of Huysmans, particularly at this point in his career, when, like Flaubert, he forced himself to contemplate and to analyse the more mediocre manifestations of *la bêtise humaine*.

There is a certain perversity in this furious contemplation of stupidity, this fanatical insistence on the exasperating attraction of the sordid and the disagreeable; and it is by such stages that we come to *A Rebours*. But on the way we have to note a volume of *Croquis Parisiens* (1880), in which the virtuoso who is a part of the artist in Huysmans has executed some of his most astonishing feats; and a volume on *L'Art Moderne* (1883), in which the most modern of artists in literature has applied himself to the criticism – the revelation, rather – of modernity in art. In the latter, Huysmans was the first to declare the supremacy of Degas – 'the greatest artist that we possess to-day in France' – while announcing with no less fervour the remote, reactionary, and intricate genius of Gustave Moreau. He was the first to discover Raffaëlli, 'the painter of poor people and the open sky – a sort of Parisian Millet,' as he called him; the first to discover Forain, 'le véritable peintre de la fille'; the first to discover Odilon Redon, to do justice to Pissaro and Paul Gauguin. No literary artist since Baudelaire has made so valuable a contribution to art criticism, and the *Curiosités Esthétiques* are, after all, less exact in their actual study, less revolutionary, and less really significant in their critical judgments, than *L'Art Moderne*. The *Croquis Parisiens*, which, in its first edition, was illustrated by etchings of Forain and Raffaëlli, is simply the attempt to do in words what those artists have done in aquafortis or in pastel. There are the same Parisian types – the omnibus-conductor, the washerwoman, the man who sells hot chestnuts – the same impressions of a sick and sorry landscape, La Bièvre, for preference, in all its desolate and lamentable attraction; there is a marvellously minute series of studies of that typically Parisian music-hall, the Folies-Bergère. Huysmans' faculty of description is here seen at its fullest stretch of agility; precise, suggestive, with all the outline and colour of actual brush-work, it might even be compared with the art of

Degas, only there is just that last touch wanting, that breath of palpitating life, which is what we always get in Degas, what we never get in Huysmans.

In *L'Art Moderne*, speaking of the water-colours of Forain, Huysmans attributes to them 'a specious and *cherché* art, demanding, for its appreciation, a certain initiation, a certain special sense.' To realise the full value, the real charm, of *A Rebours*, some such initiation might be deemed necessary. In its fantastic unreality, its exquisite artificiality, it is the natural sequel of *En Ménage* and *A Vau-l'Eau*, which are so much more acutely sordid than the most sordid kind of real life; it is the logical outcome of that hatred and horror of human mediocrity, of the mediocrity of daily existence, which we have seen to be the special form of Huysmans' *névrose*. The motto, taken from a thirteenth-century mystic, Rusbroeck the Admirable, is a cry for escape, for the 'something in the world that is there in no satisfying measure, or not at all': *Il faut que je me réjouisse au-dessus du temps ... quoique le monde ait horreur de ma joie et que sa grossièreté ne sache pas ce que je veux dire.* And the book is the history of a *Thebaïde raffinée* – a voluntary exile from the world in a new kind of 'Palace of Art.' Des Esseintes, the vague but typical hero, is one of those half-pathological cases which help us to understand the full meaning of the word *décadence*, which they partly represent. The last descendant of an ancient family, his impoverished blood tainted by all sorts of excesses, Des Esseintes finds himself at thirty *sur le chemin, dégrisé, seul, abominablement lassé.* He has already realised that 'the world is divided, in great part, into swaggerers and simpletons.' His one desire is to 'hide himself away, far from the world, in some retreat, where he might deaden the sound of the loud rumbling of inflexible life, as one covers the street with straw, for sick people.' This retreat he discovers, just far enough from Paris to be safe from disturbance, just near enough to be saved from the nostalgia of the unattainable. He succeeds in making his house a paradise of the artificial, choosing the tones of colour that go best with candle-light, for it need scarcely be said that Des Esseintes has effected a simple transposition of night and day. His disappearance from the world has been complete; it seems to him that the 'comfortable desert' of his exile need never cease to be just such a luxurious solitude; it seems to him that he has attained his desire, that he has attained to happiness.

Disturbing physical symptoms harass him from time to time, but they pass. It is an effect of nerves that now and again he is haunted by remembrance; the recurrence of a perfume, the reading of a book, brings back a period of life when his deliberate perversity was exercised actively in matters of the senses. There are his fantastic banquets, his fantastic amours: the *repas de deuil*, Miss Urania the acrobat, the episode of the ventriloquist-woman and the reincarnation of the Sphinx and the Chimæra of Flaubert, the episode of the boy *chez* Madame Laure. A casual recollection brings up the schooldays of his childhood with the Jesuits, and with that the beliefs of childhood, the fantasies of the Church, the Catholic abnegation of the *Imitatio* joining so strangely with the final philosophy of Schopenhauer. At times his brain is haunted by social theories – his dull hatred of the ordinary in life taking form in the region of ideas. But in the main he feeds himself, with something of the satisfaction of success, on the strange food for the sensations with which he has so laboriously furnished himself. There are his books, and among these a special library of the Latin writers of the Decadence. Exasperated by Virgil, profoundly contemptuous of Horace, he tolerates Lucan (which is surprising), adores Petronius (as well he might), and delights in the neologisms and the exotic novelty of Apuleius. His curiosity extends to the later Christian poets – from the coloured verse of Claudian down to the verse which is scarcely verse of the incoherent ninth century. He is, of course, an amateur of exquisite printing, of beautiful bindings, and possesses an incomparable Baudelaire (*édition tirée à un exemplaire*), a unique Mallarmé. Catholicism being the adopted religion of the Decadence – for its venerable age, valuable in such matters as the age of an old wine,

its vague excitation of the senses, its mystical picturesqueness –
Des Esseintes has a curious collection of the later Catholic
literature, where Lacordaire and the Comte de Falloux, Veuillot
and Ozanam, find their place side by side with the half-prophetic,
half-ingenious Hello, the amalgam of a monstrous mysticism and
a casuistical sensuality, Barbey d'Aurevilly. His collection of
'profane' writers is small, but it is selected for the qualities of
exotic charm that have come to be his only care in art – for the
somewhat diseased, or the somewhat artificial beauty that alone
can strike a responsive thrill from his exacting nerves.
'Considering within himself, he realised that a work of art, in
order to attract him, must come to him with that quality of
strangeness demanded by Edgar Poe; but he fared yet further
along this route, and sought for all the Byzantine flora of the
brain, for complicated deliquescences of style; he required a
troubling indecision over which he could muse, fashioning it after
his will to more of vagueness or of solid form, according to the
state of his mind at the moment. He delighted in a work of art,
both for what it was in itself and for what it could lend him; he
would fain go along with it, thanks to it, as though sustained by
an adjuvant, as though borne in a vehicle, into a sphere where his
sublimated sensations would wake in him an unaccustomed stir,
the cause of which he would long and vainly seek to determine.'
So he comes to care supremely for Baudelaire, 'who, more than
any other, possessed the marvellous power of rendering, with a
strange sanity of expression, the most fleeting, the most wavering
morbid states of exhausted minds, of desolate souls.' In Flaubert
he prefers *La Tentation de Saint-Antoine*; in Goncourt, *La Faustin*; in
Zola, *La Faute de l'Abbé Mouret* – the exceptional, the most remote
and *recherché* outcome of each temperament. And of the three it is
the novel of Goncourt that appeals to him with special intimacy –
that novel which, more than any other, seems to express, in its
exquisitely perverse charm, all that decadent civilisation of which
Des Esseintes is the type and symbol. In poetry he has discovered
the fine perfume, the evanescent charm, of Paul Verlaine, and

near that great poet (forgetting, strangely, Arthur Rimbaud) he places two poets who are curious – the disconcerting, tumultuous Tristan Corbière, and the painted and bejewelled Théodore Hannon. With Edgar Poe he has the instinctive sympathy which drew Baudelaire to the enigmatically perverse Decadent of America; he delights, sooner than all the world, in the astonishing, unbalanced, unachieved genius of Villiers de l'Isle-Adam. Finally, it is in Stéphane Mallarmé that he finds the incarnation of 'the decadence of a literature, irreparably affected in its organism, weakened in its ideas by age, exhausted by the excesses of syntax, sensitive only to the curiosity which fevers sick people, and yet hastening to say everything, now at the end, torn by the wish to atone for all its omissions of enjoyment, to bequeath its subtlest memories of sorrow on its death-bed.'

But it is not on books alone that Des Esseintes nurses his sick and craving fancy. He pushes his delight in the artificial to the last limits, and diverts himself with a bouquet of jewels, a concert of flowers, an orchestra of liqueurs, an orchestra of perfumes. In flowers he prefers the real flowers that imitate artificial ones. It is the monstrosities of nature, the offspring of unnatural adulteries, that he cherishes in the barbarically coloured flowers, the plants with barbaric names, the carnivorous plants of the Antilles – morbid horrors of vegetation, chosen, not for their beauty, but for their strangeness. And his imagination plays harmonies on the sense of taste, like combinations of music, from the flute-like sweetness of anisette, the trumpet-note of kirsch, the eager yet velvety sharpness of curaçao, the clarionet. He combines scents, weaving them into odorous melodies, with effects like those of the refrains of certain poems, employing, for example, the method of Baudelaire in L'Irréparable and Le Balcon, where the last line of the stanza is the echo of the first, in the languorous progression of the melody. And above all he has his few, carefully chosen pictures, with their diverse notes of strange beauty and strange terror – the two Salomés of Gustave Moreau, the 'Religious Persecutions' of Jan Luyken, the opium-dreams of Odilon Redon. His favourite artist is Gustave Moreau, and it is on this superb and disquieting picture that he cares chiefly to dwell.

A throne, like the high altar of a cathedral, rose beneath innumerable arches springing from columns, thick-set as Roman pillars, enamelled with vari-coloured bricks, set with mosaics, incrusted with lapis lazuli and sardonyx, in a palace like the basilica of an architecture at once Mussulman and Byzantine. In the centre of the tabernacle surmounting the altar, fronted with rows of circular steps, sat the Tetrarch Herod, the tiara on his head, his legs pressed together, his hands on his knees. His face was yellow, parchment-like, annulated with wrinkles, withered with age; his long beard floated like a white cloud on the jewelled stars that constellated the robe of netted gold across his breast. Around this statue, motionless, frozen in the sacred pose of a Hindu god, perfumes burned, throwing out clouds of vapour, pierced, as by the phosphorescent eyes of animals, by the fire of precious stones set in the sides of the throne; then the vapour mounted, unrolling itself beneath arches where the blue smoke mingled with the powdered gold of great sunrays, fallen from the domes.

In the perverse odour of perfumes, in the overheated atmosphere of this church, Salomé, her left arm extended in a gesture of command, her bent right arm holding at the level of the face a great lotus, advances slowly to the sound of a guitar, thrummed by a woman who crouches on the floor.

With collected, solemn, almost august countenance, she begins the lascivious dance that should waken the sleeping senses of the aged Herod; her breasts undulate, become rigid at the contact of the whirling necklets; diamonds sparkle on the dead whiteness of her skin, her bracelets, girdles, rings, shoot sparks; on her triumphal robe, sewn with pearls, flowered with silver, sheeted with gold, the jewelled breast-plate, whose every stitch is a precious stone, bursts into flame, scatters in snakes of fire, swarms on the ivory-toned, tea-rose flesh, like splendid insects with dazzling wings, marbled with carmine, dotted with morning gold, diapered with steel-blue, streaked with peacock-green.

•

In the work of Gustave Moreau, conceived on no Scriptural data, Des Esseintes saw at last the realisation of the strange, superhuman Salomé that he had dreamed. She was no more the mere dancing-girl who, with the corrupt torsion of her limbs, tears a cry of desire from an old man; who, with her eddying breasts, her palpitating body, her quivering thighs, breaks the energy, melts the will, of a king; she has become the symbolic deity of indestructible Lust, the goddess of

❀ 193

immortal Hysteria, the accursed Beauty, chosen among many by the catalepsy that has stiffened her limbs, that has hardened her muscles; the monstrous, indifferent, irresponsible, insensible Beast, poisoning, like Helen of old, all that go near to her, all that look upon her, all that she touches.

It is in such a 'Palace of Art' that Des Esseintes would recreate his already over-wrought body and brain, and the monotony of its seclusion is only once broken by a single excursion into the world without. This one episode of action, this one touch of realism, in a book given over to the artificial, confined to a record of sensation, is a projected voyage to London, a voyage that never occurs. Des Esseintes has been reading Dickens, idly, to quiet his nerves, and the violent colours of those ultra-British scenes and characters have imposed themselves upon his imagination. Days of rain and fog complete the picture of that *pays de brume et de boue*, and suddenly, stung by the unwonted desire for change, he takes the train to Paris, resolved to distract himself by a visit to London. Arrived in Paris before his time, he takes a cab to the office of *Galignani's Messenger*, fancying himself, as the rain-drops rattle on the roof and the mud splashes against the windows, already in the midst of the immense city, its smoke and dirt. He reaches *Galignani's Messenger*, and there, turning over Baedekers and Murrays, loses himself in dreams of an imagined London. He buys a Baedeker, and, to pass the time, enters the 'Bodéga' at the corner of the Rue de Rivoli and the Rue Castiglione. The wine-cellar is crowded with Englishmen: he sees, as he drinks his port, and listens to the unfamiliar accents, all the characters of Dickens – a whole England of caricature; as he drinks his Amontillado, the recollection of Poe puts a new horror into the good-humoured faces about him. Leaving the 'Bodéga,' he steps out again into the rain-swept street, regains his cab, and drives to the English tavern of the Rue d'Amsterdam. He has just time for dinner, and he finds a place beside the *insulaires*, with 'their porcelain eyes, their crimson cheeks,' and orders a heavy English dinner, which he washes down with ale and porter, seasoning his coffee, as he imagines we do in England, with gin. As time passes, and the hour of the train draws near, he begins to reflect vaguely on his project; he recalls the disillusion of the visit he had once paid to Holland. Does not a similar disillusion await him in London? 'Why travel, when one can travel so splendidly in a chair? Was he not at London already, since its odours, its atmosphere, its inhabitants, its food, its utensils, were all about him?' The train is due, but he does not stir. 'I have felt and seen,' he says to himself, 'what I wanted to feel and see. I have been saturated with English life all this time; it would be madness to lose, by a clumsy change of place, these imperishable sensations.' So he gathers together his luggage, and goes home again, resolving never to abandon the 'docile phantasmagoria of the brain' for the mere realities of the actual world. But his nervous malady, one of whose symptoms had driven him forth and brought him back so spasmodically, is on the increase. He is seized by hallucinations, haunted by sounds: the hysteria of Schumann, the morbid exaltation of Berlioz, communicate themselves to him in the music that besieges his brain. Obliged at last to send for a doctor, we find him, at the end of the book, ordered back to Paris, to the normal life, the normal conditions, with just that chance of escape from death or madness. So suggestively, so instructively, closes the record of a strange, attractive folly – in itself partly a serious ideal (which indeed is Huysmans' own), partly the caricature of that ideal. Des Esseintes, though studied from a real man, who is known to those who know a certain kind of society in Paris, is a type rather than a man: he is the offspring of the Decadent art that he adores, and this book a sort of breviary for its worshippers. It has a place of its own in the literature of the day, for it sums up, not only a talent, but a spiritual epoch.

A Rebours is a book that can only be written once, and since that date Huysmans has published a short story, Un Dilemme (1887), which is merely a somewhat lengthy anecdote; two novels, En Rade (1887) and Là-Bas (1891), both of which are interesting experiments, but neither of them an entire success; and a volume of art criticism, *Certains* (1890), notable for a single splendid essay, that on Félicien Rops, the etcher of the fantastically erotic. *En Rade* is a sort of deliberately exaggerated record – vision rather than record – of the disillusions of a country sojourn, as they affect the disordered nerves of a town *névrose*. The narrative is punctuated by nightmares, marvellously woven out of nothing, and with no psychological value – the human part of the book being a sort of picturesque pathology at best, the representation of a series of states of nerves, sharpened by the tragic ennui of the country. There is a cat which becomes interesting in its agonies; but the long boredom of the man and woman is only too faithfully shared with the reader. *Là-Bas* is a more artistic creation, on a more solid foundation. It is a study of Satanism, a dexterous interweaving of the history of Gilles de Retz (the traditional Bluebeard) with the contemporary manifestations of the Black Art. 'The execration of impotence, the hate of the mediocre – that is perhaps one of the most indulgent definitions of Diabolism,' says Huysmans, somewhere in the book, and it is on this side that one finds the link of connection with the others of that series of pessimist studies in life. *Un naturalisme spiritualiste*, he defines his own art at this point in its development; and it is in somewhat the 'documentary' manner that he applies himself to the study of these strange problems, half of hysteria, half of a real mystical corruption that does actually exist in our midst. I do not know whether the monstrous tableau of the Black Mass – so marvellously, so revoltingly described in the central episode of the book – is still enacted in our days, but I do know that all but the most horrible practices of the sacrilegious magic of the Middle Ages are yet performed, from time to time, in a secrecy which is all but absolute. The character of Madame Chantelouve is an attempt, probably the first in literature, to diagnose a case of Sadism in a woman. To say that it is successful would be to assume that the thing is possible, which one hesitates to do. The book is even more disquieting, to the normal mind, than *A Rebours*. But it is not, like that, the study of an exception which has become a type.

It is the study of an exception which does not profess to be anything but a disease.

Huysmans' place in contemporary literature is not quite easy to estimate. There is a danger of being too much attracted, or too much repelled, by those qualities of deliberate singularity which make his work, sincere expression as it is of his own personality, so artificial and *recherché* in itself. With his pronounced, exceptional characteristics, it would have been impossible for him to write fiction impersonally, or to range himself, for long, in any school, under any master. Interrogated one day as to his opinion of Naturalism, he had but to say in reply: *Au fond, il y a des écrivains qui ont du talent et d'autres qui n'en ont pas, qu'ils soient naturalistes, romantiques, décadents, tout ce que vous voudrez, ça m'est égal! il s'agit pour moi d'avoir du talent, et voilà tout!* But, as we have seen, he has undergone various influences, he has had his periods. From the first he has had a style of singular pungency, novelty, and colour; and, even in *Le Drageoir à Epices*, we find such daring combinations as this (*Camaïeu Rouge*) – *Cette fanfare de rouge m'étourdissait; cette gamme d'une intensité furieuse, d'une violence inouïe, m'aveuglait.* Working upon the foundation of Flaubert and of Goncourt, the two great modern stylists, he has developed an intensely personal style of his own, in which the sense of rhythm is entirely dominated by the sense of colour. He manipulates the French language with a freedom sometimes barbarous, 'dragging his images by the heels or the hair' (in the admirable phrase of Léon Bloy) 'up and down the worm-eaten staircase of terrified syntax,' gaining, certainly, the effects at which he aims. He possesses, in the highest degree, that *style tacheté et faisandé* – high-flavoured and spotted with corruption – that he attributes to Goncourt and Verlaine. And with this audacious and barbaric profusion of words – chosen always for their colour and their vividly expressive quality – he is able to describe the essentially modern aspects of things as no one had ever described them before. No one before him had ever so realised the perverse charm of the sordid, the perverse charm of the artificial. Exceptional always, it is for such qualities as these, rather than for the ordinary qualities of the novelist, that he is remarkable. His stories are without incident, they are constructed to go on until they stop, they are almost without characters. His psychology is a matter of the sensations, and chiefly the visual sensations. The moral nature is ignored, the emotions resolve themselves for the most part into a sordid ennui, rising at times into a rage at existence. The protagonist of every book is not so much a character as a bundle of impressions and sensations – the vague outline of a single consciousness, his own. But it is that single consciousness – in this morbidly personal writer – with which we are concerned. For Huysmans' novels, with all their strangeness, their charm, their repulsion, typical too, as they are, of much beside himself, are certainly the expression of a personality as remarkable as that of any contemporary writer.

1892.

TWO SYMBOLISTS

Un livre comme je ne les aime pas, says Mallarmé characteristically (*ceux épars et privés d'architecture*) of this long expected first volume of collected prose, *Divagations,* in which we find the prose poems of early date; medallion or full-length portraits of Villiers de l'Isle-Adam, Verlaine, Rimbaud, Poe, Whistler, and others; the marvellous, the unique, studies in the symbolism of the ballet and the theatrical spectacle, comparatively early in date; *Richard Wagner: rêverie d'un Poète français, Le Mystère dans les Lettres*; and, under various titles, the surprising *Variations sur un Sujet.* The hesitation of a lifetime having been, it would seem, overcome, we are at last able to read Mallarmé's 'doctrine,' if not altogether as he would have us read it. And we are at last able, without too much injustice, to judge him as a writer of prose.

In saying that this volume is the most beautiful and the most valuable which has found its way into my hands for I know not how long, I shall not pretend to have read it with ease, or to have understood every word of it. *D'exhiber les choses à un imperturbable premier plan, en camelots, activés par la pression de l'instant, d'accord – écrire, dans le cas pourquoi, indûment, sauf pour étaler la banalité; plutôt que tendre le nuage, précieux, flottant sur l'intime gouffre de chaque pensée, vu que vulgaire l'est ce à quoi on décerne, pas plus, un caractère immédiat.* No, it has always been to that *labyrinthe illuminé par des fleurs* that Mallarmé has felt it due to their own dignity to invite his readers. To their own dignity, and also to his. Mallarmé is obscure, not so much because he writes differently as because he thinks differently from other people. His mind is elliptical, and (relying on the intelligence of his readers) he emphasises the effect of what is unlike other people in his mind by resolutely ignoring even the links of connection that exist between them. Never having aimed at popularity, he has never needed, as most writers need, to make the first advances. He has made neither intrusion upon nor concession to those who after all need not read him. And when he has spoken he has not considered it needful or seemly to listen in order that he might hear whether he was heard. To the charge of obscurity he replies, with sufficient disdain, that there are many who do not know how to read – except the newspapers, he adds, in one of those disconcerting, oddly printed parentheses, which make his work, to those who can rightly apprehend it, so full of wise limitations, so safe from hasty or seemingly final conclusions. No one in our time has more significantly vindicated the supreme right of the artist in the aristocracy of letters; wilfully, perhaps, not always wisely, but nobly, logically. Has not every artist shrunk from that making of himself 'a motley to the view,' that handing over of his naked soul to the laughter of the multitude? but who in our time has wrought so subtle a veil, shining on this side, where the few are, a thick cloud on the other, where are the many? The oracles have always had the wisdom to hide their secret in the obscurity of double meanings or of what has seemed meaningless; and might it not after all be the finest epitaph for a self-respecting man of letters to be able to say, even after the writing of many books: I have kept my secret, I have not betrayed myself to the crowd?

It has been the distinction of Mallarmé that he has always aspired after an impossible liberation of the soul of literature from what is fretting and constraining in 'the body of that death,' which is the mere literature of words. Words, he has realised, are of value only as notations of the free breath of the spirit; words, therefore, must be employed with an extreme care in their choice and adjustment, in setting them to reflect and chime upon one another; yet least of all things for their own sake, for the sake of what they can never, except by suggestion, express. Thus an artificiality, even, in the use of words – that seeming artificiality which comes from using words as if they had never been used before, that chimerical search after the virginity of language – is but the paradoxical outward sign of an extreme discontent with even the best of their service. Writers who use words fluently, seeming to disregard their importance, do so from an unconscious confidence in their expressiveness, which the scrupulous thinker, the precise dreamer, can never place in the most carefully chosen among them. To evoke, by some elaborate, instantaneous magic of language, without the formality of an after all impossible description; to be, in fact, rather than to express; that is what Mallarmé has consistently, and from the first, sought in verse and prose. And he has sought this wandering, illusive, beckoning butterfly, the soul of dreams, over more and more entangled ground; and it has led him into the depths of many forests, far from the sunlight. He would be the last to permit me to say that he has found what he sought; but (is it possible to avoid saying?) how heroic a search, and what marvellous discoveries, by the way!

Yes, all these, he admits perhaps proudly, are divagations, and the secret, eternal, and only beauty is not yet found. Is it, perhaps, in a mood, a momentary mood, really of discouragement, that he has consented to the publication – the 'showing off,' within covers, as of goods in a shop-window: it is his own image – of these fragmentary suggestions towards a complete Æsthetic? Beautiful and invaluable I find them; here and there final; and always, in form, hieratic.

Certain writers, in whom the artist's contempt for common things has been carried to its utmost limit, should only be read in books of beautiful and slightly unusual form. Perhaps of all modern writers Villiers and Mallarmé have most carefully sought the most remote ideal, and seem most to require some elaborate presentation to the reader. Mallarmé, indeed, delighted in heaping up obstacles in the reader's way, not only in the concealment of his meaning by style, but in a furtive, fragmentary, and only too luxurious method of publication, which made it difficult for most people to get his books at all, even for unlimited money. Villiers, on the contrary, after publishing his first book, the *Premières Poésies* of 1859, in the delicate type of Perrin of Lyons, on ribbed paper, with old gold covers, became careless as to how his books appeared, and has to be read in a disorderly crowd of volumes, some of them as hideous as the original edition of *L'Eve Future*, with its red stars and streaks, its Apollo and Cupid and grey city landscape. It is therefore with singular pleasure that one finds the two beautiful books which have lately been published by M. Deman, the well-known publisher of Rops: one, the fullest collection of Mallarmé's poems which has ever been published, the other a selection of twenty stories by Villiers. The Mallarmé is white and red, the poems printed in italics, a frontispiece by Rops; the Villiers is a large square volume in shimmering dark green and gold, with headpieces and tailpieces, in two tints, by Th. van Rysselberghe. These scrolls and titles are done with a sort of reverent self-suppression, as if, for once, decoration existed for a book and not the book for the decoration, which is hardly the quality for which modern decorators are most conspicuous.

In the *Poésies* we have, no doubt, Mallarmé's final selection from his own poems. Some of it is even new. The magnificent and mysterious fragment of *Hérodiade*, his masterpiece, perhaps, is, though not indeed completed, more than doubled in length by the addition of a long passage on which he was at work almost to the time of his death. It is curious to note that the new passage is written in exactly the style of the older passage, though in the interval between the writing of the one and the writing of the other Mallarmé had completely changed his style. By an effort of will he had thought himself back into an earlier style, and the two fragments join without an apparent seam. There were, it appears, still a hymn or lyric spoken by St. John and a concluding monologue, to be added to the poem; but we have at least the whole of the dialogue between Hérodiade and the Nurse, certainly a poem sufficiently complete in itself. The other new pieces are in the latest manner, mainly without punctuation; they would scarcely be alluring, one imagines, even if punctuated. In the course of a few centuries, I am convinced, every line of Mallarmé will have become perfectly clear, as a corrupt Greek text becomes clear in time. Even now a learned commentator could probably do much to explain them, at the cost of a life-long labour; but scholars only give up their lives to the difficult authors of a remote past. Mallarmé can afford to wait; he will not be forgotten; and for us of the present there are the clear and lovely early poems, so delightfully brought together in the white and red book.

L'insensibilité de l'azur et des pierres: a serene and gem-like quality, entirely his own, is in all these poems, in which a particular kind of French verse realises its ideal. Mallarmé is the poet of a few, a limited poet, perfect within his limits as the Chinese artist of his own symbol. In a beautiful poem he compares himself to the painter of tea-cups who spends his life in painting a strange flower

Sur ses tasses de neige à la lune ravie,

a flower which has perfumed his whole existence, since, as a child, he had felt it graft itself upon the 'blue filigree of his soul.'

A very different image must be sought if we wish to sum up the characteristics of Villiers de l'Isle-Adam. An uncertain artist, he was a man of passionate and lofty genius, and he has left us a great mass of imperfect work, out of which we have to form for ourselves whatever notion we can of a man greater than his work. My first impression, on looking at the twenty stories which make up the present selection, was that the selection had been badly made. Where is *Les Demoiselles de Bienfilâtre*? I asked myself, remembering that little ironical masterpiece; where is *Le Convive des Dernières Fêtes*, with its subtlety of horror; *Sentimentalisme*, with its tragic and tender modernity; *La Reine Ysabeau*, with its sombre and taciturn intensity? Story after story came into my mind, finer, it seemed to me, in the artistic qualities of the story than many of those selected. Second thoughts inclined me to think that the selection could scarcely have been better. For it is a selection made after a plan, and it shows us, not indeed always Villiers at his best as a story-teller, but, throughout, Villiers at his highest point of elevation; the man whom we are always trying to see through his work, and the man as he would have seen himself. There is not a collection of stories in French of greater nobility than these *Histoires Souveraines* in which a regal pomp of speech drapes a more than regal sovereignty of soul. The Villiers who mocked mean things and attacked base things is no longer there; the idealist is at home in his own world, among his ideals.

1897, 1899.

CHARLES BAUDELAIRE

Baudelaire is little known and much misunderstood in England. Only one English writer has ever done him justice, or said anything adequate about him. As long ago as 1862 Swinburne introduced Baudelaire to English readers: in the columns of the *Spectator*, it is amusing to remember. In 1868 he added a few more words of just and subtle praise in his book on Blake, and in the same year wrote the magnificent elegy on his death, *Ave atque Vale*. There have been occasional outbreaks of irrelevant abuse or contempt, and the name of Baudelaire (generally mis-spelled) is the journalist's handiest brickbat for hurling at random in the name of respectability. Does all this mean that we are waking up, over here, to the consciousness of one of the great literary forces of the age, a force which has been felt in every other country but ours?

It would be a useful influence for us. Baudelaire desired perfection, and we have never realised that perfection is a thing to aim at. He only did what he could do supremely well, and he was in poverty all his life, not because he would not work, but because he would work only at certain things, the things which he could hope to do to his own satisfaction. Of the men of letters of our age he was the most scrupulous. He spent his whole life in writing one book of verse (out of which all French poetry has come since his time), one book of prose in which prose becomes a fine art, some criticism which is the sanest, subtlest, and surest which his generation produced, and a translation which is better than a marvellous original. What would French poetry be to-day if Baudelaire had never existed? As different a thing from what it is as English poetry would be without Rossetti. Neither of them is quite among the greatest poets, but they are more fascinating than the greatest, they influence more minds. And Baudelaire was an equally great critic. He discovered Poe, Wagner, and Manet. Where even Sainte-Beuve, with his vast materials, his vast general talent for criticism, went wrong in contemporary judgments, Baudelaire was infallibly right. He wrote neither verse nor prose with ease, but he would not permit himself to write either without inspiration. His work is without abundance, but it is without waste. It is made out of his whole intellect and all his nerves. Every poem is a train of thought and every essay is the record of sensation. This 'romantic' had something classic in his moderation, a moderation which becomes at times as terrifying as Poe's logic. To 'cultivate one's hysteria' so calmly, and to affront the reader (*Hypocrite lecteur, mon semblable, mon frère*) as a judge rather than as a penitent; to be a casuist in confession; to be so much a moralist, with so keen a sense of the ecstasy of evil: that has always bewildered the world, even in his own country, where the artist is allowed to live as experimentally as he writes. Baudelaire lived and died solitary, secret, a confessor of sins who has never told the whole truth, *le mauvais moine* of his own sonnet, an ascetic of passion, a hermit of the brothel.

To understand, not Baudelaire, but what we can of him, we must read, not only the four volumes of his collected works, but every document in Crépet's *Œuvres Posthumes*, and, above all, the letters, and these have only now been collected into a volume, under the care of an editor who has done more for Baudelaire than any one since Crépet. Baudelaire put into his letters only what he cared to reveal of himself at a given moment: he has a different angle to distract the sight of every observer; and let no one think that he knows Baudelaire when he has read the letters to Poulet-Malassis, the friend and publisher, to whom he showed his business side, or the letters to la Présidente, the touchstone of his *spleen et idéal*, his chief experiment in the higher sentiments. Some of his carefully hidden virtues peep out at moments, it is true, but nothing that everybody has not long been aware of. We hear of his ill-luck with money, with proof-sheets, with his own health. The tragedy of the life which he chose, as he chose all things (poetry, Jeanne Duval, the 'artificial paradises') deliberately, is made a little clearer to us; we can moralise over it if we like. But the man remains baffling, and will probably never be discovered.

As it is, much of the value of the book consists in those glimpses into his mind and intentions which he allowed people now and then to see. Writing to Sainte-Beuve, to Flaubert, to Soulary, he sometimes lets out, through mere sensitiveness to an intelligence capable of understanding him, some little interesting secret. Thus it is to Sainte-Beuve that he defines and explains the origin and real meaning of the *Petits Poèmes en Prose: Faire cent bagatelles laborieuses qui exigent une bonne humeur constante (bonne humeur nécessaire, même pour traiter des sujets tristes), une excitation bizarre qui a besoin de spectacles, de foules, de musiques, de réverbères même, voilà ce que j'ai voulu faire!* And, writing to some obscure person, he will take the trouble to be even more explicit, as in this symbol of the sonnet: *Avez-vous observé qu'un morceau de ciel aperçu par un soupirail, ou entre deux cheminées, deux rochers, ou par une arcade, donnait une idée plus profonde de l'infini que le grand panorama vu du haul d'une montagne?* It is to another casual person that he speaks out still more intimately (and the occasion of his writing is some thrill of gratitude towards one who had at last done 'a little justice,' not to himself, but to Manet): *Eh bien! on m'accuse, moi, d'imiter Edgar Poe! Savez-vous pourquoi j'ai si patiemment traduit Poe? Parce qu'il me ressemblait. La première fois que j'ai ouvert un livre de lui, j'ai vu avec épouvante et ravissement, non seulement des sujets rêvés par moi, mais des phrases, pensées par moi, et écrites par lui, vingt ans auparavant.* It is in such glimpses as these that we see something of Baudelaire in his letters.

1906.

WALTER PATER

Writing about Botticelli, in that essay which first interpreted Botticelli to the modern world, Pater said, after naming the supreme artists, Michelangelo or Leonardo:

> But, besides these great men, there is a certain number of artists who have a distinct faculty of their own by which they convey to us a peculiar quality of pleasure which we cannot get elsewhere; and these, too, have their place in general culture, and must be interpreted to it by those who have felt their charm strongly, and are often the objects of a special diligence and a consideration wholly affectionate, just because there is not about them the stress of a great name and authority.

It is among these rare artists, so much more interesting, to many, than the very greatest, that Pater belongs; and he can only be properly understood, loved, or even measured by those to whom it is 'the delicacies of fine literature' that chiefly appeal. There have been greater prose-writers in our language, even in our time; but he was, as Mallarmé called him, 'le prosateur ouvragé par excellence de ce temps.' For strangeness and subtlety of temperament, for rarity and delicacy of form, for something incredibly attractive to those who felt his attraction, he was as unique in our age as Botticelli in the great age of Raphael. And he, too, above all to those who knew him, can scarcely fail to become, not only 'the object of a special diligence,' but also of 'a consideration wholly affectionate,' not lessened by the slowly increasing 'stress of authority' which is coming to be laid, almost by the world in general, on his name.

In the work of Pater, thought moves to music, and does all its hard work as if in play. And Pater seems to listen for his thought, and to overhear it, as the poet overhears his song in the air. It is like music, and has something of the character of poetry, yet, above all, it is precise, individual, thought filtered through a temperament; and it comes to us as it does because the style which clothes and fits it is a style in which, to use some of his own words, 'the writer succeeds in saying what he *wills.*'

The style of Pater has been praised and blamed for its particular qualities of colour, harmony, weaving; but it has not always, or often, been realised that what is most wonderful in the style is precisely its adaptability to every shade of meaning or intention, its extraordinary closeness in following the turns of thought, the waves of sensation, in the man himself. Everything in Pater was in harmony, when you got accustomed to its particular forms of expression: the heavy frame, so slow and deliberate in movement, so settled in repose; the timid and yet scrutinising eyes; the mannered, yet so personal, voice; the precise, pausing speech, with its urbanity, its almost painful conscientiousness of utterance; the whole outer mask, in short, worn for protection and out of courtesy, yet moulded upon the inner truth of nature like a mask moulded upon the features which it covers. And the books are the man, literally the man in many accents, turns of phrase; and, far more than that, the man himself, whom one felt through his few, friendly, intimate, serious words: the inner life of his soul coming close to us, in a slow and gradual revelation.

He has said, in the first essay of his which we have:

The artist and he who has treated life in the spirit of art desires only to be shown to the world as he really is; as he comes nearer and nearer to perfection, the veil of an outer life, not simply expressive of the inward, becomes thinner and thinner.

And Pater seemed to draw up into himself every form of earthly beauty, or of the beauty made by men, and many forms of knowledge and wisdom, and a sense of human things which was neither that of the lover nor of the priest, but partly of both; and his work was the giving out of all this again, with a certain labour to give it wholly. It is all, the criticism, and the stories, and the writing about pictures and places, a confession, the *vraie vérité* (as he was fond of saying) about the world in which he lived. That world he thought was open to all; he was sure that it was the real blue and green earth, and that he caught the tangible moments as they passed. It was a world into which we can only look, not enter, for none of us have his secret. But part of his secret was in the gift and cultivation of a passionate temperance, an unrelaxing attentiveness to whatever was rarest and most delightful in passing things.

In Pater logic is of the nature of ecstasy, and ecstasy never soars wholly beyond the reach of logic. Pater is keen in pointing out the liberal and spendthrift weakness of Coleridge in his thirst for the absolute, his 'hunger for eternity,' and for his part he is content to set all his happiness, and all his mental energies, on a relative basis, on a valuation of the things of eternity under the form of time. He asks for no 'larger flowers' than the best growth of the earth; but he would choose them flower by flower, and for himself. He finds life worth just living, a thing satisfying in itself, if you are careful to extract its essence, moment by moment, not in any calculated 'hedonism,' even of the mind, but in a quiet, discriminating acceptance of whatever is beautiful, active, or illuminating in every moment. As he grew older he added something more like a Stoic sense of 'duty' to the old, properly and severely Epicurean doctrine of 'pleasure.' Pleasure was never, for Pater, less than the essence of all knowledge, all experience, and not merely all that is rarest in sensation; it was religious from the first, and had always to be served with a strict ritual. 'Only be sure it is passion,' he said of that spirit of divine motion to which he appealed for the quickening of our sense of life, our sense of ourselves; be sure, he said, 'that it does yield you this fruit of a quickened, multiplied consciousness.' What he cared most for at all times was that which could give 'the highest quality to our moments as they pass'; he differed only, to a certain extent, in his estimation of what that was. 'The herb, the wine, the gem' of the preface to the *Renaissance* tended more and more to become, under less outward symbols of perfection, 'the discovery, the new faculty, the privileged apprehension' by which 'the imaginative regeneration of the world' should be brought about, or even, at times, a brooding over 'what the soul passes, and must pass, through, *aux abois* with nothingness, or with those offended mysterious powers that may really occupy it.'

•

When I first met Pater he was nearly fifty. I did not meet him for about two years after he had been writing to me, and his first letter reached me when I was just over twenty-one. I had been writing verse all my life, and what Browning was to me in verse Pater, from about the age of seventeen, had been to me in prose. Meredith made the third; but his form of art was not, I knew never could be, mine. Verse, I suppose, requires no teaching, but it was from reading Pater's *Studies in the History of the Renaissance*, in its first edition on ribbed paper (I have the feel of it still in my fingers), that I realised that prose also could be a fine art. That book opened a new world to me, or, rather, gave me the key or secret of the world in which I was living. It taught me that there was a beauty besides the beauty of what one calls inspiration, and comes and goes, and cannot be caught or followed; that life (which had seemed to me of so little moment) could be itself a work of art; from that book I realised for the first time that there was anything interesting or vital in the world besides poetry and music. I caught from it an unlimited curiosity, or, at least, the direction of curiosity into definite channels.

The knowledge that there was such a person as Pater in the world, an occasional letter from him, an occasional meeting, and, gradually, the definite encouragement of my work in which, for some years, he was unfailingly generous and attentive, meant more to me, at that time, than I can well indicate, or even realise, now. It was through him that my first volume of verse was published; and it was through his influence and counsels that I trained myself to be infinitely careful in all matters of literature. Influence and counsel were always in the direction of sanity, restraint, precision.

I remember a beautiful phrase which he once made up, in his delaying way, with 'wells' and 'no doubts' in it, to describe, and to describe supremely, a person whom I had seemed to him to be disparaging. 'He does,' he said meditatively, 'remind me of, well, of a steam-engine stuck in the mud. But he is so enthusiastic!' Pater liked people to be enthusiastic, but, with him, enthusiasm was an ardent quietude, guarded by the wary humour that protects the sensitive. He looked upon undue earnestness, even in outward manner, in a world through which the artist is bound to go on a wholly 'secret errand,' as bad form, which shocked him as much in persons as bad style did in books. He hated every form of extravagance, noise, mental or physical, with a temperamental hatred: he suffered from it, in his nerves and in his mind. And he had no less dislike of whatever seemed to him either morbid or sordid, two words which he often used to express his distaste for things and people. He never would have appreciated writers like Verlaine, because of what seemed to him perhaps unnecessarily 'sordid' in their lives. It pained him, as it pains some people, perhaps only because they are more acutely sensitive than others, to walk through mean streets, where people are poor, miserable, and hopeless.

And since I have mentioned Verlaine, I may say that what Pater most liked in poetry was the very opposite of such work as that of Verlaine, which he might have been supposed likely to like. I do not think it was actually one of Verlaine's poems, but something done after his manner in English, that some reviewer once quoted, saying: 'That, to our mind, would be Mr. Pater's ideal of poetry.' Pater said to me, with a sad wonder, 'I simply don't know what he meant.' What he liked in poetry was something even more definite than can be got in prose; and he valued poets like Dante and like Rossetti for their 'delight in concrete definition,' not even quite seeing the ultimate magic of such things as *Kubla Khan*, which he omitted in a brief selection from the poetry of Coleridge. In the most interesting letter which I ever had from him, the only letter which went to six pages, he says:

12 Earl's Terrace,
Kensington, W.,
Jan. 8, 1888.

My dear Mr. Symons, – I feel much flattered at your choosing me as an arbiter in the matter of your literary work, and thank you for the pleasure I have had in reading carefully the two poems you have sent me. I don't use the word 'arbiter' loosely for 'critic'; but suppose a real controversy, on the question whether you shall spend your best energies in writing verse, between your poetic aspirations on the one side, and prudence (calculating results) on the other. Well! judging by these two pieces, I should say that you have a poetic talent remarkable, especially at the present day, for precise and intellectual grasp on the matter it deals with. Rossetti, I believe, said that the value of every artistic product was in direct proportion to the amount of purely intellectual force that went to the initial conception of it: and it is just this intellectual conception which seems to me to be so conspicuously wanting in what, in some ways, is the most characteristic verse of our time, especially that of our secondary poets. In your own pieces, particularly in your MS. 'A Revenge,' I find Rossetti's requirement fulfilled, and should anticipate great things from one who has the talent of conceiving his motive with so much firmness and tangibility – with that close logic, if I may say so, which is an element in any genuinely imaginative process. It is clear to me that you aim at this, and it is what gives your verses, to my mind, great interest. Otherwise, I think the two pieces of unequal excellence, greatly preferring 'A Revenge' to 'Bell in Camp.' Reserving some doubt whether the watch, as the lover's gift, is not a little bourgeois, I think this piece worthy of any poet. It has that aim of concentration and organic unity which I value greatly both in prose and verse. 'Bell in Camp' pleases me less, for the same reason which makes me put Rossetti's 'Jenny,' and some of Browning's pathetic-satiric pieces, below the rank which many assign them. In no one of the poems I am thinking of, is the inherent sordidness of everything in the persons supposed, except the one poetic trait then under treatment, quite forgotten.

Otherwise, I feel the pathos, the humour, of the piece (in the full sense of the word humour) and the skill with which you have worked out your motive therein. I think the present age an unfavourable one to poets, at least in England. The young poet comes into a generation which has produced a large amount of first-rate poetry, and an enormous amount of good secondary poetry. You know I give a high place to the literature of prose as a fine art, and therefore hope you won't think me brutal in saying that the admirable qualities of your verse are those also of imaginative prose; as I think is the case also with much of Browning's finest verse. I should say, make prose your principal *métier*, as a man of letters, and publish your verse as a more intimate gift for those who already value you for your pedestrian work in literature. I should think you ought to find no difficulty in finding a publisher for poems such as those you have sent to me.

I am more than ever anxious to meet you. Letters are such poor means of communication. Don't come to London without making an appointment to come and see me here. – Very sincerely yours,

Walter Pater.

'Browning, one of my best-loved writers,' is a phrase I find in his first letter to me, in December 1886, thanking me for a little book on Browning which I had just published. There is, I think, no mention of any other writer except Shakespeare (besides the reference to Rossetti which I have just quoted) in any of the fifty or sixty letters which I have from him. Everything that is said about books is a direct matter of business: work which he was doing, of which he tells me, or which I was doing, about which he advises and encourages me.

In practical things Pater was wholly vague, troubled by their persistence when they pressed upon him. To wrap up a book to send by post was an almost intolerable effort, and he had another reason for hesitating. 'I take your copy of Shakespeare's sonnets with me,' he writes in June 1889, 'hoping to be able to restore it to you there lest it should get bruised by transit through the post.' He wrote letters with distaste, never really well, and almost always with excuses or regrets in them: 'Am so over-burdened (my time, I mean) just now with pupils, lectures, and the making thereof'; or, with hopes for a meeting: 'Letters are such poor means of communication: when are we to meet?' or, as a sort of hasty makeshift: 'I send this prompt answer, for I know by experience that when I delay my delays are apt to be lengthy.' A review took him sometimes a year to get through; and remained in the end, like his letters, a little cramped, never finished to the point of ease, like his published writings. To lecture was a great trial to him. Two of the three lectures which I have heard in my life were given by Pater, one on Mérimée, at the London Institution, in November 1890, and the other on Raphael, at Toynbee Hall, in 1892. I never saw a man suffer a severer humiliation. The act of reading his written lecture was an agony which communicated itself to the main part of the audience. Before going into the hall at Whitechapel he had gone into a church to compose his mind a little, between the discomfort of the underground railway and the distress of the lecture-hall.

In a room, if he was not among very intimate friends, Pater was rarely quite at his ease, but he liked being among people, and he made the greater satisfaction overcome the lesser reluctance. He was particularly fond of cats, and I remember one evening, when I had been dining with him in London, the quaint, solemn, and perfectly natural way in which he took up the great black Persian, kissed it, and set it down carefully again on his way upstairs. Once at Oxford he told me that M. Bourget had sent him the first volume of his *Essais de Psychologie Contemporaine*, and that the cat had got hold of the book and torn up the part containing the essay on Baudelaire, 'and as Baudelaire was such a lover of cats I thought she might have spared him!'

We were talking once about fairs, and I had been saying how fond I was of them. He said: 'I am fond of them, too. I always go to fairs. I am getting to find they are very similar.' Then he began to tell me about the fairs in France, and I remember, as if it were an unpublished fragment in one of his stories, the minute, coloured impression of the booths, the little white horses of the 'roundabouts,' and the little wild beast shows, in which what had most struck him was the interest of the French peasant in the wolf, a creature he might have seen in his own woods. 'An English clown would not have looked at a wolf if he could have seen a tiger.'

I once asked Pater if his family was really connected with that of the painter, Jean-Baptiste Pater. He said: 'I think so, I believe so, I always say so.' The relationship has never been verified, but one would like to believe it; to find something lineally Dutch in the English writer. It was, no doubt, through this kind of family interest that he came to work upon Goncourt's essay and the contemporary *Life of Watteau* by the Count de Caylus, printed in the first series of *L'Art du XVIIIe Siècle*, out of which he has made certainly the most living of his *Imaginary Portraits*, that *Prince of Court Painters* which is supposed to be the journal of a sister of Jean-Baptiste Pater, whom we see in one of Watteau's portraits in the Louvre. As far back as 1889[4] Pater was working towards a second volume of *Imaginary Portraits*, of which *Hippolytus Veiled* was to have been one. He had another subject in Moroni's *Portrait of a Tailor* in the National Gallery, whom he was going to make a Burgomaster; and another was to have been a study of life in the time of the Albigensian persecution. There was also to be a modern study: could this have been *Emerald Uthwart*? No doubt *Apollo in Picardy*, published in 1893, would have gone into the volume. *The Child in the House*, which was printed as an *Imaginary Portrait*, in *Macmillans Magazine* in 1878, was really meant to be the first chapter of a romance which was to show 'the poetry of modern life,' something, he said, as *Aurora Leigh* does. There is much personal detail in it, the red hawthorn, for instance, and he used to talk to me of the old house at Tunbridge, where his great-aunt lived, and where he spent much of his time when a child. He remembered the gipsies there, and their caravans, when they came down for the hop-picking; and the old lady in her large cap going out on the lawn to do battle with the surveyors who had come to mark out a railway across it; and his terror of the train, and of 'the red flag, which meant *blood*.' It was because he always dreamed of going on with it that he did not reprint this imaginary portrait in the book of *Imaginary Portraits*; but he did not go on with it because, having begun the long labour of *Marius*, it was out of his mind for many years, and when, in 1889, he still spoke of finishing it, he was conscious that he could never continue it in the same style, and that it would not be satisfactory to rewrite it in his severer, later manner. It remains, perhaps fortunately, a fragment, to which no continuation could ever add a more essential completeness.

Style, in Pater, varied more than is generally supposed, in the course of his development, and, though never thought of as a thing apart from what it expresses, was with him a constant preoccupation. Let writers, he said, 'make time to write English more as a learned language.' It has been said that Ruskin, De Quincey, and Flaubert were among the chief 'origins' of Pater's style; it is curiously significant that matter, in Pater, was developed before style, and that in the bare and angular outlines of the earliest fragment, *Diaphanéité*, there is already the substance which is to be clothed upon by beautiful and appropriate flesh in the *Studies in the Renaissance*. Ruskin, I never heard him mention, but I do not doubt that there, to concern himself with beauty in art and literature, was at least a quickening influence. Of De Quincey he spoke with an admiration which I had difficulty in sharing, and I remember his showing me with pride a set of his works bound in half-parchment, with pale gold lettering on the white backs, and with the cinnamon edges which he was so fond of. Of Flaubert we rarely met without speaking. He thought *Julien l'Hospitalier* as perfect as anything he had done. *L'Education Sentimentale* was one of the books which he advised me to read; that, and *Le Rouge et le Noir* of Stendhal; and he spoke with particular admiration of two episodes in the former, the sickness and the death of the child. Of the Goncourts he spoke with admiration tempered by dislike. Their books often repelled him, yet their way of doing things seemed to him just the way things should be done; and done before almost any one else. He often read *Madame Gervaisais*, and he spoke of *Chérie* (for all its 'immodesty') as an admirable thing, and a model for all such studies.

Once, as we were walking in Oxford, he pointed to a window and said, with a slow smile: 'That is where I get my Zolas.' He was always a little on his guard in respect of books; and, just as he read Flaubert and Goncourt because they were intellectual neighbours, so he could read Zola for mere pastime, knowing that there would be nothing there to distract him. I remember telling him about *The Story of an African Farm*, and of the wonderful human quality in it. He said, repeating his favourite formula: 'No doubt you are quite right; but I do not suppose I shall ever read it.' And he explained to me that he was always writing something, and that while he was writing he did not allow himself to read anything which might possibly affect him too strongly, by bringing a new current of emotion to bear upon him. He was quite content that his mind should 'keep as a solitary prisoner its own dream of a world'; it was that prisoner's dream of a world that it was his whole business as a writer to remember, to perpetuate.

1906.

FOOTNOTE

4. In this same year he intended to follow the *Appreciations* by a volume of *Studies of Greek Remains*, in which he then meant to include the studies in Platonism, not yet written; and he had thought of putting together a volume of 'theory,' which was to include the essay on Style. In two or three years' time, he thought, *Gastom de Latour* would be finished.

THE GONCOURTS

My first visit to Edmond de Goncourt was in May 1892. I remember my immense curiosity about that 'House Beautiful,' at Auteuil, of which I had heard so much, and my excitement as I rang the bell, and was shown at once into the garden, where Goncourt was just saying good-bye to some friends. He was carelessly dressed, without a collar, and with the usual loosely knotted large white scarf rolled round his neck. He was wearing a straw hat, and it was only afterwards that I could see the fine sweep of the white hair, falling across the forehead. I thought him the most distinguished-looking man of letters I had ever seen; for he had at once the distinction of race, of fine breeding, and of that delicate artistic genius which, with him, was so intimately a part of things beautiful and distinguished. He had the eyes of an old eagle; a general air of dignified collectedness; a rare, and a rarely charming, smile, which came out, like a ray of sunshine, in the instinctive pleasure of having said a witty or graceful thing to which one's response had been immediate. When he took me indoors, into that house which was a museum, I noticed the delicacy of his hands, and the tenderness with which he handled his treasures, touching them as if he loved them, with little, unconscious murmurs: *Quel goût! quel goût!* These rose-coloured rooms, with their embroidered ceilings, were filled with cabinets of beautiful things, Japanese carvings, and prints (the miraculous

'Plongeuses'!), always in perfect condition (*Je cherche le beau*); albums had been made for him in Japan, and in these he inserted prints, mounting others upon silver and gold paper, which formed a sort of frame. He showed me his eighteenth-century designs, among which I remember his pointing out one (a Chardin, I think) as the first he had ever bought; he had been sixteen at the time, and he bought it for twelve francs.

When we came to the study, the room in which he worked, he showed me all his own first editions, carefully bound, and first editions of Flaubert, Baudelaire, Gautier, with those, less interesting to me, of the men of later generations. He spoke of himself and his brother with a serene pride, which seemed to me perfectly dignified and appropriate; and I remember his speaking (with a parenthetic disdain of the *brouillard scandinave*, in which it seemed to him that France was trying to envelop herself; at the best it would be but *un mauvais brouillard*) of the endeavour which he and his brother had made to represent the only thing worth representing, *la vie vécue, la vraie vérité*. As in painting, he said, all depends on the way of seeing, *l'optique*: out of twenty-four men who will describe what they have all seen, it is only the twenty-fourth who will find the right way of expressing it. 'There is a true thing I have said in my journal,' he went on. 'The thing is, to find a lorgnette' (and he put up his hands to his eyes, adjusting them carefully) 'through which to see things. My brother and I invented a lorgnette, and the young men have taken it from us.'

How true that is, and how significantly it states just what is most essential in the work of the Goncourts! It is a new way of seeing, literally a new way of seeing, which they have invented; and it is in the invention of this that they have invented that 'new language' of which purists have so long, so vainly, and so thanklessly complained. You remember that saying of Masson, the mask of Gautier, in *Charles Demailly*: 'I am a man for whom the visible world exists.' Well, that is true, also, of the Goncourts; but in a different way.

'The delicacies of fine literature,' that phrase of Pater always comes into my mind when I think of the Goncourts; and indeed Pater seems to me the only English writer who has ever handled language at all in their manner or spirit. I frequently heard Pater refer to certain of their books, to *Madame Gervaisais*, to *L'Art du XVIII Siècle*, to *Chérie*; with a passing objection to what he called the 'immodesty' of this last book, and a strong emphasis in the assertion that 'that was how it seemed to him a book should be written.' I repeated this once to Goncourt, trying to give him some idea of what Pater's work was like; and he lamented that his ignorance of English prevented him from what he instinctively realised would be so intimate an enjoyment. Pater was of course far more scrupulous, more limited, in his choice of epithet, less feverish in his variations of cadence; and naturally so, for he dealt with another subject-matter and was careful of another kind of truth. But with both there was that passionately intent pre-occupation with 'the delicacies of fine literature'; both achieved a style of the most personal sincerity: *tout grand écrivain de tous les temps*, said Goncourt, *ne se reconnaît absolument qu'à cela, c'est qu'il a une langue personnelle, une langue dont chaque page, chaque ligne, est signée, pour le lecteur lettré, comme si son nom était au bas de cette page, de cette ligne*: and this style, in both, was accused, by the 'literary' criticism of its generation, of being insincere, artificial, and therefore reprehensible.

It is difficult, in speaking of Edmond de Goncourt, to avoid attributing to him the whole credit of the work which has so long borne his name alone. That is an error which he himself would never have pardoned. *Mon frère et moi* was the phrase constantly on his lips, and in his journal, his prefaces, he has done full justice to the vivid and admirable qualities of that talent which, all the same, would seem to have been the lesser, the more subservient, of the two. Jules, I think, had a more active sense of life, a more generally human curiosity; for the novels of Edmond, written since his brother's death, have, in even that excessively specialised world of their common observation, a yet more specialised choice and direction. But Edmond, there is no doubt, was in the strictest sense the writer; and it is above all for the qualities of its writing that the work of the Goncourts will live. It has been largely concerned with truth – truth to the minute details of human character, sensation, and circumstance, and also of the document, the exact words, of the past; but this devotion to fact, to the curiosities of fact, has been united with an even more persistent devotion to the curiosities of expression. They have invented a new language: that was the old reproach against them; let it be their distinction. Like all writers of an elaborate carefulness, they have been accused of sacrificing both truth and beauty to a deliberate eccentricity. Deliberate their style certainly was; eccentric it may, perhaps, sometimes have been; but deliberately eccentric, no. It was their belief that a writer should have a personal style, a style as peculiar to himself as his handwriting; and indeed I seem to see in the handwriting of Edmond de Goncourt just the characteristics of his style. Every letter is formed carefully, separately, with a certain elegant stiffness; it is beautiful, formal, too regular in the 'continual slight novelty' of its form to be quite clear at a glance: very personal, very distinguished writing.

It may be asserted that the Goncourts are not merely men of genius, but are perhaps the typical men of letters of the close of our century. They have all the curiosities and the acquirements, the new weaknesses and the new powers, that belong to our age; and they sum up in themselves certain theories, aspirations, ways of looking at things, notions of literary duty and artistic conscience, which have only lately become at all actual, and some of which owe to them their very origin. To be not merely novelists (inventing a new kind of novel), but historians; not merely historians, but the historians of a particular century, and of what was intimate and what is unknown in it; to be also discriminating, indeed innovating, critics of art, but of a certain section of art, the eighteenth century, in France and in Japan; to collect pictures and *bibelots*, beautiful things, always of the French and Japanese eighteenth century: these excursions in so many directions, with their audacities and their careful limitations, their bold novelty and their scrupulous exactitude in detail, are characteristic of what is the finest in the modern, conception of culture and the modern ideal in art. Look, for instance, at the Goncourts' view of history. *Quand les civilisations commencent, quand les peuples se forment, l'histoire est drame ou geste... Les siècles qui ont précédé notre siècle ne demandaient à l'historien que le personnage de l'homme, et le portrait de son génie... Le XIXe siècle demande l'homme qui était cet homme d'État, cet homme de guerre, ce poète, ce peintre, ce grand homme de science ou de métier. L'âme qui était en cet acteur, le cœur qui a vécu derrière cet esprit, il les exige et les réclame; et s'il ne peut recueillir tout cet être moral, toute la vie intérieure, il commande du moins qu'on lui en apporte une trace, un jour, un lambeau, une relique.* From this theory, this conviction, came that marvellous series of studies in the eighteenth century in France (*La Femme au XVIIIe Siècle, Portraits intimes du XVIIIe Siècle, La du Barry,* and the others), made entirely out of documents, autograph letters, scraps of costume, engravings, songs, the unconscious self-revelations of the time, forming, as they justly say, *l'histoire intime; c'est ce roman vrai que la postérité appellera peut-être un jour l'histoire humaine.* To be the bookworm and the magician; to give the actual documents, but not to set barren fact by barren fact; to find a soul and a voice in documents, to make them more living and more charming than the charm of life itself: that is what the Goncourts have done. And it is through this conception of history that they have found their way to that new conception of the novel which has revolutionised the entire art of fiction.

Aujourd'hui, they wrote, in 1864, in the preface to *Germinie Lacerteux, que le Roman s'élargit et grandit, qu'il commence à être la grande forme sérieuse, passionnée, vivante, de l'étude littéraire et de l'enquête sociale, qu'il devient, par l'analyse et par la recherche psychologique, l'Histoire morale contemporaine, aujourd'hui que le Roman s'est imposé les études et les devoirs de la science, il pent en revendiquer les libertés et les franchises. Le public aime les romans faux,* is another brave declaration in the same preface; *ce roman est un roman vrai.* But what, precisely, is it that the Goncourts understood by *un roman vrai?* The old notion of the novel was that it should be an entertaining record of incidents or adventures told for their own sake; a plain, straightforward narrative of facts, the aim being to produce as nearly as possible an effect of continuity, of nothing having been omitted, the statement, so to speak, of a witness on oath; in a word, it is the same as the old notion of history, *drame ou geste.* That is not how the Goncourts apprehend life, or how they conceive it should be rendered. As in the study of history they seek mainly the *inédit,* caring only to record that, so it is the *inédit* of life that they conceive to be the main concern, the real 'inner history.' And for them the *inédit* of life consists in the noting of the sensations; it is of the sensations that they have resolved to be the historians; not of action, nor of emotion, properly speaking, nor of moral conceptions, but of an inner life which is all made up of the perceptions of the senses. It is scarcely too paradoxical to say that they are psychologists for whom the soul does not exist. One thing, they know, exists: the sensation flashed through the brain, the image on the mental retina. Having found that, they bodily omit all the rest as of no importance, trusting to their instinct of selection, of retaining all that really matters. It is the painter's method, a selection made almost visually; the method of the painter who accumulates detail on detail, in his patient, many-sided observation of his subject, and then omits everything which is not an essential part of the *ensemble* which he sees. Thus the new conception of what the real truth of things consists in has brought with it, inevitably, an entirely new form, a breaking-up of the plain, straightforward narrative into chapters, which are generally quite disconnected, and sometimes of less than a page in length. A very apt image for this new, curious manner of narrative has been found, somewhat maliciously, by M. Lemaître. *Un homme qui marche à l'intérieur d'une maison, si nous regardons du dehors, apparaît successivement à chaque fenêtre, et dans les intervalles nous échappe. Ces fenêtres, ce sont les chapitres de MM. de Goncourt. Encore,* he adds, *y a-t-il plusieurs de ces fenêtres où l'homme que nous attendions ne passe point.* That, certainly, is the danger of the method. No doubt the Goncourts, in their passion for the *inédit*, leave out certain things because they are obvious, even if they are obviously true and obviously important; that is the defect of their quality. To represent life by a series of moments, and to choose these moments for a certain subtlety and rarity in them, is to challenge grave perils. Nor are these the only perils which the Goncourts have constantly before them. There are others, essential to their natures, to their preferences. And, first of all, as we may see on every page of that miraculous *Journal*, which will remain, doubtless, the truest, deepest, most poignant piece of human history that they have ever written, they are sick men, seeing life through the medium of diseased nerves. *Notre œuvre entier*, writes Edmond de Goncourt, *repose sur la maladie nerveuse; les peintures de la maladie, nous les avons tirées de nous-mêmes, et, à force de nous disséquer, nous sommes arrivés à une sensitivité supra-aiguë que blessaient les infiniment petits de la vie.* This unhealthy sensitiveness explains much, the singular merits as well as certain shortcomings or deviations, in their work. The Goncourts' vision of reality might almost be called an exaggerated sense of the truth of things; such a sense as diseased nerves inflict upon one, sharpening the acuteness of every sensation; or somewhat such a sense as one derives from haschisch, which simply intensifies, yet in a veiled and fragrant way, the charm or the disagreeableness of outward things, the notion of time, the notion of space. What the Goncourts paint is the subtler poetry of reality, its unusual aspects, and they evoke it, fleetingly, like Whistler; they do not render it in hard outline, like Flaubert, like Manet. As in the world of Whistler, so in the world of the Goncourts, we see cities in which there are always fireworks at Cremorne, and fair women reflected beautifully and curiously in mirrors. It is a world which is extraordinarily real; but there is choice, there is curiosity, in the aspect of reality which it presents.

Compare the descriptions, which form so large a part of the work of the Goncourts, with those of Théophile Gautier, who may reasonably be said to have introduced the practice of eloquent writing about places, and also the exact description of them. Gautier describes miraculously, but it is, after all, the ordinary observation carried to perfection, or, rather, the ordinary pictorial observation. The Goncourts only tell you the things that Gautier leaves out; they find new, fantastic points of view, discover secrets in things, curiosities of beauty, often acute, distressing, in the aspects of quite ordinary places. They see things as an artist, an ultra-subtle artist of the impressionist kind, might see them; seeing them indeed always very consciously with a deliberate attempt upon them, in just that partial, selecting, creative way in which an artist looks at things for the purpose of painting a picture. In order to arrive at their effects, they shrink from no sacrifice, from no excess; slang, neologism, forced construction, archaism, barbarous epithet, nothing comes amiss to them, so long as it tends to render a sensation. Their unique care is that the phrase should live, should palpitate, should be alert, exactly expressive, super-subtle in expression; and they prefer indeed a certain perversity in their relations with language, which they would have not merely a passionate and sensuous thing, but complex with all the curiosities of a delicately depraved instinct. It is the accusation of the severer sort of French critics that the Goncourts have invented a new language; that the language which they use is no longer the calm and faultless French of the past. It is true; it is their distinction; it is the most wonderful of all their inventions: in order to render new sensations, a new vision of things, they have invented a new language.

1894, 1896.

COVENTRY PATMORE

There are two portraits of Coventry Patmore by Mr. Sargent. One, in the National Portrait Gallery, gives us the man as he ordinarily was: the straggling hair, the drooping eyelid, the large, loose-lipped mouth, the long, thin, furrowed throat, the whole air of gentlemanly ferocity. But the other, a sketch of the head in profile, gives us more than that; gives us, in the lean, strong, aquiline head, startlingly, all that was abrupt, fiery, and essential in the genius of a rare and misunderstood poet. There never was a man less like the popular idea of him than the writer of *The Angel in the House.* Certainly an autocrat in the home, impatient, intolerant, full of bracing intellectual scorn, not always just, but always just in intention, a disdainful recluse, judging all human and divine affairs from a standpoint of imperturbable omniscience, Coventry Patmore charmed one by his whimsical energy, his intense sincerity, and, indeed, by the childlike egoism of an absolutely self-centred intelligence. Speaking of Patmore as he was in 1879, Mr. Gosse says, in his admirable memoir:

> Three things were in those days particularly noticeable in the head of Coventry Patmore: the vast convex brows, arched with vision; the bright, shrewd, bluish-grey eyes, the outer fold of one eyelid permanently and humorously drooping; and the wilful, sensuous mouth. These three seemed ever at war among themselves; they spoke three different tongues; they proclaimed a man of dreams, a canny man of business, a man of vehement determination. It was the

harmony of these in apparently discordant contrast which made the face so fascinating; the dwellers under this strange mask were three, and the problem was how they contrived the common life.

That is a portrait which is also an interpretation, and many of the pages on this 'angular, vivid, discordant, and yet exquisitely fascinating person,' are full of a similar insight. They contain many of those anecdotes which indicate crises, a thing very different from the merely decorative anecdotes of the ordinary biographer. The book, written by one who has been a good friend to many poets, and to none a more valuable friend than to Patmore, gives us a more vivid sense of what Patmore was as a man than anything except Mr. Sargent's two portraits, and a remarkable article by Mr. Frederick Greenwood, published after the book, as a sort of appendix, which it completes on the spiritual side.

To these portraits of Patmore I have nothing of importance to add; and I have given my own estimate of Patmore as a poet in an essay published in 1897, in *Studies in Two Literatures*. But I should like to supplement these various studies by a few supplementary notes, and the discussion of a few points, chiefly technical, connected with his art as a poet. I knew Patmore only during the last ten years of his life, and never with any real intimacy; but as I have been turning over a little bundle of his letters, written with a quill on greyish-blue paper, in the fine, careless handwriting which had something of the distinction of the writer, it seems to me that there are things in them characteristic enough to be worth preserving.

The first letter in my bundle is not addressed to me, but to the friend through whom I was afterwards to meet him, the kindest and most helpful friend whom I or any man ever had, James Dykes Campbell. Two years before, when I was twenty-one, I had written an *Introduction to the Study of Browning*. Campbell had been at my elbow all the time, encouraging and checking me; he would send back my proof-sheets in a network of criticisms and suggestions, with my most eloquent passages rigorously shorn, my pet eccentricities of phrase severely straightened. At the beginning of 1888 Campbell sent the book to Patmore. His opinion, when it came, seemed to me, at that time, crushing; it enraged me, I know, not on my account, but on Browning's. I read it now with a clearer understanding of what he meant, and it is interesting, certainly, as a more outspoken and detailed opinion on Browning than Patmore ever printed.

> My Dear Mr. Campbell, – I have read enough of Mr. Arthur Symons' clever book on Browning to entitle me to judge of it as well as if I had read the whole. He does not seem to me to be quite qualified, as yet, for this kind of criticism. He does not seem to have attained to the point of view from which all great critics have judged poetry and art in general. He does not see that, in art, the style in which a thing is said or done is of more importance than the thing said or done. Indeed, he does not appear to know what style means. Browning has an immense deal of mannerism – which in art is always bad; – he has, in his few best passages, manner, which as far as it goes is good; but of style – that indescribable reposeful 'breath of a pure and unique individuality' – I recognise no trace, though I find it distinctly enough in almost every other English poet who has obtained so distinguished a place as Browning has done in the estimation of the better class of readers. I do not pretend to say absolutely that style does not exist in Browning's work; but, if so, its 'still small voice' is utterly overwhelmed, for me, by the din of the other elements. I think I can see, in Browning's poetry, all that Mr. Symons sees, though not perhaps all that he fancies he sees. But I also discern a want of which he appears to feel nothing; and those defects of manner which he acknowledges, but thinks little of, are to me most distressing, and fatal to all enjoyment of the many brilliant qualities they are mixed up with. – Yours very truly,
>
> Coventry Patmore.

Campbell, I suppose, protested in his vigorous fashion against the criticism of Browning, and the answer to that letter, dated May 7, is printed on p. 264 of the second volume of Mr. Basil Champneys' *Life of Patmore*. It is a reiteration, with further explanations, such as that

When I said that manner was more important than matter in poetry, I really meant that the true matter of poetry could only be expressed by the manner. I find the brilliant thinking and the deep feeling in Browning, but no true individuality – though of course his manner is marked enough.

Another letter in the same year, to Campbell, after reading the proofs of my first book of verse, *Days and Nights*, contained a criticism which I thought, at the time, not less discouraging than the criticism of my *Browning*. It seems to me now to contain the truth, the whole truth, and nothing but the truth, about that particular book, and to allow for whatever I may have done in verse since then. The first letter addressed to me is a polite note, dated March 16, 1889, thanking me for a copy of my book, and saying 'I send herewith a little volume of my own, which I hope may please you in some of your idle moments.' The book was a copy of *Florilegium Amantis*, a selection of his own poems, edited by Dr. Garnett. Up to that time I had read nothing of Patmore except fragments of *The Angel in the House*, which I had not had the patience to read through. I dipped into these pages, and as I read for the first time some of the odes of *The Unknown Eros*, I seemed to have made a great discovery: here was a whole glittering and peaceful tract of poetry which was like a new world to me. I wrote to him full of my enthusiasm; and, though I heard nothing then in reply, I find among my books a copy of *The Unknown Eros* with this inscription: 'Arthur Symons, from Coventry Patmore, July 23, 1890.'

The date is the date of his sixty-seventh birthday, and the book was given to me after a birthday-dinner at his house at Hastings, when, I remember, a wreath of laurel had been woven in honour of the occasion, and he had laughingly, but with a quite naïve gratification, worn it for a while at the end of dinner. He was one of the very few poets I have seen who could wear a laurel wreath and not look ridiculous.

In the summer of that year I undertook to look after the

Academy for a few weeks (a wholly new task to me) while Mr. Cotton, the editor, went for a holiday. The death of Cardinal Newman occurred just then, and I wrote to Patmore, asking him if he would do an obituary notice for me. He replied, in a letter dated August 13, 1890:

> I should have been very glad to have complied with your request, had I felt myself at all able to do the work effectively; but my acquaintance with Dr. Newman was very slight, and I have no sources of know-ledge about his life, but such as are open to all. I have never taken much interest in contemporary Catholic history and politics. There are a hundred people who could do what you want better than I could, and I can never stir my lazy soul to take up the pen, unless I fancy that I have something to say which makes it a matter of conscience that I should say it.

Failing Patmore, I asked Dr. Greenhill, who was then living at Hastings, and Patmore wrote on August 16:

> Dr. Greenhill will do your work far better than I could have done it. What an intellect we have lost in Newman – so delicately capable of adjustment that it could crush a Hume or crack a Kingsley! And what an example both in literature and in life. But that we have not lost.

Patmore's memory was retentive of good phrases which had once come up under his pen, as that witty phrase about crushing and cracking had come up in the course of a brief note scribbled on a half-sheet of paper. The phrase reappears five years after-wards, elaborated into an impressive sentence, in the preface to *The Rod, the Root, and the Flower*, dated Lymington, May 1895:

> The steam-hammer of that intellect which could be so delicately adjusted to its task as to be capable of either crushing a Hume or cracking a Kingsley is no longer at work, that tongue which had the weight of a hatchet and the edge of a razor is silent; but its mighty task of so representing truth as to make it credible to the modern mind, when not interested in unbelief, has been done.

In the same preface will be found a phrase which Mr. Gosse

quotes from a letter of June 17, 1888, in which Patmore says that the reviewers of his forthcoming book, *Principle in Art*, 'will say, or at least feel, "Ugh, Ugh! the horrid thing! It's alive!" and think it their duty to set their heels on it accordingly.' By 1895 the reviewers were replaced by 'readers, zealously Christian,' and the readers, instead of setting their heels on it, merely 'put aside this little volume with a cry.'

I find no more letters, beyond mere notes and invitations, until the end of 1893, but it was during these years that I saw Patmore most often, generally when I was staying with Dykes Campbell at St. Leonards. When one is five-and-twenty, and writing verse, among young men of one's own age, also writing verse, the occasional companionship of an older poet, who stands aside, in a dignified seclusion, acknowledged, respected, not greatly loved or, in his best work at least, widely popular, can hardly fail to be an incentive and an invigoration. It was with a full sense of my privilege that I walked to and fro with Coventry Patmore on that high terrace in his garden at Hastings, or sat in the house watching him smoke cigarette after cigarette, or drove with him into the country, or rowed with him round the moat of Bodiam Castle, with Dykes Campbell in the stern of the boat; always attentive to his words, learning from him all I could, as he talked of the things I most cared for, and of some things for which I cared nothing. Yes, even when he talked of politics, I listened with full enjoyment of his bitter humour, his ferocious gaiety of onslaught; though I was glad when he changed from Gladstone to St. Thomas Aquinas, and gladder still when he spoke of that other religion, poetry. I think I never heard him speak long without some reference to St. Thomas Aquinas, of whom he has written so often and with so great an enthusiasm. It was he who first talked to me of St. John of the Cross, and when, eight years later, at Seville, I came upon a copy of the first edition of the *Obras Espirituales* on a stall of old books in the Sierpes, and began to read, and to try to render in English, that extraordinary verse which remains, with that of S. Teresa, the finest lyrical verse which Spain has produced, I understood how much the mystic of the prose and the poet of *The Unknown Eros* owed to the *Noche Escura* and the *Llama de Amor Viva*. He spoke of the Catholic mystics like an explorer who has returned from the perils of far countries, with a remembering delight which he can share with few.

If Mr. Gosse is anywhere in his book unjust to Patmore it is in speaking of the later books of prose, the *Religio Poetae* and *The Rod, the Root, and the Flower*, some parts of which seem to him 'not very important except as extending our knowledge of' Patmore's 'mind, and as giving us a curious collection of the raw material of his poetry.' To this I can only reply in some words which I used in writing of the *Religio Poetae*, and affirm with an emphasis which I only wish to strengthen, that, here and everywhere, and never more than in the exquisite passage which Mr. Gosse only quotes to depreciate, the prose of Patmore is the prose of a poet; not prose 'incompletely executed,' and aspiring after the 'nobler order' of poetry, but adequate and achieved prose, of a very rare kind. Thought, in him, is of the very substance of poetry, and is sustained throughout at almost the lyrical pitch. There is, in these essays, a rarefied air as of the mountain-tops of meditation; and the spirit of their sometimes remote contemplation is always in one sense, as Pater has justly said of Wordsworth, impassioned. Only in the finest of his poems has he surpassed these pages of chill and ecstatic prose.

But if Patmore spoke, as he wrote, of these difficult things as a traveller speaks of the countries from which he has returned, when he spoke of poetry it was like one who speaks of his native country. At first I found it a little difficult to accustom myself to his permanent mental attitude there, with his own implied or stated pre-eminence (Tennyson and Barnes on the lower slopes, Browning vaguely in sight, the rest of his contemporaries nowhere), but, after all, there was an undisguised simplicity in it, which was better, because franker, than the more customary 'pride that apes humility,' or the still baser affectation of indifference. A man of genius, whose genius, like Patmore's, is of an intense and narrow kind, cannot possibly do justice to the work which has every merit but his own. Nor can he, when he is conscious of its equality in technical skill, be expected to discriminate between what is more or less valuable in his own work; between, that is, his own greater or less degree of inspiration. And here I may quote a letter which Patmore wrote to me, dated Lymington, December 31, 1893, about a review of mine in which I had greeted him as 'a poet, one of the most essential poets of our time,' but had ventured to say, perhaps petulantly, what I felt about a certain part of his work.

> I thank you for the copy of the *Athenæum*, containing your generous and well-written notice of 'Religio Poetae.' There is much in it that must needs be gratifying to me, and nothing that I feel disposed to complain of but your allusion to the 'dinner-table domesticities of the "Angel in the House."' I think that you have been a little misled – as almost everybody has been – by the differing characters of the metres of the 'Angel' and 'Eros.' The meats and wines of the two are, in very great part, almost identical in character; but, in one case, they are served on the deal table of the octo-syllabic quatrain, and, in the other, they are spread on the fine, irregular rock of the free tetrameter.

In his own work he could see no flaw; he knew, better than any one, how nearly it answered almost everywhere to his own intention; and of his own intentions he could be no critic. It was from this standpoint of absolute satisfaction with what he had himself done that he viewed other men's work; necessarily, in the case of one so certain of himself, with a measure of dissatisfaction. He has said in print fundamentally foolish things about writers living and dead; and yet remains, if not a great critic, at least a great thinker on the first principles of art. And, in those days when I used to listen to him while he talked to me of the basis of poetry, and of metres and cadences, and of poetical methods, what meant more to me than anything he said, though not a word was without its value, was the profound religious gravity with which he treated the art of poetry, the sense he conveyed to one of his own reasoned conception of its immense importance, its divinity.

It was partly, no doubt, from this reverence for his art that Patmore wrote so rarely, and only under an impulse which could not be withstood. Even his prose was written with the same ardour and reluctance, and a letter which he wrote to me from Lymington, dated August 7, 1894, in answer to a suggestion that he should join some other writers in a contemplated memorial to Walter Pater, is literally exact in its statement of his own way of work, not only during his later life:

> I should have liked to make one of the honourable company of commentators upon Pater, were it not that the faculty of writing, or, what amounts to the same thing, interest in writing, has quite deserted me. Some accidental motive wind comes over me, once in a year or so, and I find myself able to write half a dozen pages in an hour or two: but all the rest of my time is hopelessly sterile.

To what was this curious difficulty or timidity in composition due? In the case of the poetry, Mr. Gosse attributes it largely to the fact of a poet of lyrical genius attempting to write only philosophical or narrative poetry; and there is much truth in the suggestion. Nothing in Patmore, except his genius, is so conspicuous as his limitations. Herrick, we may remember from his essay on Mrs. Meynell, seemed to him but 'a splendid insect'; Keats, we learn from Mr. Champneys' life, seemed to him 'to be greatly deficient in first-rate imaginative power'; Shelley 'is all unsubstantial splendour, like the transformation scene of a pantomime, or the silvered globes hung up in a gin-palace'; Blake is 'nearly all utter rubbish, with here and there not so much a gleam as a trick of genius.' All this, when he said it, had a queer kind of delightfulness, and, to those able to understand him, never seemed, as it might have seemed in any one else, mere arrogant bad taste, but a necessary part of a very narrow and very intense nature. Although Patmore was quite ready to give his opinion on any subject, whether on 'Wagner, the musical impostor,' or on 'the grinning woman, in every canvas of

Leonardo,' he was singularly lacking in the critical faculty, even in regard to his own art; and this was because, in his own art, he was a poet of one idea and of one metre. He did marvellous things with that one idea and that one metre, but he saw nothing beyond them; all thought must be brought into relation with nuptial love, or it was of no interest to him, and the iambic metre must do everything that poetry need concern itself about doing.

In a memorandum for prayer made in 1861, we read this petition:

> That I may be enabled to write my poetry from immediate perception of the truth and delight of love at once divine and human, and that all events may so happen as shall best advance this my chief work and probable means of working out my own salvation.

In his earlier work, it is with human love only that he deals; in his later, and inconceivably finer work, it is not with human love only, but with 'the relation of the soul to Christ as his betrothed wife': 'the burning heart of the universe,' as he realises it. This conception of love, which we see developing from so tamely domestic a level to so incalculable a height of mystic rapture, possessed the whole man, throughout the whole of his life, shutting him into a 'solitude for two' which has never perhaps been apprehended with so complete a satisfaction. He was a married monk, whose monastery was the world; he came and went in the world, imagining he saw it more clearly than any one else; and, indeed, he saw things about him clearly enough, when they were remote enough from his household prejudices. But all he really ever did was to cultivate a little corner of a garden, where he brought to perfection a rare kind of flower, which some thought too pretty to be fine, and some too colourless to be beautiful, but in which he saw the seven celestial colours, faultlessly mingled, and which he took to be the image of the flower most loved by the Virgin in heaven.

Patmore was a poet profoundly learned in the technique of his art, and the *Prefatory Study on English Metrical Law*, which fills the first eighty-five pages of the *Amelia* volume of 1878, is among the subtlest and most valuable of such studies which we have in English. In this essay he praises the simplest metres for various just reasons, but yet is careful to define the 'rhyme royal,' or stanza of seven ten-syllable lines, as the most heroic of measures; and to admit that blank verse, which he never used, 'is, of all recognised English metres, the most difficult to write well in.' But, in his expressed aversion for trochaic and dactylic measures, is he not merely recording his own inability to handle them? and, in setting more and more rigorous limits to himself in his own dealing with iambic measures, is he not accepting, and making the best of, a lack of metrical flexibility? It is nothing less than extraordinary to note that, until the publication of the nine *Odes* in 1868, not merely was he wholly tied to the iambic measure, but even within those limits he was rarely quite so good in the four-line stanza of eights and sixes as in the four-line stanza of eights; that he was usually less good in the six-line than in the four-line stanza of eights and sixes; and that he was invariably least good in the stanza of three long lines which, to most practical intents and purposes, corresponds with this six-line stanza. The extremely slight licence which this rearrangement into longer lines affords was sufficient to disturb the balance of his cadences, and nowhere else was he capable of writing quite such lines as:

> One friend was left, a falcon, famed for beauty, skill and size,
> Kept from his fortune's ruin, for the sake of its great eyes.

All sense, not merely of the delicacy, but of the correctness of rhythm, seems to have left him suddenly, without warning.

And then, the straightening and tightening of the bonds of metre having had its due effect, an unprecedented thing occurred. In the *Odes* of 1868, absorbed finally into *The Unknown Eros* of 1877, the iambic metre is still used; but with what a new freedom, and at the summons of how liberating an inspiration! At the same time Patmore's substance is purged and his speech loosened, and, in throwing off that burden of prose stuff which had tied down the very wings of his imagination, he finds himself rising on a different movement. Never was a development in metre so spiritually significant.

In spite of Patmore's insistence to the contrary, as in the letter which I have already quoted, there is no doubt that the difference between *The Angel in the House* and *The Unknown Eros* is the difference between what is sometimes poetry in spite of itself, and what is poetry alike in accident and essence. In all his work before the *Odes* of 1868, Patmore had been writing down to his conception of what poetry ought to be; when, through I know not what suffering, or contemplation, or actual inner illumination, his whole soul had been possessed by this new conception of what poetry could be, he began to write as finely, and not only as neatly, as he was able. The poetry which came, came fully clothed, in a form of irregular but not lawless verse, which Mr. Gosse states was introduced into English by the *Pindarique Odes* of Cowley, but which may be more justly derived, as Patmore himself, in one of his prefaces, intimates, from an older and more genuine poet, Drummond of Hawthornden. Mr. Gosse is cruel enough to say that Patmore had 'considerable affinities' with Cowley, and that 'when Patmore is languid and Cowley is unusually felicitous, it is difficult to see much difference in the form of their odes.' But Patmore, in his essay on metre, has said,

> If there is not sufficient motive power of passionate thought, no
> typographical aids will make anything of this sort of verse but
> metrical nonsense – which it nearly always is – even in Cowley,
> whose brilliant wit and ingenuity are strangely out of harmony with
> most of his measures;

and it seems to me that he is wholly right in saying so. The difference between the two is an essential one. In Patmore the cadence follows the contours of the thought or emotion, like a transparent garment; in Cowley the form is a misshapen burden, carried unsteadily. It need not surprise us that to the ears of

Cowley (it is he who tells us) the verse of Pindar should have sounded 'little better than prose.' The fault of his own 'Pindarique' verse is that it is so much worse than prose. The pauses in Patmore, left as they are to be a kind of breathing, or pause for breath, may not seem to be everywhere faultless to all ears; but they *are* the pauses in breathing, while in Cowley the structure of his verse, when it is irregular, remains as external, as mechanical, as the couplets of the *Davideis*.

> Whether Patmore ever acknowledged it or no, or indeed whether [says Mr. Gosse] the fact has ever been observed, I know not, but the true analogy of the *Odes* is with the Italian lyric of the early Renaissance. It is in the writings of Petrarch and Dante, and especially in the *Canzoniere* of the former, that we must look for examples of the source of Patmore's later poetic form.

Here again, while there may be a closer 'analogy,' at least in spirit, there is another, and even clearer difference in form. The canzoni of Petrarch are composed in stanzas of varying, but in each case uniform, length, and every stanza corresponds precisely in metrical arrangement with every other stanza in the same canzone. In English the *Epithalamion* and the *Prothalamion* of Spenser (except for their refrain) do exactly what Petrarch had done in Italian; and whatever further analogy there may be between the spirit of Patmore's writing and that of Spenser in these two poems, the form is essentially different. The resemblance with *Lycidas* is closer, and closer still with the poems of Leopardi, though Patmore has not followed the Italian habit of mingling rhymed and non-rhymed verse, nor did he ever experiment, like Goethe, Heine, Matthew Arnold, and Henley, in wholly unrhymed irregular lyrical verse.

Patmore's endeavour, in *The Unknown Eros*, is certainly towards a form of *vers libre*, but it is directed only towards the variation of the normal pause in the normal English metre, the iambic 'common time,' and is therefore as strictly tied by law as a metre can possibly be when it ceases to be wholly regular. Verse literally 'free,' as it is being attempted in the present day in France, every measure being mingled, and the disentangling of them left wholly to the ear of the reader, has indeed been attempted by great metrists in many ages, but for the most part only very rarely and with extreme caution. The warning, so far, of all these failures, or momentary half-successes, is to be seen in the most monstrous and magnificent failure of the nineteenth century, the *Leaves of Grass* of Walt Whitman. Patmore realised that without law there can be no order, and thus no life; for life is the result of a harmony between opposites. For him, cramped as he had been by a voluntary respect for far more than the letter of the law, the discovery of a freer mode of speech was of incalculable advantage. It removed from him all temptation to that 'cleverness' which Mr. Gosse rightly finds in the handling of 'the accidents of civilised life,' the unfortunate part of his subject-matter in *The Angel in the House*; it allowed him to abandon himself to the poetic ecstasy, which in him was almost of the same nature as philosophy, without translating it downward into the terms of popular apprehension; it gave him a choice, formal, yet flexible means of expression for his uninterrupted contemplation of divine things.

1906.

SAROJINI NAIDU

It was at my persuasion that *The Golden Threshold* was published. The earliest of the poems were read to me in London in 1896, when the writer was seventeen; the later ones were sent to me from India in 1904, when she was twenty-five; and they belong, I think, almost wholly to those two periods. As they seemed to me to have an individual beauty of their own, I thought they ought to be published. The writer hesitated. 'Your letter made me very proud and very sad,' she wrote. 'Is it possible that I have written verses that are "filled with beauty," and is it possible that you really think them worthy of being given to the world? You know how high my ideal of Art is; and to me my poor casual little poems seem to be less than beautiful – I mean with that final enduring beauty that I desire.' And, in another letter, she writes: 'I am not a poet really. I have the vision and the desire, but not the voice. If I could write just one poem full of beauty and the spirit of greatness, I should be exultantly silent for ever; but I sing just as the birds do, and my songs are as ephemeral.' It is for this bird-like quality of song, it seems to me, that they are to be valued. They hint, in a sort of delicately evasive way, at a rare temperament, the temperament of a woman of the East, finding expression through a Western language and under partly Western influences. They do not express the whole of that temperament; but they express, I think, its essence; and there is an Eastern magic in them.

Sarojini Chattopâdhyây was born at Hyderabad on February 13, 1879. Her father, Dr. Aghorenath Chattopâdhyây, is descended from the ancient family of Chattorajes of Bhramangram, who were noted throughout Eastern Bengal as patrons of Sanskrit learning, and for their practice of Yoga. He took his degree of Doctor of Science at the University of Edinburgh in 1877, and afterwards studied brilliantly at Bonn. On his return to India he founded the Nizam College at Hyderabad, and has since laboured incessantly, and at great personal sacrifice, in the cause of education.

Sarojini was the eldest of a large family, all of whom were taught English at an early age. 'I,' she writes, 'was stubborn and refused to speak it. So one day, when I was nine years old, my father punished me – the only time I was ever punished – by shutting me in a room alone for a whole day. I came out of it a full-blown linguist. I have never spoken any other language to him, or to my mother, who always speaks to me in Hindustani. I don't think I had any special hankering to write poetry as a little child, though I was of a very fanciful and dreamy nature. My training under my father's eye was of a sternly scientific character. He was determined that I should be a great mathematician or a scientist, but the poetic instinct, which I inherited from him and also from my mother (who wrote some lovely Bengali lyrics in her youth), proved stronger. One day, when I was eleven, I was sighing over a sum in algebra; it *wouldn't* come right; but instead a whole poem came to me suddenly. I wrote it down.

'From that day my "poetic career" began. At thirteen I wrote a long poem *à la* "Lady of the Lake" – 1300 lines in six days. At thirteen I wrote a drama of 2000 lines, a full-fledged passionate thing that I began on the spur of the moment, without forethought, just to spite my doctor, who said I was very ill and must not touch a book. My health broke down permanently about this time, and, my regular studies being stopped, I read voraciously. I suppose the greater part of my reading was done between fourteen and sixteen. I wrote a novel, I wrote fat volumes of journals: I took myself very seriously in those days.'

Before she was fifteen the great struggle of her life began. Dr. Govindurajulu Naidu, now her husband, is, though of an old and honourable family, not a Brahmin. The difference of caste roused an equal opposition, not only on the side of her family, but of his; and in 1895 she was sent to England, against her will, with a special scholarship from the Nizam. She remained in England, with an interval of travel in Italy, till 1898, studying first at King's College, London, then, till her health again broke down, at Girton. She returned to Hyderabad in September 1898, and in the December of that year, to the scandal of all India, broke through the bonds of caste, and married Dr. Naidu. 'Do you know I have some very beautiful poems floating in the air,' she wrote to me in 1904; 'and if the gods are kind I shall cast my soul like a net and capture them, this year. If the gods are kind – and grant me a little measure of health. It is all I need to make my life perfect, for the very "Spirit of Delight" that Shelley wrote of dwells in my little home; it is full of the music of birds in the garden and children in the long-arched verandah.' There are songs about the children in this book; they are called the Lord of Battles, the Sun of Victory, the Lotus-born, and the Jewel of Delight.

'My ancestors for thousands of years,' I find written in one of her letters, 'have been lovers of the forest and mountain caves, great dreamers, great scholars, great ascetics. My father is a dreamer himself, a great dreamer, a great man whose life has been a magnificent failure. I suppose in the whole of India there are few men whose learning is greater than his, and I don't think there are many men more beloved. He has a great white beard, and the profile of Homer, and a laugh that brings the roof down. He has wasted all his money on two great objects: to help others, and on alchemy. He holds huge courts every day in his garden of all the learned men of all religions – Rajahs and beggars and saints, and downright villains, all delightfully mixed up, and all treated as one. And then his alchemy! Oh dear, night and day the experiments are going on, and every man who brings a new prescription is welcome as a brother. But this alchemy is, you know, only the material counterpart of a poet's craving for Beauty, the eternal Beauty. "The makers of gold and the makers of verse," they are the twin creators that sway the world's secret desire for mystery; and what in my father is the genius of curiosity – the very essence of all scientific genius – in me is the desire for beauty. Do you remember Pater's phrase about Leonardo da Vinci, "curiosity and the desire of beauty"?'

It was the desire of beauty that made her a poet; her 'nerves of delight' were always quivering at the contact of beauty. To those who knew her in England, all the life of the tiny figure seemed to concentrate itself in the eyes; they turned towards beauty as the sunflower turns towards the sun, opening wider and wider until one saw nothing but the eyes. She was dressed always in clinging dresses of Eastern silk, and, as she was so small, and her long black hair hung straight down her back, you might have taken her for a child. She spoke little, and in a low voice, like gentle music; and she seemed, wherever she was, to be alone.

Through that soul I seemed to touch and take hold upon the East. And first there was the wisdom of the East. I have never known any one who seemed to exist on such 'large draughts of intellectual day' as this child of seventeen, to whom one could tell all one's personal troubles and agitations, as to a wise old woman. In the East maturity comes early; and this child had already lived through all a woman's life. But there was something else, something hardly personal, something which belonged to a consciousness older than the Christian, which I realised, wondered at, and admired, in her passionate tranquillity of mind, before which everything mean and trivial and temporary caught fire and burnt away in smoke. Her body was never without suffering, or her heart without conflict; but neither the body's weakness nor the heart's violence could disturb that fixed contemplation, as of

Buddha on his lotus-throne.

And along with this wisdom, as of age or of the age of a race, there was what I can hardly call less than an agony of sensation. Pain or pleasure transported her, and the whole of pain or pleasure might be held in a flower's cup or the imagined frown of a friend. It was never found in those things which to others seemed things of importance. At the age of twelve she passed the Matriculation of the Madras University, and awoke to find herself famous throughout India. 'Honestly,' she said to me, 'I was not pleased; such things did not appeal to me.' But here, in a letter from Hyderabad, bidding one 'share a March morning' with her, there is, at the mere contact of the sun, this outburst: 'Come and share my exquisite March morning with me: this sumptuous blaze of gold and sapphire sky; these scarlet lilies that adorn the sunshine; the voluptuous scents of neem and champak and serisha that beat upon the languid air with their implacable sweetness; the thousand little gold and blue and silver breasted birds bursting with the shrill ecstasy of life in nesting time. All is hot and fierce and passionate, ardent and unashamed in its exulting and importunate desire for life and love. And, do you know that the scarlet lilies are woven petal by petal from my heart's blood, these little quivering birds are my soul made incarnate music, these heavy perfumes are my emotions dissolved into aerial essence, this flaming blue and gold sky is the "very me," that part of me that incessantly and insolently, yes, and a little deliberately, triumphs over that other part – a thing of nerves and tissues that suffers and cries out, and that must die to-morrow perhaps, or twenty years hence.'

Then there was her humour, which was part of her strange wisdom, and was always awake and on the watch. In all her letters, written in exquisite English prose, but with an ardent imagery and a vehement sincerity of emotion which make them, like the poems, indeed almost more directly, un-English, Oriental, there was always this intellectual, critical sense of humour, which could laugh at one's own enthusiasm as frankly as that enthusiasm had been set down. And partly the humour, like the delicate reserve of her manner, was a mask or a shelter. 'I have taught myself,' she writes to me from India, 'to be common-place and like everybody else superficially. Every one thinks I am so nice and cheerful, so "brave," all the banal things that are so comfortable to be. My mother knows me only as "such a tranquil child, but so strong-willed." A tranquil child!' And she writes again, with deeper significance: 'I too have learnt the subtle philosophy of living from moment to moment. Yes, it is a subtle philosophy though it appears merely an epicurean doctrine: "Eat, drink, and be merry, for to-morrow we die." I have gone through so many yesterdays when I strove with Death that I have realised to its full the wisdom of that sentence; and it is to me not merely a figure of speech, but a literal fact. Any to-morrow I might die. It is scarcely two months since I came back from the grave: is it worth while to be anything but radiantly glad? Of all things that life or perhaps my temperament has given me I prize the gift of laughter as beyond price.'

Her desire, always, was to be 'a wild free thing of the air like the birds, with a song in my heart.' A spirit of too much fire in too frail a body, it was rarely that her desire was fully granted. But in Italy she found what she could not find in England, and from Italy her letters are radiant. 'This Italy is made of gold,' she writes from Florence, 'the gold of dawn and daylight, the gold of the stars, and, now dancing in weird enchanting rhythms through this magic month of May, the gold of fireflies in the perfumed darkness – "aerial gold." I long to catch the subtle music of their fairy dances and make a poem with a rhythm like the quick irregular wild flash of their sudden movements. Would it not be wonderful? One black night I stood in a garden with fireflies in my hair like darting restless stars caught in a mesh of darkness. It gave me a strange sensation, as if I were not human at all, but an elfin spirit. I wonder why these little things move me so deeply? It is because I have a most "unbalanced intellect," I suppose.' Then, looking out on Florence, she cries, 'God! how beautiful it is, and how glad I am that I am alive to-day!' And she tells me that she is drinking in the beauty like wine, 'wine, golden and scented, and shining, fit for the gods; and the gods have drunk it, the dead gods of Etruria, two thousand years ago. Did I say dead? No, for the gods are immortal, and one might still find them loitering in some solitary dell on the grey hillsides of Fiesole. Have I seen them? Yes, looking with dreaming eyes, I have found them sitting under the olives, in their grave, strong, antique beauty – Etruscan gods!'

In Italy she watches the faces of the monks, and at one moment longs to attain to their peace by renunciation, longs for Nirvana; 'then, when one comes out again into the hot sunshine that warms one's blood, and sees the eager hurrying faces of men and women in the street, dramatic faces over which the disturbing experiences of life have passed and left their symbols, one's heart thrills up into one's throat. No, no, no, a thousand times no! how can one deliberately renounce this coloured, unquiet, fiery human life of the earth?' And, all the time, her subtle criticism is alert, and this woman of the East marvels at the women of the West, 'the beautiful worldly women of the West,' whom she sees walking in the Cascine, 'taking the air so consciously attractive in their brilliant toilettes, in the brilliant coquetry of their manner!' She finds them 'a little incomprehensible,' 'profound artists in all the subtle intricacies of fascination,' and asks if these 'incalculable frivolities and vanities and coquetries and caprices' are, to us, an essential part of their charm? And she watches them with amusement as they flutter about her, petting her as if she were a nice child, a child or a toy, not dreaming that she is saying to herself sorrowfully: 'How utterly empty their lives must be of all spiritual beauty *if* they are nothing more than they appear to be.'

She sat in our midst, and judged us, and few knew what was passing behind that face 'like an awakening soul,' to use one of her own epithets. Her eyes were like deep pools, and you seemed to fall through them into depths below depths.

1905.

WELSH POETRY

There is certainly a reason for at least suggesting to those who concern themselves, for good or evil, with Celtic literature, what Celtic literature really is when it is finest; what a 'reaction against the despotism of fact' really means; what 'natural magic' really means, and why the phrase 'Celtic glamour' is perhaps the most unfortunate that could well have been chosen to express the character of a literature which is above all things precise, concrete, definite.

Lamartine, in the preface to the *Méditations*, describes the characteristics of Ossian, very justly, as *le vague, la rêverie, l'anéantissement dans la contemplation, le regard fixé sur des apparitions confuses dans le lointain*; and it is those very qualities, still looked upon by so many as the typically Celtic qualities, which prove the spuriousness of Ossian. That gaze fixed on formless and distant shadows, that losing of oneself in contemplation, that vague dreaminess, which Lamartine admired in Ossian, will be found nowhere in the *Black Book of Carmarthen*, in the *Book of Taliesin*, in the *Red Book of Hergest*, however much a doubtful text, uncertain readings, and confusing commentators may leave us in uncertainty as to the real meaning of many passages. Just as the true mystic is the man who sees obscure things clearly, so the Welsh poets (whom I take for the moment as representing the 'Celtic note,' the quality which we find in the work of primitive races) saw everything in the universe, the wind itself, under the images of mortality, hands and feet and the ways and motions of men. They filled human life with the greatness of their imagination, they ennobled it with the pride of their expectancy of noble things, they were boundless in praising and in cursing; but poetical excitement, in them, only taught them the amplitude and splendour of real things. A chief is an eagle, a serpent, the bull of battle, an oak; he is the strength of the ninth wave, an uplifted pillar of wrath, impetuous as the fire through a chimney; the ruddy reapers of war are his desire. The heart of Cyndyllan was like the ice of winter, like the fire of spring; the horses of Geraint are ruddy ones, with the assault of spotted eagles, of black eagles, of red eagles, of white eagles; an onset in battle is like the roaring of the wind against the ashen spears. These poets are the poets of 'tumults, shouting, swords, and men in battle-array.' The sound of battle is heard in them; they are 'where the ravens screamed over blood'; they are among 'crimsoned hair and clamorous sorrow'; they praise 'war with the shining wing,' and they know all the piteousness of the death of heroes, the sense of the 'delicate white body,' 'the lovely, slender, blood-stained body,' that will be covered with earth, and sand, and stones, and nettles, and the roots of the oak. They know too the piteousness of the hearth left desolate, the hearth that will be covered with nettles, and slender brambles, and thorns, and dock-leaves, and scratched up by fowls, and turned up by swine. And they praise the gentleness of strength and courage: 'he was gentle, with a hand eager for battle.' Women are known chiefly as the widows and the 'sleepless' mothers of heroes; rarely so much esteemed as to be a snare, rarely a desire, rarely a reward; 'a soft herd.' They praise drunkenness for its ecstasy, its uncalculating generosity, and equal with the flowing of blood in battle, and the flowing of mead in the hall, is the flowing of song. They have the haughtiness of those who, if they take rewards, 'ale for the drinking, and a fair homestead, and beautiful clothing,' give rewards: 'I am Taliesin, who will repay thee thy banquet.'

And they have their philosophy, always a close, vehemently definite thing, crying out for precise images, by which alone it can apprehend the unseen. Taliesin knows that 'man is oldest when he is born, and is younger and younger continually.' He wonders where man is when he is sleeping, and where the night waits until the passing of day. He is astonished that books have not found out the soul, and where it resides, and the air it breathes, and its form and shape. He thinks, too, of the dregs of the soul, and debates what is the best intoxication for its petulance and wonder and mockery. And, in a poem certainly late, or interpolated with fragments of a Latin hymn, he uses the eternal numeration of the mystics, and speaks of 'the nine degrees of the companies of heaven, and the tenth, saints a preparation of sevens'; numbers that are 'clean and holy.' And even in poems plainly Christian there is a fine simplicity of imagination; as when, at the day of judgment, an arm reaches out, and hides the sea and the stars; or when Christ, hanging on the cross, laments that the bones of his feet are stretched with extreme pain.

It is this sharp physical apprehension of things that really gives its note to Welsh poetry; a sense of things felt and seen, so intense, that the crutch on which an old man leans becomes the symbol of all the bodily sorrow of the world. In the poem attributed to Llywarch Hen there is a fierce, loud complaint, in which mere physical sickness and the intolerance of age translate themselves into a limitless hunger, and into that wisdom which is the sorrowful desire of beauty. The cuckoos at Aber Cuawg, singing 'clamorously' to the sick man: 'there are that hear them that will not hear them again!' the sound of the large wave grating sullenly on the pebbles, –

> The birds are clamorous; the strand is wet:
> Clear is the sky; large the wave:
> The heart is palsied with longing:

all these bright, wild outcries, in which wind and wave and leaves and the song of the cuckoo speak the same word, as if all came from the same heart of things; and, through it all, the remembrance: 'God will not undo what he is doing'; have indeed, and supremely, the 'Celtic note.' 'I love the strand, but I hate the sea,' says the *Black Book of Carmarthen*, and in all these poems we find a more than mediæval hatred of winter and cold (so pathetic, yet after all so temperate, in the Latin students' songs), with a far more unbounded hatred of old age and sickness and the disasters which are not bred in the world, but are a blind part of the universe itself; older than the world, as old as chaos, out of which the world was made.

Yet, wild and sorrowful as so much of this poetry is, with its praise of slaughter and its lament over death, there is much also of a gentle beauty, a childlike saying over of wind and wave and the brightness in the tops of green things, as a child counts over its toys. In the 'Song of Pleasant Things' there is no distinction between the pleasantness of sea-gulls playing, of summer and slow long days, of the heath when it is green, of a horse with a thick mane in a tangle, and of 'the word that utters the Trinity.' 'The beautiful I sang of, I will sing,' says Taliesin; and with him the seven senses become in symbol 'fire and earth, and water and air, and mist and flowers, and southerly wind.' And touches of natural beauty come irrelevantly into the most tragical places, like the 'sweet apple-tree of delightful branches' in that song of battles and of the coming of madness, where Myrddin says: 'I have been wandering so long in darkness and among spirits that it is needless now for darkness and spirits to lead me astray.' The same sense of the beauty of earth and of the elements comes into those mysterious riddle-rhymes, not so far removed from the riddle-rhymes which children say to one another in Welsh cottages to this day: 'I have been a tear in the air, I have been the dullest of stars; I was made of the flower of nettles, and of the water of the ninth wave; I played in the twilight, I slept in purple; my fingers are long and white, it is long since I was a herdsman.'

And now, after looking at these characteristics of Welsh poetry, look at Ossian, and that 'gaze fixed on formless and distant shadows,' which seemed so impressive and so Celtic to Lamartine. 'In the morning of Saturday,' or 'On Sunday, at the time of dawn, there was a great battle'; that is how the Welsh poet tells you what he had to sing about. And he tells you, in his definite way, more than that; he tells you: 'I have been where the warriors were slain, from the East to the North, and from the East to the South: I am alive, they are in their graves!' It is human emotion reduced to its elements; that instinct of life and death, of the mystery of all that is tangible in the world, of its personal meaning, to one man after another, age after age, which in every age becomes more difficult to feel simply, more difficult to say simply. 'I am alive, they are in their graves!' and nothing remains to be said in the face of that immense problem. Well, the Welsh poet leaves you with his thought, and that simple emphasis of his seems to us now so large and remote and impressive, just because it was once so passionately felt, and set down as it was felt. And so with his sense for nature, with that which seems like style in him; it is a wonderful way of trusting instinct, of trusting the approaches of natural things. He says, quite simply: 'I was told by a sea-gull that had come a great way,' as a child would tell you now. And when he tells you that 'Cynon rushed forward with the green dawn,' it is not what we call a figure of speech: it is his sensitive, literal way of seeing things. More definite, more concrete, closer to the earth and to instinctive emotion than most other poets, the Welsh poet might have said of himself, in another sense than that in which he said it of Alexander: 'What he desired in his mind he had from the world.'

1898.

A NOTE ON ARTHUR SYMONS

By Jeremy Mark Robinson

Arthur William Symons (Feb 28, 1865, Milford Haven, Wales - Jan 22, 1945, Wittersham, Kent) is best-known now for his poetry and criticism, and his contributions to the evaluation of modernist and Symbolist poetry (which influenced Eliot, Joyce, Pound, Yeats *et al*). Symons' literary studies included monographs on Aubrey Beardsley, Joseph Conrad, Algernon Swinburne, Robert Browning, William Blake, Dante Gabriel Rossetti, Elizabethan drama, Charles Baudelaire and Walter Pater. Symons also wrote extensively on painting, art, theatre and music (and topics such as Leonardo da Vinci, Auguste Rodin, Impressionism and Symbolism). He was associated with several magazines of the late 19th century period, including the *Yellow Book*, the *Athenaeum,* the *Saturday Review,* the *Fortnightly Review* and the short-lived *Savoy* (which he edited). He was a member of the Rhymer's Club (poets in the group included the founder W.B. Yeats, Lionel Johnson and Ernest Dowson).

Arthur Symons grew up in Wales (his parents were Cornish, and his father was a minister), was educated in Devon, and moved to London at 16. He was educated privately (and somewhat sporadically). Symons was known as the 'blond angel', a vagabond poet, clearly in the Bohemian/ French tradition of

Baudelaire, Verlaine and Rimbaud (Verlaine was a strong influence on his poetry). It's no surprise that Symons gravitated towards living in France and Italy – his passion for French culture (and for Parisian life) is obvious in any of his critical studies. In Paris he attended the famous Tuesday evenings with Stéphane Mallarmé.

Arthur Symons knew many of the key artists and writers of the day, including Aubrey Beardsley, Joseph Conrad, W.B. Yeats, Edmund Gosse and Walter Pater. Symons bought a house (Island Cottage) in Wittersham, Kent, a pleasant village on the Kent-Sussex border, in 1906 (where he died in 1945).

Arthur Symons suffered a major breakdown in 1908, when he was living in Italy (it took two years for him to recover; some say he never fully recovered, and it affected his literary reputation). He later wrote about the experience in the 1930 book *Confessions: A Study In Pathology*.

In his books of literary criticism, Arthur Symons discussed many figures of the late 19th century and early 20th century, including Baudelaire, Pater, Rossetti, Verlaine, Rimbaud, Mallarmé, Conrad, Poe, Ibsen, Patmore, Hardy, Meredith, Zola, Flaubert, Villiers and Maeterlinck. Symons was especially fond of French literature, and Symbolist and Decadent poetry in particular: Verlaine, Rimbaud, Laforgue, Baudelaire, Lautréamont, and Symbolist/ *fin de siècle* authors such as Wilde, Rossetti, Swinburne and Huysmans. Symons' 1899 book *The Symbolist Movement In Literature*[1] was an important early study of *fin de siècle* poetry.

Arthur Symons' poetry included books such as *Days and Nights* (his first book of poetry, published in 1889), *Silhouettes* (1892), *London Nights* (1895), *Amor Victima* (1897), *Images of Good and Evil* (1899), *Poems* (1902), *Lyrics* (1903), *The Fool of the World* (1906), *Poems By Arthur Symons* (1911), *Knave of Hearts* (1913) and *Jezebel Mort* (1931). Symons also translated a good deal of poetry, including Verlaine, Baudelaire, Verhaeren, D'Annunzio,

[1] It developed out of an essay published in *Harper's Magazine* in Nov, 1893: *The Decadent Movement In Literature*.

Mallarmé, etc. Symons' plays included *The Minister's Call* (1892), *The Toy Cart* (1916), and *Tristan and Iseult* (1917).

FURTHER READING

K. Beckson. *Arthur Symons*, Oxford University Press, 1987
N. Freeman. *Arthur Symons*, Modern Humanities Research Association, Cambridge, 2017
S. Hayes. *Arthur Symons*, Brimstone, Shaftesbury, 2007
J. Munro. *Arthur Symons*, Twayne, New York, 1969
J. Wainwright. *Poets On Poets*, Carcanet Press, Manchester, 1997

CRESCENT MOON PUBLISHING

web: www.crmoon.com e-mail: cresmopub@yahoo.co.uk

ARTS, PAINTING, SCULPTURE

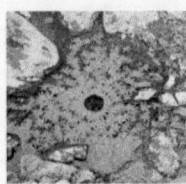

The Art of Andy Goldsworthy
Andy Goldsworthy: Touching Nature
Andy Goldsworthy in Close-Up
Andy Goldsworthy: Pocket Guide
Andy Goldsworthy In America
Land Art: A Complete Guide
The Art of Richard Long
Richard Long: Pocket Guide
Land Art In the UK
Land Art in Close-Up
Land Art In the U.S.A.
Land Art: Pocket Guide
Installation Art in Close-Up
Minimal Art and Artists In the 1960s and After
Colourfield Painting
Land Art DVD, TV documentary
Andy Goldsworthy DVD, TV documentary
The Erotic Object: Sexuality in Sculpture From Prehistory to the Present Day
Sex in Art: Pornography and Pleasure in Painting and Sculpture
Postwar Art
Sacred Gardens: The Garden in Myth, Religion and Art
Glorification: Religious Abstraction in Renaissance and 20th Century Art
Early Netherlandish Painting
Leonardo da Vinci
Piero della Francesca
Giovanni Bellini

Fra Angelico: Art and Religion in the Renaissance
Mark Rothko: The Art of Transcendence
Frank Stella: American Abstract Artist
Jasper Johns
Brice Marden

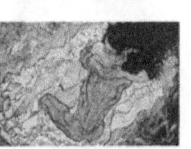

Alison Wilding: The Embrace of Sculpture
Vincent van Gogh: Visionary Landscapes
Eric Gill: Nuptials of God
Constantin Brancusi: Sculpting the Essence of Things
Max Beckmann

Caravaggio
Gustave Moreau
Egon Schiele: Sex and Death In Purple Stockings
Delizioso Fotografico Fervore: Works In Process 1
Sacro Cuore: Works In Process 2
The Light Eternal: J.M.W. Turner
The Madonna Glorified: Karen Arthurs

LITERATURE

J.R.R. Tolkien: The Books, The Films, The Whole Cultural Phenomenon
J.R.R. Tolkien: Pocket Guide
Tolkien's Heroic Quest
The *Earthsea* Books of Ursula Le Guin
Beauties, Beasts and Enchantment: Classic French Fairy Tales
German Popular Stories by the Brothers Grimm
Philip Pullman and *His Dark Materials*
Sexing Hardy: Thomas Hardy and Feminism
Thomas Hardy's *Tess of the d'Urbervilles*
Thomas Hardy's *Jude the Obscure*
Thomas Hardy: The Tragic Novels
Love and Tragedy: Thomas Hardy
The Poetry of Landscape in Hardy
Wessex Revisited: Thomas Hardy and John Cowper Powys
Wolfgang Iser: Essays and Interviews
Petrarch, Dante and the Troubadours
Maurice Sendak and the Art of Children's Book Illustration
Andrea Dworkin
Cixous, Irigaray, Kristeva: The *Jouissance* of French Feminism
Julia Kristeva: Art, Love, Melancholy, Philosophy, Semiotics and Psychoanalysis
Hélène Cixous I Love You: The *Jouissance* of Writing
Luce Irigaray: Lips, Kissing, and the Politics of Sexual Difference
Peter Redgrove: Here Comes the Flood
Peter Redgrove: Sex-Magic-Poetry-Cornwall
Lawrence Durrell: Between Love and Death, East and West
Love, Culture & Poetry: Lawrence Durrell
Cavafy: Anatomy of a Soul
German Romantic Poetry: Goethe, Novalis, Heine, Hölderlin
Feminism and Shakespeare
Shakespeare: Love, Poetry & Magic
The Passion of D.H. Lawrence
D.H. Lawrence: Symbolic Landscapes
D.H. Lawrence: Infinite Sensual Violence
Rimbaud: Arthur Rimbaud and the Magic of Poetry
The Ecstasies of John Cowper Powys
Sensualism and Mythology: The Wessex Novels of John Cowper Powys
Amorous Life: John Cowper Powys and the Manifestation of Affectivity (H.W. Fawkner)
Postmodern Powys: New Essays on John Cowper Powys (Joe Boulter)
Rethinking Powys: Critical Essays on John Cowper Powys
Paul Bowles & Bernardo Bertolucci
Rainer Maria Rilke
Joseph Conrad: *Heart of Darkness*
In the Dim Void: Samuel Beckett
Samuel Beckett Goes into the Silence
André Gide: Fiction and Fervour
Jackie Collins and the Blockbuster Novel
Blinded By Her Light: The Love-Poetry of Robert Graves
The Passion of Colours: Travels In Mediterranean Lands
Poetic Forms

POETRY

Ursula Le Guin: Walking In Cornwall
Peter Redgrove: Here Comes The Flood
Peter Redgrove: Sex-Magic-Poetry-Cornwall
Dante: Selections From the Vita Nuova
Petrarch, Dante and the Troubadours
William Shakespeare: Sonnets
William Shakespeare: Complete Poems
Blinded By Her Light: The Love-Poetry of Robert Graves
Emily Dickinson: Selected Poems
Emily Brontë: Poems
Thomas Hardy: Selected Poems
Percy Bysshe Shelley: Poems
John Keats: Selected Poems
Joh n Keats: Poems of 1820
D.H. Lawrence: Selected Poems
Edmund Spenser: Poems
Edmund Spenser: Amoretti
John Donne: Poems
Henry Vaughan: Poems
Sir Thomas Wyatt: Poems
Robert Herrick: Selected Poems
Rilke: Space, Essence and Angels in the Poetry of Rainer Maria Rilke
Rainer Maria Rilke: Selected Poems
Friedrich Hölderlin: Selected Poems
Arseny Tarkovsky: Selected Poems
Arthur Rimbaud: Selected Poems
Arthur Rimbaud: A Season in Hell
Arthur Rimbaud and the Magic of Poetry
Novalis: Hymns To the Night
German Romantic Poetry
Paul Verlaine: Selected Poems
Elizaethan Sonnet Cycles
D.J. Enright: By-Blows
Jeremy Reed: Brigitte's Blue Heart
Jeremy Reed: Claudia Schiffer's Red Shoes
Gorgeous Little Orpheus
Radiance: New Poems
Crescent Moon Book of Nature Poetry
Crescent Moon Book of Love Poetry
Crescent Moon Book of Mystical Poetry
Crescent Moon Book of Elizabethan Love Poetry
Crescent Moon Book of Metaphysical Poetry
Crescent Moon Book of Romantic Poetry
Pagan America: New American Poetry

MEDIA, CINEMA, FEMINISM and CULTURAL STUDIES

J.R.R. Tolkien: The Books, The Films, The Whole Cultural Phenomenon
J.R.R. Tolkien: Pocket Guide
The *Lord of the Rings* Movies: Pocket Guide
The Cinema of Hayao Miyazaki
Hayao Miyazaki: *Princess Mononoke*: Pocket Movie Guide
Hayao Miyazaki: *Spirited Away*: Pocket Movie Guide
Tim Burton : Hallowe'en For Hollywood
Ken Russell
Ken Russell: *Tommy*: Pocket Movie Guide
The Ghost Dance: The Origins of Religion
The Peyote Cult

Cixous, Irigaray, Kristeva: The *Jouissance* of French Feminism
Julia Kristeva: Art, Love, Melancholy, Philosophy, Semiotics and Psychoanalysis
Luce Irigaray: Lips, Kissing, and the Politics of Sexual Difference
Hélene Cixous I Love You: The *Jouissance* of Writing
Andrea Dworkin
'Cosmo Woman': The World of Women's Magazines
Women in Pop Music
HomeGround: The Kate Bush Anthology
Discovering the Goddess (Geoffrey Ashe)
The Poetry of Cinema
The Sacred Cinema of Andrei Tarkovsky
Andrei Tarkovsky: Pocket Guide
Andrei Tarkovsky: *Mirror*: Pocket Movie Guide
Andrei Tarkovsky: *The Sacrifice*: Pocket Movie Guide
Walerian Borowczyk: Cinema of Erotic Dreams
Jean-Luc Godard: The Passion of Cinema
Jean-Luc Godard: *Hail Mary*: Pocket Movie Guide
Jean-Luc Godard: *Contempt*: Pocket Movie Guide
Jean-Luc Godard: *Pierrot le Fou*: Pocket Movie Guide
John Hughes and Eighties Cinema
Ferris Bueller's Day Off: Pocket Movie Guide
Jean-Luc Godard: Pocket Guide
The Cinema of Richard Linklater
Liv Tyler: Star In Ascendance
Blade Runner and the Films of Philip K. Dick
Paul Bowles and Bernardo Bertolucci
Media Hell: Radio, TV and the Press
An Open Letter to the BBC
Detonation Britain: Nuclear War in the UK
Feminism and Shakespeare
Wild Zones: Pornography, Art and Feminism
Sex in Art: Pornography and Pleasure in Painting and Sculpture
Sexing Hardy: Thomas Hardy and Feminism

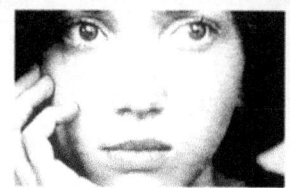

The Light Eternal is a model monograph, an exemplary job. The subject matter of the book is beautifully
organised and dead on beam. (Lawrence Durrell)
It is amazing for me to see my work treated with such passion and respect. (Andrea Dworkin)

CRESCENT MOON PUBLISHING
P.O. Box 1312, Maidstone, Kent, ME14 5XU, Great Britain. www.crmoon.com

cresmopub@yahoo.co.uk   www.crescentmoon.org.uk